A GUIDE TO
London's
BEST
Restaurants

Virgin

Virgin Books

PATRICK CLOONAN — THE ILLUSTRATOR
Patrick Cloonan is a freelance illustrator.

ACKNOWLEDGEMENTS
Virgin Books would like to thank London Transport for their help in compiling this guide. Without their tireless efforts the invaluable transport sections of the guide could never have been completed.

We would also like to thank Peter Shaw and Jane Wintersgill for their contributions to the section on pubs and wine bars with food.

First published in Great Britain in 1982 by Virgin Books Ltd., 61-63 Portobello Road, London W11 3DD.

Copyright © 1982 Virgin Books Ltd.

ISBN 0/907080/48/0

Printed in Great Britain by Richard Clay Ltd., Suffolk
Typesetting by Portobello Typesetting Ltd.
Designed by Cooke Key
Illustrated by Patrick Cloonan
Production services by Book Production Consultants, Cambridge
Cover design by Ray Hyden
Distributed by Hamlyn Paperbacks.

THE AUTHORS

HELEN ALEXANDER
is home sales manager for a book publisher. She eats out regularly, both on business and for pleasure, and also enjoys cooking at her home in Camden. She has lived in London on and off for many years, and comes from quite a greedy family.

DINAH AYOTT
is middle-aged and greedy, but discerning with it. She has lived within a mile of St Paul's for the past 26 years, so Holborn, the City, Islington and the East End are not unfamiliar to her; her only regret is that most of her wealthy city connections would rather eat in their own directors' dining rooms than accompany her.

ROBYN BOWMAN
*was born in Sydney in 1946, and has lived in London since 1972, where she has ample opportunity to indulge the two senses that really matter to her: those of sight and taste. The former led her to co-publish and co-edit the design magazine, **VIZ**; the latter to restaurant and recipe writing.*

CATHERINE CARDWELL
lives in Putney and dines out frequently in the area. She was helped by Malcolm Bowden, who once ate a hundred fish fingers and won a Birds Eye T-shirt.

SUE DENIM
is a glutton. She lives in Bayswater and rides a bicycle.

CHARLOTTE DuCANN
ex-waitress, much enjoys being on the other side of the menu. When she is not out to lunch, she is a freelance journalist.

HENRIETTA GREEN
*is known for her healthy taste in food, and her discerning choice of dinner companions. She writes on food for **The Sunday Express** magazine and for **Company.***

MUIR MACKEAN
is a widely-travelled journalist whose parents first turned him on to food.

MAREK RYMASZEWSKI
is a 29 year old singer-songwriter, who considers 'value for money' restaurants as important as civilised cinema audiences, and decently pressed records...and almost as vital as women who can cope with his monumental ego.

PUBLISHER'S NOTE

The compiling of a guide under the title 'A Guide to London's Best' is bound to be a subjective and at times seemingly arbitrary exercise. We hope, however, that after countless hours of footwork and telephone checking, we have provided a reasonable selection of those restaurants in London that are worth travelling some distance to visit.

For the purpose of this guide London has been divided into sixteen areas, and the areas have been ordered according to their geographical position, i.e. We start with **The West End** and then travel west to **Marylebone** and **Bayswater** and **Notting Hill**, turn south to **Fulham** and then go east to **Chelsea** and on to **East of the City** before turning north and west to **Islington**, **Camden** and **Hampstead**; finally south of the river is covered in two parts — **east** and **west**. Within each area the restaurants have been listed alphabetically. For each restaurant the following information has been given: name, address, telephone number, opening times, the average cost of a meal for two, and the average price of a bottle of wine. Prices were all correct at the time of going to press, although it is expected that there will be some increases towards the summer, of as much as 15 per cent. Each area is self-contained and completed with an introduction and illustration, and transport information. We originally intended to provide maps for all the areas, but so assiduous were our reviewers we have had to omit them, in order to include all the restaurants.

Within the various areas the restaurants have been sub-divided according to price into three groups: Budget, Mid-Price and Luxury. This does vary slightly according to the area covered, but roughly Budget means a meal for two, excluding wine, for less than £10; Mid-Price less than £25; and Luxury everything else. Following the area section there are a number of special features dealing with places to have breakfast and tea (including hotels); wine bars and pubs with good food; latenight eating places; and restaurants with music.

Needless to say there will be errors, both of omission and of commission. If you know of a restaurant or wine bar that we have failed to include but is worthy of mention, or disagree with those that we have included, or what has been written about them, please write and let us know. There is a form on the next page.

Food prices are the average price of a three-course meal for two including coffee but excluding service and wine. Wine prices are the average cost of a bottle of house wine.

READERS RESPONSE FORM

To: Catherine Ledger
    'A Guide to London's BEST RESTAURANTS'
    Virgin Books
    61/63 Portobello Road,   LONDON W11 3DD

Name: ....

Address: ....

Telephone: ....

Comment: ....

....

....

....

....

....

....

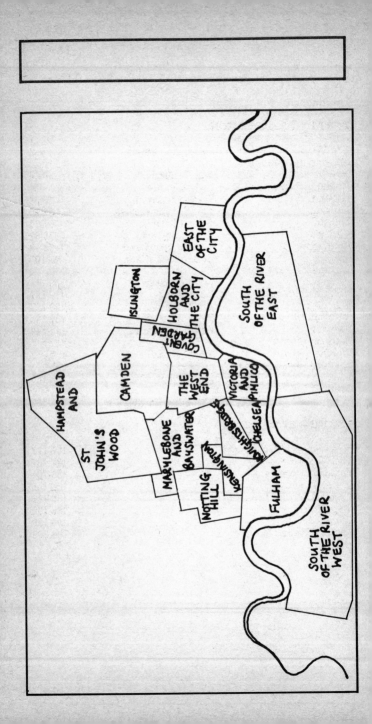

Introduction

PART I — AREA SECTION

PART II — FEATURES

INTRODUCTION

It is a fact of life that we must eat in order to survive, and since this is so we may as well enjoy it. Brillat-Savarin once remarked: 'Animals feed, man eats; wise men alone know how to eat'.

Eating well is more a matter of resource than resources, and it has been our intention in writing this guide to search out those restaurants of special merit, where eating can be both pleasurable and good value.

The guide has been divided into sections, area by area, with special attention paid to the particular characteristics of each area. Since the reviewers are all familiar with a specific area, it is hoped that this will result in a more comprehensive listing of restaurants, showing the extraordinary variety of eating possibilities in London, so that eating out may never again be a disappointing experience.

The prime object of the guide is to make known those restaurants our critics have found particularly gratifying; and although it is unlikely that all, or even most, of the restaurants reviewed will be new to the reader, we trust that many will be entirely novel.

Writing the guide has been most palatable; restaurateurs have been helpful, and we look forward to updating the guide next year. It is an entirely individual collection, and we would, therefore, welcome your comments, both on those eating-houses we have included and those we have, inadvertently perhaps, excluded.

A GUIDE TO London's BEST Restaurants

PART I

MANZIS

The pull of the West End has slackened. Once it was 'the thing' to go to town for a night out on the tiles, now people stay in the suburbs or parade the Piazza of Covent Garden. Nonetheless there are still plenty of restaurants which are worth the trip; cheap and cheerful, fast and friendly, ritzy and relaxed — you'll find them all there in the centre of the big smoke. The West End abounds in ethnic eateries: Chinese in Chinatown, Greek in Charlotte Street and Italian in Soho. So one thing is certain, whatever your mood, you'll find a restaurant to suit in the West End.

LUXURY

Antoine's (Wheeler's)
40 Charlotte St, W1 (636 2817)
FISH
Mon-Fri, and Sun 12
noon-2.30, 6.00-10.30.
Food £29. Wine £3.95.
Wheeler's has discreetly
colonized the West End with
its chain of restaurants. Other
branches are: Wheeler's at 19
Old Brompton St; Braganza at
56 Frith St; Sovereign at 17
Hertford St; and Vendome at
20 Dover St. Each one is run as
a separate domain, although
there is a certain sameness,
both in terms of decor (oak
tables and leaded glass
windows) and of food. It's all
fish — poached, grilled, fried,
steamed. The fish is always
fresh and excellently
prepared, but some of the
sauces could do with a touch
of imagination.

Apicella
4 Mill St, W1 (499 1308)
ITALIAN
Mon-Sat 12 noon-3.00, 7.00-12
midnight; closed Sat lunch.
Food £25. Wine £4.60.
Apicella, the 'in' Italian
restaurant for '82 is to
lunchtime what Langan's is to
the evenings. Why the people
— dubbed 'Vogue Gulch' by
Nicholas Coleridge in an
article on Apicella's — who
know and care about such
things descend on one place
rather than another, mystifies
me. But it does offer a very
good meal — a wide selection
of home-made pastas,
delicious fresh mediterranean
prawns and a very tasty

Carpaccio au Poivre Vert
(wafer thin slices of smoked
beef with a green pepper
sauce) — but you may be so
busy media gazing that you
won't even notice the food.

Cafe Jardin
10 Lancashire Court, 1223
New Bond St, W1 (493 2896)
FRENCH
Mon-Sat 12 noon-2.30,
7.00-11.30; closed Sat lunch.
Food £30. Wine £4.75.
Recently opened and
decorated herbaceously as its
name implies, Cafe Jardin has
a strong fish bias. The menu
read like a dream but the
reality was far more down to
earth. The Cassolette de
Queues d'Ecrevisses au
Vouvray a la Creme (crayfish
cooked in cream and Vouvray
in a pastry case) was over rich
and the pastry soggy; Oeuf
Poche en surprise a
l'Armoricaine (chopped
lobster served under a lightly
poached egg topped with a
cheese souffle) was a success
and well-timed. Mousseline de
Sole lacked flavour although
the texture was beautifully
velvety and Fricasse d'agneau
au Basilic (noisettes of lamb
with sweetbreads and kidneys
in a white wine and basil
sauce) were by no means as
interesting as they promised.
They are trying hard but there
is room for improvement.

Cecconis
5a Burlington Gdns, W1 (434
1509)
ITALIAN
Mon-Sat 12.30-2.30, 7.30-11.00;
closed Sat lunch.
Food £37. Wine £5.50.

Pointed out by the fickle finger of fashion, Cecconis was once the haunt for the trendy trattoria crowd. But beckoned elsewhere (namely Apicella) they moved on. Cecconis seem to have risen above such a minor disaster; they are still packed out every day. The food is still excellent, the pasta still freshly made daily, but at the prices they charge it certainly should be.

Chaopraya
22 St Christopher's Pl, W1 (486 0777)
THAI
Mon-Sat 12 noon-3.00, 6.30-11.00.
Food £26. Wine £4.00.
Named after a river in Bangkok, it's a pretty restaurant decked out in indigenous cane. Thai food is similar to Chinese, only hotter; if you've never tried it before stick to the set menu. It includes Beef Sateh, fried chicken with asparagus, fried squid with garlic and pepper and beef with curry paste, and will certainly give you a general picture of what it is all about. If, however, you want a real baptism of fire try Poh Tack, a mixed seafood soup flavoured with hot pepper and lemon grass. Coffee comes with coconut sweets wrapped in banana leaves — much more chic than After Eights.

The Connaught Restaurant
Connaught Hotel, Carlos Place, W1 (499 7070)
FRENCH
Mon-Sun 12.30-2.30, set lunch from £14; 6.30-10.30, set dinner from £14.80.

Food £41.25. Wine £5.50.
The Connaught is a diner's dream. Panelled walls, crystal chandeliers, attentive service and, most important, exquisite food. Michel Bourdin, the world renowned chef, cooks faultlessly; his Coulibiac de Saumon is justly famous and cannot be bettered. The menu changes weekly but you can rest assured that everything is cooked to perfection with original sauces and is always of the highest quality. You may have to starve for a week in order to pay the bill, but it's worth it.

Dorchester Grill Room
Park Lane, W1 (629 8888)
FRENCH
Mon-Sat 12 noon-3.00, 6.00-11.00; Sun 12.30-2.30, 7.00-11.00.
Food £30. Wine £4.40 (Set lunch £10.50 incl wine)
Anton Mosimann, the maitre chef d'hotel, is one of Britain's best chefs (actually he is Swiss but as he has adopted this country, it doesn't really count). The food, under his guidance, is superb — beautifully cooked and stunningly presented — the Terrine de Covent Garden, a layered mousse of supreme de volaille with rows of vegetables is bliss and his Rendez-vous de Fruits de Mer a sensation. In fact if you follow nouvelle cuisine, his version cannot be faulted.

WEST END

L'Escargot
48 Greek St, W1 (437 2679)
FRENCH
Mon-Sat 12noon-2.30,
6.00-11.00.
Food £25. Wine £4.25.
There are two things really worth mentioning about L'Escargot — the lovely Eleana, everyone's favourite manageress, and the superb carpet with its border of woven snails. The food is not terrific; the puff pastry for Escargot Feuilletage was soggy, the skate in its black butter and caper sauce overcooked and the sauce with the turbot insipid. The mille feuille was heavy and the passion fruit sorbet more ice than passion. But they are to be commended for a pretty place, a bustling brasserie downstairs where you can eat if you don't want a full meal, and warm friendly service. With so much going, they really should improve the food.

L'Etoile
30 Charlotte St, W1 (636 7189)
FRENCH
Mon-Sat 12.30-2.30, 6.30- 10.00.
Food £30. Wine £5.35.
L'Etoile doesn't shine as bright as it did in former years. Once it had a reputation for fine classical French food but it has since dimmed. Service was sloppy and unfriendly (we arrived late and were chastised like naughty school children) and the meal was indifferent. The starters Loup au mayonnaise and Salade Nicoise were unmemorable, the best end of lamb charred although it had distinctly been

ordered pink and the steak erred on the side of tough. Puddings were of a similar standard. Peaches in a sickly sweet syrup and Black Forest gateau textured like glutinous cotton are just not good enough from a restaurant which claims to care about food.

Le Gavroche
43 Upper Brook St, W1 (408 0881)
FRENCH
Mon-Fri 12 noon-2.00, 7.00-10.00.
Food £80 (set lunch £16.50, set dinner £30). Wine £10.
The only restaurant in Britain to have been awarded three stars by the Guide Michelin, Le Gavroche is the ne plus ultra. The Roux brothers have created here everything one would expect from a supremely sophisticated French restaurant of the 'nouvelle cuisine' school; and one pays accordingly. So luxurious is it in fact that one may find it hard to keep an eye on the bill.

The Gay Hussar
2 Greek St, W1 (437 0973)
HUNGARIAN
Mon-Sat 12.30-2.30, 5.30-11.00.
Food £28. Wine £4.50.
The lunch-time haunt of many a Fleet Street editor and politician (Michael Foot can sometimes be spotted hanging up the coat), it offers genuine Hungarian cooking. We tried the chilled wild cherry soup which was certainly unusual but a little sweet, and Csuka Csiki Martassal, a pike mousse with beetroot sauce which had

14

a coarse texture but a refined flavour. The Borju Porkolt, a veal Goulash with dumplings, was full bodied and there was nothing stodgy about the dumplings (my school cook could learn a thing or two here), and Csirke Pejacsevics (chicken in paprika with a cucumber sauce) was an amazing contrast of flavours. We shared a Turos Gomboc (sweet cheese dumplings) as they are too good to miss, although after such a rich meal we barely had room.

Lacy's
26 Whitfield St, W1 (636 2411)
FRENCH
Mon-Sat 12.30-2.30, 7.30-11.00.; closed Sat lunch.
Food £28. Wine £4.00.
Run by the eponymous Bill Lacy and his wife Marguerite Costa of cookery writer fame, it is to be found in a subterranean basement and has as much charm as a catacomb. Its reputation has dimmed recently and it's no longer consistently good — some nights it can be brilliant but there is no way of knowing if you will strike lucky.

Mirabelle
56 Curzon St, W1 (499 4636)
FRENCH
Mon-Sat 12noon-2.30, 7.00-12 midnight.
Food £32. Wine £6.50.
The Mirabelle once had a reputation as one of the finest restaurants in London — it ought to look to its laurels, or should I say rosettes? The menu is dull and they seem totally oblivious to any

changes or developments in the culinary world. The prices are outrageous — £2.50 for a grapefruit or £3.50 for an artichoke — but the place was packed so they probably can't see any reason to change.

The Ritz
Piccadilly W1 (493 8181)
INTERNATIONAL
Mon-Sat 12 noon-2.30, 6.30-11.00; Sun 6.30-10.30.
Food £37. Wine £3.95 (1/2 litre carafe).
Michael Quinn has newly arrived to give the gracious grill room a much needed food-lift. Things were rather slack (and that's some understatement) but he promises to put it right. If he works the same miracles as at Gravetye Manor, it's going to be very good indeed. Watch this space for further announcements, perhaps even news, next year, of their first Michelin star.

Scott's
20 Mount St, W1 (629 5248)
FISH
Mon-Sat 12.30-2.45, 6.00-10.45; Sun 7.00-10.00.
Food £32. Wine £5.25.
I remember tucking into oysters years ago in their slightly scruffy Oyster bar just off Piccadilly Circus. Since then they have moved to the heart of Mayfair and become extremely elegant. It has been decorated very tastefully — rag-rolled in a subtle shade of apricot, and with a thick pile carpet. Recently they extended the menu — 'In honour of the Royal Wedding' — so I felt obliged to try the Quennelle

de Turbotin Royal (mousseline of turbot poached in white wine with truffles), and it was a triumph. My friend's Fruit de Mer a la Facon de Chef (sauteed sea food with tomatoes, mushrooms and peppers) paled into insignificance by comparison, but we were both well pleased with our puddings, a refreshing lemon sorbet and a crunchy meringue glacee.

Tiberio
22 Queen St, W1 (629 3561)
ITALIAN
Mon-Sat 12.00-3.00,
7.00-2.00am; closed Sat lunch.
Food £30. Wine £5.75.
Tiberio is expense account Italian populated by the suited businessman. The place is discreetly restrained; tables are set far enough apart so no-one will overhear the latest business deal, service is most attentive and although there is dancing every night — it's definitely not music to let your hair down to. A thoughtful, if expensive, touch are the daily fresh orchids on every table.

MID-PRICE

Amalfi
24-31 Old Compton St, W1
(437 7284)
ITALIAN
Mon-Sat 12 noon-3.00,
6.00-11.00.
Food £12. Wine £3.15.
The Amalfi is half restaurant, half coffee bar/pasticerria. The former is open for restaurant hours (see above) whereas the latter opens at ten in the

morning and keeps going all day; but if you don't want to stand propping up the bar, no-one seems to mind if you nip into the restaurant with your coffee etc, provided they're not busy. Pastries are their speciality (they even open on Sundays to sell them) but their food comes a strong second. The menu is traditional Italian — pasta, a good choice of veal and chicken dishes and, to round off the meal, strong expresso and one of their delicious pastries.

Anemos
32-34 Charlotte St, W1 (636 2289)
GREEK
Mon-Sat 12noon-3.00, 6.00-12 midnight.
Food £12.50. Wine £4.50.
The manager informed me above the babble of bazoukis that his customers come 'More to let their hair down than to eat!' So if you want to relive those package tour memories of carefree nights spent in tolerant tavernas — head over to Anemos. There are plates to be thrown, chairs to dance on, sitaki to practise and plenty of noise. The food is standard Greek — taramosalata, sheftalia, bastourma (garlic sausages), baklava and all those other sticky cakes — but to echo the manager 'It's not for the eats — but for the enjoy!'.

Aunties
126 Cleveland St, W1 (387 3226)
ENGLISH
Mon-Sat 12.30-1.45, 7.30-9.30;
closed Sat lunch.

Food £13.90. Wine £4.25.
Auntie's is sensible, no-nonsense English food, the sort of thing our mothers should have taught us to cook — that is if they had ever learnt themselves. It's a quaint restaurant brimming over with bric-a-brac and English character. There is a set price for three wholesome courses; first a choice of soup, smoked mackerel or pate; then a choice of pies — steak and kidney, beef in Guinness, fishermans, Elizabethan (pigeon and beef) — and earthy meat dishes. Puddings followed in the same vein — apple and blackberry pie for instance, but for those already full up, you could always try a home-made ice cream.

Bentleys
11 Swallow St, W1 (734 4756)
FISH
Mon-Sat 12noon-2.45,
6.00-10.45.
Food £24. Wine £5.60.
I must have hit an off day when I went to Bentleys. We ate upstairs — the oyster bar sadly was crowded out — and from beginning to end it was a disappointment. the service was slack, the wine tepid and the oysters washed, which gave them a distinct tap-water flavour and did nothing to dignify their delicate flavour. The lobster bisque was heavy on the paprika, the crab salad seafresh but short on greenery and the hollandaise sauce, accompanying my companion's turbot, tasted as if it had been hanging around for hours. Bentleys have their own oyster bed which gives them a starter for ten in fish restaurant one-upmanship, but after our meal they had lost most of their points.

Bertorelli Brothers
19 Charlotte St, W1 (636 4174)
ITALIAN
Mon-Sat 12noon-2.30,
6.00-10.00.
Food £15. Wine £3.80.
There's nothing modern about Bertorelli's, it's just as it has been for the last fifty years; cavernous rooms, crisp white tablecloths, handwritten menus, bright lights and bustling waiters and waitresses serving you assiduously. It boasts a huge selection of dishes which change daily; but the food is not the real reason for going (it's pleasant but not terribly memorable). You just have to soak up the atmosphere for yourself.

Boulevard
56-59 Wigmore St, W1 (935 3152)
AMERICAN
Mon-Sun 12 noon-12 midnight.
Food £12. Wine £3.50.
Boulevard has undergone a transformation and is now Garfunkels (whoever he may be) at Boulevard. It is wondrous in its bad taste; a cascade of lamps tinkle down the far wall. The bright lights generally do not encourage you to linger but then Garfunkels/Boulevard is dedicated to fast food and they do it very well. The menu is extensive; fat juicy hamburgers, plenty of chicken and pasta, although my Chic Fettucine was not very aptly

17

named as it came dowdily dressed in a plain tomato sauce. Their children's menu is a good idea (small portions for small prices) and it's worth remembering that they're open all day, so you can escape the crowds of Oxford Street for a quiet cup of tea.

Carrolls
32 Great Windmill St, W1 (437 2747)
JEWISH
Mon-Sat 12 noon-10.30.
Food £12. No licence.
Carrolls has just had a face-lift and is looking extremely smart. Don't worry though — the picture of shining and fading stars are still there and the salt beef is still as good as ever. Afficionados will know all about its delights but for those of you who haven't discovered it yet, let me tell you about the best latkes in town. Crisp, freshly fried to a rich brown, they are a never-to-be-forgotten experience. Carrolls has all the other treats of mid-European Jewish food, chopped or schmultz herring, chopped liver and of course, salt beef. The standard is excellent so give it a whirl.

Le Chateaubriand
Mayfair Hotel, Stratton St, W1 (629 7777)
FRENCH
Mon-Fri 12.30-2.30, 6.30-10.30;
Sun 12.30-2.30, 7.00-10.30.
Food £21. Wine £4.75.
Although it looks and is luxurious — thick pile carpets, attentive waiters, and the most comfy chairs — the Chateaubriand is not that expensive provided you stick

to their set menu. There's still plenty of choice; about eight main dishes which determine the price you pay, plus a good selection of hors d'oeuvres and puddings or cheese. They also have occasional regional fortnights with celebrated chefs from France cooking their specialities and an excellent Sunday lunch with half price for children under fourteen.

Chez Gerard
5 Charlotte St, W1 (636 4975)
FRENCH
Mon-Sun 12.30-2.30, 6.30-11.00;
closed Sat lunch.
Food £17.50. Wine £4.20.
Chez Gerard specialises in steaks cooked on their charcoal grill — and they are amongst the best in town. Their secret, they claim, is to buy best Scotch beef and to hang it for at least ten days (butchers would do well to revive this practise). The menu is not extensive but what's there is most agreeable; for a starter try either their rough pate or Soupe de Poisson with ladles of rouille and croutons. Main courses all come piled high with real pommes frites, thinly sliced, golden brown and very crisp; puddings change daily but there's often a good tarte lurking around. Angus Steak Houses should watch out!

Chez Victor
45 Wardour St, W1 (437 6523)
FRENCH
Mon-Sat 12 noon-3.00, 6.00-12 midnight; closed Sat lunch.
Food £20. Wine £5.
Chez Victor is more French

than the French. It has a tatty air as if to imply that serious eaters are never distracted by the decor, so why make the effort. But I do enjoy my sorties here and once inside I feel as if I'm in Paris. The meals are always excellent; the snails tender and garlicky, the onion soup crusted with croutons and cheese, the steaks 'exactement comme il faut', the steak tartare suitably spiced, the salads tossed in virgin green olive oil and the roquefort sharp and crumbly. As you may have gathered, it's one of my favourite restaurants.

The China Garden
66 Brewer St, W1 (437 6500)
CHINESE
Mon-Sun 12 noon-2.30, 6.00-11.30; closed Sun lunch.
Food £17.50. Wine £5.50.
It's very theatrical: black walls, white floors (how do they keep them clean?) and larger-than-life, subtly spotlit bronze storks dotted about the room. The food is Pekinese — mashed prawns on sesame toast, the inevitable Peking Duck complete with pancakes etc and plenty of stir-fried vegetables. I've always thought the acid test of any Chinese restaurant was to count how many Chinese were actually eating there. I am sad to say that there wasn't one all evening.

Coconut Grove
3-5 Barrett St, W1 (486 5269)
AMERICAN
Mon-Sun 12 noon-12.30am.
Food £17. Wine £4.75.
Sleek and steely with glass

wall windows, Coconut Grove is still popular with high fashion trendies. The food is genuine American, gargantuan portions served with verve. Potato Skins — deep fried with a sour cream and chives dip — are delicious but the sauce accompanying the Peel and Eat Spiced Shrimps was ordinary pre-packaged. Salads are a good bet, enormous bowls crammed full and my Caesar Salad was suitably salty; but it was tempting to think in the case of the 8oz Sirlion Steak that quality had been sacrificed for quantity. Cream teas are served in the afternoon and cocktails before or with your meal.

Diamond Restaurant
23 Lisle St, WC2 (437 2517)
CHINESE
Mon-Sun 12 noon-3.30am.
Food £13. Wine £5.
There are two very good reasons for coming here. Firstly, they have the most sensational crab and ginger, and, secondly, you can eat here up until 3.30 in the morning. Otherwise you can take your pick from the literally hundreds of Chinese restaurants crowded together in Chinatown, the area lying between Shaftesbury Avenue and Leicester Square. I certainly cannot claim to have tried them all.

Efes Kebab House
80 Great Titchfield St, W1 (636 1953)
TURKISH
Mon-Sat 11.30am-11.30.
Food £12. Wine £3.40 (litre).

Turkish food is not that dissimilar to Greek, but it's spicier and certainly less run of the mill as it's quite rare in London. Efes offers a take-away service and a small, dimly lit restaurant in the back. There you can gorge Muska Borek, a crisp fried pastry parcel stuffed with melted cheese and parsley, Cerkez Tavagu chicken in a creamy walnut sauce and a variety of kebabs including Bobrek Izgara, tender spiced kidneys. There's an irresistible pudding — Suthi Borek — which is similar to strudel but filled with an almond flavoured custard instead of the more down to earth apples.

L'Epicure
28 Frith St, W1 (437 2829)
FRENCH
Mon-Sat 12 noon-2.30, 6.00-11.15; closed Sat lunch.
Food £17.50. Wine £4.30.
They are very keen on flames here. Outside are flaming torches; inside almost everything is flambeed. I've never been convinced about 'lamp cooking' — it's over-rated and a danger to the eyebrows — but these waiters have it well under control. If you choose carefully you can avoid the horrors of fire; otherwise it's omelettes, steak (flambeed with a choice of four sauces) kidneys, liver etc. For pudding they seem prepared to flambe just about every fruit imaginable.

Foleys
23 Foley St, W1 (636 2718)
FISH

Mon 12 noon-3.00; Tue-Sat 12 noon-3.00, 6.00-11.00; closed Sat lunch.
Food £14. Wine £4.25.
I'm delighted to see that there are a few recently-opened fish restaurants. Up until now they've either been stuffy and expensive or very basic fish 'n' chips. Not so Foley's; it's an attractive restaurant with a relaxed atmosphere (pretty pink tables and terracotta tiled floors). The menu is original with a good choice of fish — brill, tuna, halibut and monkfish to name but a few — and they are freshly cooked to order and imaginatively served. Carp steamed on a bed of Spinach and Mint was promising and the Shark with Pernod sounded tempting if you had the courage to try it.

The Fountain
Fortnum & Mason
181, Piccadilly, W1 (734 8040)
INTERNATIONAL
Mon-Sat 9.30am-11.30.
Food £13. Wine £3.65.
The Fountain hasn't changed much over the years, the chandeliers still tinkle, hatted ladies clutching their shopping still lunch there and Jermyn Street roues still drop in for supper after the theatre. We came hot-foot from Shaftesbury Avenue after some nondescript show and were immensely cheered up by our meal. I had a creamy lobster bisque followed by a wedge of F&M's own game pie (the pastry was a little tired) with salad. My friend had a 'satisfactory' chicken consomme with cheese straws and steak and kidney pie

which he really did
appreciate. We couldn't resist
the Sundaes, and with twelve
different ones (plus ordinary
ice creams with nine different
sauces) you're spoilt for
choice.

Gaylord
16 Albemarle St, W1 (629
9802)
INDIAN
Mon-Sun 12 noon-3.00,
6.00-11.30.
Food £17. Wine £5.60 (litre).
Apart from the usual list of
Tandoori cooked food,
Gaylord also offers several
Kashmiri and Mughlai
specialities. They have a
distinct, creamy flavour as the
ingredients are usually
simmered in milk or yoghurt
and have the advantage for
spice-wary customers of only
being mildly seasoned. We
chose the Almond Korma, a
delicate stew of tender lamb
cooked in milk with almonds
and Chicken Muglai which is
cooked in a rich mixture of
butter (ghee) and cream. The
meat dishes were splendid but
the various accompaniments, a
disappointment. The rice was
overcooked and the
vegetables rather impalatable.
The sweet trolley offered
various ethnic surprises which
left us with the feeling that
they must be an acquired
taste. Gaylord has two
branches in the West End —
the other is at 79-81 Mortimer
St, W1 (636 0808).

Gennaros
44-45 Dean St, W1 (437 3950)
ITALIAN
Mon-Sun 12 noon-3.00,

6.00-11.30.
Food £21. Wine £4.75.
One of the oldest Italian
restaurants, it was first
established in 1903. They've
moved about a bit since then
finally ending up in their
present suitably distinguished
surroundings. You can either
eat a la carte or set price (at £8
or £9) and although the choice
is not enormous, there are
plenty of unusual dishes,
including a stunning Quaglie
alla Grappa con Crostini,
quails cooked in grappa. All
the main dishes are served
with polenta, a rare treat
although probably not one you
could stomach too often. Don't
miss out on the cheeses — a
selection of indigenous Bel
Paese, Gorgonzola, Fontina
and Pecorina, and all in prime
condition.

Hard Rock Cafe
150 Park Lane, W1 (629 0382)
AMERICAN
Mon-Thu 12 noon-12.15am; Fri,
Sat 12 noon-12.45am; Sun
noon-12 midnight.
Food £15. Wine £3.75.
Wrap up warmly and take
earplugs. The former is for
braving the icy winds of Hyde
Park Corner as you queue for
a place, the latter to protect
you against the deafening
music once inside. Their
thoughtfully strong cocktails
will soon take your mind off
these inconveniences; after all
this is the Hard Rock Cafe, and
it is very handy for the Park.
Devotees say it serves the best
hamburgers in town, and the
thronging masses would seem
to prove them right.

Langans Brasserie
Stratton St, W1 (493 6437)
FRENCH
Mon-Fri 12.30-2.30, 7.00-11.30;
Sat 8.00-12 midnight.
Food £24. Wine £4.50.

Langans goes from strength to strength, and under the direction of Richard Shepherd (ex-Capital Hotel) the food is still interesting and the people glittering. I started with a light delicate spinach souffle with a sharp contrasting anchovy sauce, poired in the centre, and my friend had a superb curly endive salad with bacon and a lightly poached egg. Main courses were Foie de Veau grille Lyonnaise which was presented as pink as I had requested and Langue de Boeuf Braisechoux rouge et sauce Madere which my companion revelled in. Puddings were plentiful, and the raspberry tart especially good, but I just couldn't find the room. A rare treat.

Leoni's Quo Vadis
26 Dean St, W1 (437 4809)
ITALIAN
Mon-Sat 12 noon-2.30,
6.00-11.15.
Food £22. Wine £3.80.

Famous as the building where Karl Marx once lived, one can't help wondering how he would react to this bourgeois restaurant. It has recently undergone a facelift and now looks modestly opulent — soft beige and tasteful dried flowers; not very Italian although the food is the genuine article. There's a real proletariat Tuscan Bean Soup and I enjoyed the Filetto di Bue Cornelia, a tender fillet in

a marsala wine based sauce, even if it was a trifle overcooked for my taste. Karl Marx probably wasn't concerned about such petty problems.

Little Akropolis
10 Charlotte St, W1 (636 8198)
GREEK
Mon-Sat 12 noon-2.30,
6.00-10.30; closed Sat lunch.
Food £14. Wine £5.20.

Outside there are dwarf neo-Grecian pillars, inside red flock boudoir paper — the effect is one of cosy charm. Opened in 1948, Little Akropolis probably hasn't changed much, it just carries on in its own sweet way. The menu is, however, full of surprises; an unusual aubergine pate, really more of a puree strongly flavoured with garlic and crushed nuts, is worth ordering and so is the palm heart salad, sadly only too rarely seen in England. Their Kleftico (Baked Lamb) is justifiably a speciality of the house; it is tender and moist with a faint hint of garlic. Make sure you leave plenty of room for pudding; there are delicious light pancakes with rose petal jam or, if you can't face that, try creamy goat's milk yoghurt with real Greek honey.

Manzis
1-2 Leicester St, WC2 (734 0224)
FISH
Mon-Sat 12 noon-2.30,
5.30-11.45; Sun 6.00-10.30.
Food £18. Wine £3.95.

Never, ever allow yourself to be seated upstairs even if it means waiting for hours as downstairs is the place to be. It hustles and bustles and is full of life; tables are crammed together (so don't got for an intimate dinner a deux), or you can perch at the bar. The fish is always fresh and expertly cooked: mussels, when in season, are plump and juicy and Skateau Beurre Noir, meaty and magnificent. Call in here before or after the theatre: it's only just around the corner from Leicester Square.

Martinez
25 Swallow St, W1 (734 5066)
SPANISH
Mon-Sat 12 noon-3.00, 6.15-11.30
Food £21. Wine £4.20.
Martinez boasts the most stunning collection of Spanish tiles. Hand painted in warm Mediterranean colours, they depict events in daily rural life and cover all the walls from the Sherry Bar downstairs to the large restaurant upstairs. The food claims to be typically Spanish but I couldn't help thinking that it was rather international, disguised in suitably foreign sounding names. Salmon Ahumado is Smoked Salmon and Pechuga de Pollo Aranjuez nothing more than Breast of Chicken cooked with asparagus tips. The wine list is authentic with a good choice of Riojas at very reasonable prices.

Masako
6-8 St Christopher's Pl, W1 (935 1579)
JAPANESE
Mon-Sat 12 noon-2.00,

6.00-10.00.
Food £22. Wine £1.30 (small carafe rice wine)
Divided into three, you can choose where to eat. Upstairs is conventional table and chairs and koto (Japanese harp) music on Friday and Saturday nights. Downstairs is much more fun with either a sushi (raw fish and rice) bar or individual rooms laid out with bamboo matting, very low tables and cushioned seats for reclining at your leisure (check your socks before you go as they'll insist you take your shoes off). The lighting everywhere is rather bright as you're meant to see what you are eating — half the fun of Japanese food is its appearance.

Melati
21 Great Windmill St, W1 (437 2745)
MALAYSIAN
Mon-Sat 12 noon-3.00, 6.00-11.30.
Food £12. Wine £4.
If you have a sudden urge to go Oriental but can't face another Chinese meal — why not try Indonesian/Malaysian food. It's an amalgamation of Chinese and Indian food which is quite logical when you realise that Indonesia is equidistant between the two countries. Melati offers a good choice of dishes and it's good for novices. For a start the menu is clearly set out with thorough explanations of each dish, so you know exactly what you are ordering. The food is spicy — but not overly so — and unusual; it's the first time I've ever seen, let alone tried,

coconut soup. I can heartily recommend it.

Ormonds
6 Ormond Yard, Duke of York St, SW1 (930 2842)
INTERNATIONAL
Mon-Sat 12.30-2.30, 6.30-11.30; closed Sat lunch.
Food £19. Wine £3.95.
Ormond's is new to the London scene, but it is determined to make its mark; rumour has it that they are about to open a cocktail/disco club as well. You will find it tucked away in a small mews off St James's. Inside they've hit on the idea of white walls and paintings for sale (cynics comment that it's a cheap way out but the owner insists it is a way of helping starving artists). The food is nicely, but not extraordinarily cooked; they have a seasonal menu which is supplemented with daily specials biased towards fish. We tried Crudite with Bagna Calda (anchovy and cream dip) which was delightful and Rolls of Smoked Salmon with Chilled Scrambled Eggs which was not such a good idea as it sounded — the eggs were lumpy and the salmon salty. The Medallions of Veal were tender and moist and the Calves' Liver with Avocado Guacamole an interesting combination of tastes. Altogether it is a place worth watching.

Pappagalli's Pizza Inc
7-9 Swallow St, W1 (734 5182)
AMERICAN
Mon-Sun 12 noon-12 midnight.
Food £12. Wine £3.95.
Restaurants come and go but this one is determined to stick around. I visited it two days after it had opened and they were certainly trying — let's hope they keep it up. Based loosely (although I don't think they'll thank me for mentioning it) on the Chicago Pizza Pie Factory it is devoted to pizzas → but Sicilian pizzas as opposed to its rival's deep dish ones. I'm not altogether convinced that I noticed a remarkable difference but they assured me that the Sicilian variety are lighter, fluffier and crustier — but they would! The fillings are similar; my Gourmet Pepperoni with pepperoni, peppers, tomatoes, onions and lot of melted cheese was very good and I liked the idea of pepper oil and pepper chips on hand for hotting it up.

Relais Des Amis
17b Curzon St, W1 (499 7595)
FRENCH
Mon-Sun 12 noon-3.00, 6.00-12 midnight.
Food £22. Wine £4.95.
Relais des Amis is the sister restaurant to Cafe des Amis and the Brasserie des Amis. Both have established a fair reputation but it's still a little too soon to tell whether the Relais will be as successful. It's an excessively pretty place with an airy out-of-doors feel; they have even painted a powder blue sky with fluffy clouds in the centre to confuse their customers. The menu is straight French with minor influences of nouvelle cuisine — Truite Rosee aux concombres (trout with

cucumber sauce) and Caneton aux Citron Vert (duckling in lime sauce) are suitable examples.

There are a couple of back rooms decorated as Provencal dining rooms which can be hired for private parties.

Richoux

41a South Audley St, W1 (629 5228)
ENGLISH
Mon-Fri 9.00am-11.00; Sat 10.00am-12 midnight; Sun 11.30-11.00.
Food £14. Wine £4.50.

Richoux has a refined old-fashioned air — even the waitresses are dressed up as parlour maids. You can drop in any time for brunch, English tea, a toasted sandwich snack or for a proper meal. We went for a light lunch and I was tempted by creamy Scrambled Eggs which were light and obviously freshly cooked. My friend tried the Chef's Club Sandwich (chicken, bacon, tomato and mayonnaise) which was a little skimpy on the fillings. Afterwards we threw caution to the winds and both ordered Ice Cream Specials — Dusty Road (Coffee and Chocolate with butterscotch sauce and cream) and Black Velvet (Vanilla with meringue, blackcurrants and cream). They were marvellous. They have other branches at 172 Piccadilly (on the old site of Jacksons); 86 Brompton Rd; and 360 Oxford St.

Rowleys

113 Jermyn St, SW1 (930 2707)
FRENCH
Mon-Sun 12 noon-3.00, 6.00-11.30; closed Sun lunch.
Food £18.50. Wine £5.75 (litre)

Without wishing to be accused of stating the obvious, I must mention that there isn't much of a choice at Rowley's. Like it or not, the meal comprises bread and butter, mixed salad with either vinaigrette or blue cheese dressing, charcoal grilled Entrecote and french fried potatoes. Portions are generous, the meat tender and tasty; so if you do fancy a steak this is one of the more pleasant places to eat one.

St Moritz

161 Wardour St, W1 (734 3324)
SWISS
Mon-Sat 12 noon-3.00, 6.00-11.30; closed Sat lunch.
Food £18. Wine £3.90.

Don't, whatever you do, go into the wrong St Moritz which is a cavernous disco with suspicious heavies hanging around; the right St Moritz, two doors up the road, is a cosy restaurant in neo-chalet style. As you would expect from the Swiss, fondue — either meat or cheese — features prominently; but if dipping food into a pan of boiling oil is not your idea of a fun meal, there are other things to choose from. Air cured beef, another ethnic speciality, turned out to be rather chewy but the veal cooked in cream and Pernod was most pleasing with a hint of aniseed, and the Rosti, crisply fried cakes of grated potatoes, are a must. Sadly there were no Swiss chocolates to go with the coffee.

Surprise
12 Great Marlborough St, W1 (434 2666)
AMERICAN
Mon-Sat 12 noon-3.00, 6.00-11.15; Sun 11.45am-2.45.
Food £15. Wine £4.95.
The only surprise at Surprise is its mediocrity. I had been told I could look forward to a real American Salad, you know the sort I mean, a massive bowl filled with iceberg lettuce, crisp vegetables, diced chicken or perhaps some Virginian baked ham drowned in a delicious dressing. So I tripped off to the help-yourself salad bar full of anticipation. What a disappointment; limp lettuce, woolly tomatoes, mealy potatoes — need I go on. My friends chose more wisely — the pan-fried liver was enlivened by a hint of rosemary although the halibut was fighting a loosing battle, taste-wise, with the spiced butter. We perked up for puddings; ice-cream with a dreamy hot fudge sauce, and the Surprise Dessert, chocolate fudge cake brownie topped with ice-cream and chocolate sauce had us all fighting for second tastes. On Sunday they do an all-American Brunch with Blueberry Muffins, Corn Beef Hash and Waffles which sounds a 'neat' idea.

The Swiss Centre
2 New Coventry St, W1 (734 1291)
SWISS

The Swiss Centre is confusing. There are five restaurants, all with the same Alpine look, and each offering variations on a Swiss theme — at differing prices.

The Chesa
Mon-Sun 12 noon-3.00, 6.00-12 midnight.
Food £17. Wine £5.50.
This, the most elegant of the five, serves international food, as well as more traditional Swiss dishes. Service is helpful; set menus change monthly.

Rendez-Vous, Locanda and the Taverne
Mon-Sun 11.30am-12 midnight.
The Rendez-Vous is ideal for the hurried shopper; service is brisk and efficient. The bias is to Swiss-German cuisine, with dishes such as toggeburgers, toasts with various toppings, as well as cold and hot snacks and coffee. There is a business lunch (£2.20), with a 20% discount for those who pay their bill before 12.45.
The Locanda represents the Italian area of Switzerland, serving pasta and fish dishes, and zabaglione — made in front of the customer.
The Taverne is French in style, with raclette and fondue on the menu.
The Swiss Imbiss opens at 8.30am for breakfast, serves coffee, croissants, Swiss-German sausages, and snacks, and remains open until midnight.

Tiddy Dols Eating House
2 Hertford St, W1 (499 2357)
ENGLISH

Mon-Sun 6.00-2.00am.
Food £24. Wine £3.95.
Named after the eighteenth century gingerbread man who peddled his wares in Shepherd's Market, Tiddy Dols has gone overboard with its historical connections. Set in a series of Georgian houses which have been knocked through and subsequently ruined in the process, it serves up solid British food. There's Isabella's Emerald Soup (a thick mixture of leeks, spinach, celery and onions with cream provided unless 'your waist is more important than the taste') or Quiche Lorraine, which they claim is of Anglo-Saxon origin. For the main course there's the usual selection of Roast Beef, Leg of Lamb, Cock-a-Leekie, Steak, Kidney and Mushroom Pies etc. Puddings are high on stodge; Tiddy's Original Gingerbread, Suet Pudding, Strawberry Jam Pudding, Apple Dumpling; and for those of fainter appetite tropical Fruit Salad which they can justify as the fruit that comes from 'our ex-colonies'. Tourists seem to love it, although I find it a little too expensive for what it is.

Trattoria Dei Pescatori
57 Charlotte St, W1 (580 3289)
FISH
Mon-Tue 12 noon-3.00, 6.00-10.30; Wed-Sat 12 noon-3.00, 6.00-11.30.
Food £21. Wine £4.50.
Even if you can't translate the name, there's no mistaking that this is a fish restaurant as just about everything fishy is hanging from the ceiling.

Nets, lobster pots, boats, even a massive stuffed swordfish all contribute to an air of exuberant abandon which only the Italians manage to create. The food is also rather high spirited — sea food salads heavily laced with garlic; mussels drowned in white wine, and lasagne bursting with fish and cream. The main courses are rather more subdued, a perfectly grilled sole or red mullet cooked in wine with capers or a restrained steamed turbot with Hollandaise sauce. There's plenty of choice for fish eaters but lovers of meat may be a bit disappointed — there's nothing but steak to choose from.

Trattoria Terrazza
19 Romilly St, W1 (437 3334)
ITALIAN
Mon-Sun 12 noon-2.30, 6.00-11.30.
Food £19. Wine £3.95.
This is the original trendy trattoria opened in the late sixties by Mario and Franco (remember them) and designed by Apicello. It was the precursor of what was to come in their thousands up and down the country. Look-alike restaurants sprung up complete with tiled floors, stark walls, directional lighting and informal smiling waiters. Time has marched on since then but the Terrazza hasn't changed. It's no better or worse than its clones, but you ought to go as it is a landmark in restaurant history.

Vecchia Milano
74-77 Welbeck St, W1 (935 2371)
ITALIAN
Mon-Sat 12 noon-3.00, 6.00-11.00.
Food £13. Wine £4.35 (litre).
Part of the Spaghetti House chain (although after the siege at Knightsbridge, it's not something they shout about), Vecchia Milano is divided in two. Upstairs is the proper restaurant with waitress service, comfy chairs and a not terribly original menu — antipasto, pasta etc and according to a friend of mine, the best ossobucco for miles. Downstairs is the Tavola Calda, a sort of up market self-service where promising stuffed peppers, fritto misto et al can be had at approximately two-thirds of the posh price. It seems an enterprising idea which is repeated at another branch in the West End; Tavola Calda, Villa Carlotta, 33-34 Charlotte St, W1 (636 6011).

Veeraswamy
99-101 Regent St, W1 (734 1401)
INDIAN
Mon-Sun 12 noon-3.00, 5.30-10.30.
Food £20. Wine £4.90.
Whilst the food is not terribly grandiose (tandoori, chicken and lamb vindaloo, Prawn Biriyani and all the usual run-of-the-mill dishes, albeit better cooked than normal) the place certainly is. Perching above Regent Street, it is decorated like a Maharaja's palace with exquisite tablecloths with matching napkins from Rajastan and a traditional punka (fan) made from yards of flimsy fabric, suspended from the ceiling. After all those rude jokes about bad taste Indian decor, Veeraswamy is a pleasure.

La Vie En Rose
10 Charlotte St, W1 (631 4916)
FRENCH
Mon-Sat 12 noon-2.30, 7.00-10.45; closed Sat lunch.
Food £14. Wine £3.90 red, £4.20 white.
Le patron is a great Piaf fan, hence the name, the larger-than-life portraits and the music. But don't be put off even if you can't stand the 'Little Sparrow' as the food is extremely good value especially if you stick to the set menu. There's a choice of three starters and three main courses; we tried pate which was surprisingly good and a crisp salad of french beans and potatoes dressed in olive oil, followed by pork and red cabbage which was full bodied if a little overcooked, and a perfectly pleasant chicken. Puddings are superb and homemade; creme caramel and a pear tarte with a light almond filling were 'on' that day, but they do change everything regularly.

White Tower Restaurant
1 Percy St, W1 (636 8141)
GREEK
Mon-Fri 12.30-2.30, 6.30-10.30.
Food £24. Wine £4.50 white, £5.25 red.
This is tasteful up-market Greek. Not a bousouki in sight — just a few choice prints and a painting of Byron (in his

ethnic headgear) as the only give-away signs of this restaurant's origins. The food is what we long for from every taverna but never quite get — taramasolata that actually tastes of cod's roe, moussaka which is light and crisp and lamb kebabs which are tender and lean. There are some more unusual dishes — Poussin Roti Farci au Bourgourie (Poussin stuffed with almonds, chicken livers mushrooms and flavoured with spices) and Fish Kebab a la Polita (Turbot marinated in wine, olive oil and bay leaves). The menu is a gossipy read — did you know that Aubergine Iman Bayaldi is named after an Iman who ate so many aubergines one day that he bayeldeed (passed out). Hang on to it for inter-course entertainment as service can be a little slow.

BUDGET

The Agra
135-137 Whitfield St, W1 (387 4828)
INDIAN
Mon-Sun 12 noon-3.00, 6.00-12 midnight.
Food £9. Wine £3.70.
The Agra hasn't changed much since I was a student around the corner and used to eat there regularly. It is still very good value for money. You can fill up on enormous Keema Nans and popadums for a couple of pounds or splash out on their Tandoori Chicken which is just as moist and tasty as ever. Either way

the waiters will leave you undisturbed to debate through the night.

Averofs
86 Cleveland St, W1 (387 2375)
GREEK
Mon-Sat 12 noon-3.00, 6.00-10.30.
Food £8.50. Wine £4.50.
Unless you know where you're heading you might miss Averofs. It doesn't look much from the outside, a dumpy shop front hidden in a veil of nets; but once you're in, you'll find a small homely place where you'll be made to feel most welcome. It's trad taverna, but everything is cooked to order and their loukanika (sausages) and bastourma (spiced sausages) are the freshest in town.

Cafe Creperie
26 James St, W1 (935 8480)
FRENCH
Mon-Sun 12 noon-12 midnight.
Food £10. Wine £3.95.
In summer there's heavy competition with Coconut Grove, their next-door neighbour, as they both spill onto the pavement, cluttering it with chairs and umbrellas — but it keeps both places on their toes. As its name suggests Cafe Creperie is devoted to crepes (although there are steaks/salads/dishes of the day): the crepes are substantial (if not rather too heavy) and there are plenty of imaginative fillings to choose from — 15 savoury and 12 sweet. They are liberal with the alcohol; the Martinquaise, a slightly sickly mixture of ice-cream, bananas and almonds

was drenched in creme de cacao. They open at 10.00am for continental breakfast with fresh croissants.

The Chicago Pizza Pie Factory

17 Hanover Sq, W1 (629 2669)
AMERICAN
Mon-Sat 11.45am-11.30.
Food £10. Wine £3.70.

To quote their own publicity, 'The Chicago Pizza Pie Factory is designed for people who enjoy eating good food and having a good time.' You may have to queue for your good food (they only take bookings for lunch up until 12.30) and shout above the din of Chicago radio tapes to have a good time, but who cares? The pizzas have very thick crusts and are still as good as ever. And they don't stint on the ingredients: the speciality — cheese and sausage — was fairly weighed down. One criticism is that the cheesecake doesn't live up to its promise of 'a little bit of heaven': it's oversweet and a touch synthetic.

Chuen Cheng Ku

17 Wardour St, W1 (734 3509)
CHINESE
Mon-Sun 11.00am-11.45.
Food £8. Wine £3.70.

Everyone has their favourite Chinese restaurant — this is mine. It's a vast place with endless rooms and dour-faced waiters who seem to go out of their way to be unhelpful; but the Dim Sum, make up for everything. Dim Sum are those delicate steamed dishes served on bamboo trays piled one on top of the other which are simply delicious. Actually the Chinese consider them as snacks and consequently only serve them during the day, leaving the evenings free for more serious food. Catch them between 11.00am and 5.00 and you won't be disappointed. Order a good selection; my favourites are Steamed Duck Dumplings and Stuffed Char Siu (bite-sized buns stuffed with a spiced barbecued pork). If you're still hungry fill up with the Mixed Meat Noodles - it's more of a soup than you'd expect from its description, with slices of meat (pork, duck and beef) swimming in a subtly spiced stock.

Cranks Healthfood Restaurant

8 Marshall St, W1 (437 9431)
HEALTH FOOD
Mon 10.00am-8.30; Tue-Sat 10.00am-11.30.
Food £9. Wine £3.88.

Cranks is a health food/vegetarian restaurant par excellence. Bowls of fresh salads, all organically grown, crunchy 100% wholewheat bread, home-made soups, daily savouries (usually stuffed vegetables or slightly leaden quiches) and an irresistible selection of death-to-a-diet cakes (gluttonous carrot is especially good). The only thing is that it does have the rather unfortunate image common to all restaurants of this ilk — it's just a little too serious for comfort. But to give them their credit they are trying to liven things up with candlelit evenings (Tue-Sat only).

Fatsos Pasta Joint
13 Old Compton St, W1 (437
1503)
ITALIAN
Sun-Thu 12 noon-11.30; Fri-Sat
12 noon-12.30am.
Food £9.50. Wine £3.75.
*The menu here is almost
entirely devoted to pasta, and
the portions are generous. You
can choose both the shape of
the pasta — spaghetti,
fettucine, fusilli, farfalle, and
so on — and the sauce,
peasant, meatball, clam,
prawn, to name but a few.
Vamped up in neo-diner style,
Fatsos is rather lacking in
atmosphere. It is not a place
for traditionalists.*

The Granary
39 Albermarle St, W1 (493
2978)
INTERNATIONAL
Mon-Fri 11.00am-7.00; Sat
11.00am-2.30.
Food £7.50. Wine 70p (a
glass).
*This is self-service stripped
pine with generous portions of
good, wholesome food.
Everything is home-made,
quiches, salads, pates, soups
and hot savouries and they are
justly proud of their cakes and
sweets. You can avoid the
queues if you try them at tea-
time, but be warned, the
cakes might all be gone.*

**The Gurkhas Tandoori
Restaurant**
23 Warren St, W1 (388 1640)
INDIAN
Mon-Sun 12 noon-2.45,
6.00-11.30.
Food £9. Wine £3.50.
*Just off the Euston Rd is this
cheery Nepalese restaurant,
frequented by regulars. The
food is delicious. Begin with
the Onion Bhajee and
Papadums, and then take your
pick from an extensive list of
main dishes. I especially
enjoyed the Murgh Mussalum,
mild chicken cooked in spices
with cream. I would
particularly recommend the
Lassi (a very refreshing
yoghurt drink) with the curry;
and the Mango Kulfi with
cream — quite a treat. At
lunchtime they serve spiced
tea (not on the menu). This is a
fun and lively (ghoulish
Nepalese masks affixed to very
busy wallpaper) restaurant; it
would be a good place to
come with a crowd of friends,
but as it is small booking
would be advisable.*

Justin De Blank
54 Duke St, Grosvenor Sq, W1
(629 3174)
FRENCH/ENGLISH
Mon-Sat 8.30am-3.30, 4.30-9.00.
Food £11. Wine £3.35.
*If you don't mind a touch of
the self-service, try Justin de
Blank. It's every bit as good as
his food shop but much better
value. Everything is freshly
cooked and looks most
tempting. There are plenty of
starters — soup pates, mousses
and plump mushrooms
marinaded in his own
imported olive oil which has a
superbly strong nutty flavour.
There's a choice of cold meats
with mounds of fresh salads
and about six hot dishes.
Vegetarians please note that
they always serve at least one
meatless main course.
Puddings are quite excellent,
fruit brulee or chocolate fridge*

cake — a concoction of chocolate, crumbled biscuits and chopped fruit. It's also open for breakfast — fresh croissants and brioche — and for tea, so you could always go back for a second helping of pudding.

Ley Ons
56 Wardour St, W1 (437 6465)
CHINESE
Mon-Sun 11.30am-11.30.
Food £10. Wine £4.70.
It's worth getting a group of friends together to try one of their special dinners as they are exceptionally good value. We sat down to the dinner for six; but it probably could have fed that amount (and one of us is known for a delicate appetite). We started with a thick crabmeat and sweetcorn soup, swiftly followed by crunchy prawn crackers and a splendid pork in a sweet spiced sauce. There was chicken with cashew nuts, which was a little insipid, but the Beef with Black Bean and Chilli was excellent. The Duck was heavy on fat and thin on flesh but we all pronounced Prawns with Celery, and Fishballs with stir fried Vegetables quite as good as anything we'd had before. They were more than generous with the bowls of fried rice and filled up the huge pot of Jasmine Tea endlessly.

La Perla
28 Brewer St, W1 (437 2060)
ITALIAN
Mon-Sat 11.30am-9.00.
Food £8. Wine £3.80.
Opposite Rupert St market La Perla is to be found nestling between some of Soho's more outrageous sex-shops. It's not that salubrious inside — red plastic banquettes and formica tabletops — but serious pasta eaters shouldn't be put off as it serves up some of the most imaginative sauces in town. There's tagliatelle, Marinara, a sharp, salty sauce of olives, anchovies, tomatoes and aubergines or Boscaiolo, a rich stewed sauce of mushrooms, tomatoes and herbs. Peperonata is understandably popular as it's a satisfying blend of peppers and bacon, as is the Cannelloni alla Grigliais filled with spiced beef. Another favourite based on a Sicilian recipe is Risotto al burro con Sardine e Piselli, (rice with sardines and peas) which sounds awful but actually tastes a dream.

Poons
4 Leicester St, WC2 (437 1528)
CHINESE
Mon-Sat 12 noon-11.30.
Food £8. No licence.
This is the original Poons as opposed to the more up-market one in Covent Garden (no relation). Actually they are moving in that direction in a couple of weeks (see above for new address) to what they term a 'larger and smarter room'. Let's hope it won't affect the prices or the standard. Their speciality, Wind Dried Foods — duck, pork, liver, Chinese bacon and sausages — are an acquired taste, but once you've acquired it, you'll be hooked for life.

Smiles
16-17 Jermyn St, SW1 (734 7334)
AMERICAN
Mon-Sun 10.00am-12 midnight.
Food £9.50. Wine £3.95.
Smiles — within striking distance of all the West End cinemas — is a useful place for a late meal after the movies. It's under new management and is undergoing a re-vamp (American prohibition style) and a menu change. I had a sneak preview and it looks promising — plenty of salads, Cock a Doodle Doo Nibbles (barbecued chicken wings), hamburgers and a chocolate fudge cake which purports to be 'richer than Paul Getty'.

Tudor Cafe
45 Lexington St, W1 (437 7262)
ENGLISH
Mon-Fri 7.30am-5.30; Sat 8.00am-1.30.
Food £4.60. Unlicensed
When does a caff stop being a caff and become a restaurant? If the standard of food is anything to go by, this one has arrived and I bet it's the only caff to boast a cook who once worked at the Savoy. The style is basic British; Irish stew, boiled beef and carrots although I noticed the odd plate of chilli-con-carne had crept in. Unfortunately at the moment it's only open until late afternoon, but perhaps popular demand will persuade them to stay the course through till supper.

Le Verde Valle
74 Wardour St, W1 (437 3519)
ITALIAN
Mon-Sat 12 noon-3.00, 6.00-11.30.
Food £10.50. Wine £3.75.
It's always a squash at lunchtime but the evenings are far more spacious. The menu is pretty standard but the thing to watch out for are their daily specials. They always include some form of fresh pasta and it's generally very good. We struck lucky and arrived on the Tortelino day. Tortelino, for those who have never had the good fortune to try it, are tiny round parcels of pasta stuffed with spinach and riccotta. These were quite splendid (the spinach had just a hint of nutmeg) and were cooked 'al dente' and covered in cream.

Widow Applebaum's
46 South Molton St, W1 (629 4649)
AMERICAN DELI
Mon-Fri 10.00-10.00; Sat 10.00-6.00.
Food £11. Wine £2.50.
It rates a good second to a genuine New York Deli with the best Pastrami sandwiches this side of the pond. There are some other pretty amazing stateside specials — B.L.T. (bacon, lettuce and tomato sandwich, for the uninitiated) and Salmon on 7th (smoked salmon on wholemeal bread with Russian dressing). Dustin Hoffman and other famous deli freaks always pop in when they're in town.

TRANSPORT

(All details subject to change. Phone 01-222 1234 at anytime, day or night to check details. Some routes shown do not

operate every day of the
week.)

OXFORD STREET (WEST)
Tube: Marble Arch, Bond
Street or Oxford
Circus
Buses: 1, 2, 2b, 6, 7, 8, 12, 13,
15, 16a, 23, 73, 74, 88,
113, 137, 159, 500, N89,
N91, N94.

OXFORD STREET (EAST)
Tube: Oxford Circus or
Tottenham Court Road
Buses: 1, 7, 8, 25, 73

REGENT STREET
Tube: Oxford Circus or
Piccadilly Circus
Buses: 3, 6, 12, 13, 15, 23, 53,
88, 113, 159, 500, N89,
N91, N94

BOND STREET
Tube: Bond Street or Green
Park
Buses: 25 or 1, 6, 7, 8, 12, 13,
15, 16a, 23, 73, 88, 113,
137, 159, 500, N89,
N91, N94 — to Oxford
Street or 9, 14, 22, 38,
55, N97 — to Piccadilly

SOUTH MOLTON ST/ST CHRISTOPHER'S PLACE
Tube: Bond Street
Buses: 1, 6, 7, 8, 12, 13, 15,
16a, 23, 25, 73, 88, 113,
137, 159, 500, N89, N91,
N94 — to Oxford Street

PICCADILLY
Tube: Green Park or
Piccadilly Circus
Buses: 9, 14, 22, 25, 38, 55, N97

SOHO
Tube: Piccadilly Circus,
Leicester Square or
Tottenham Court Road
Buses: 1, 7, 8, 25, 73 — to
Oxford Street (East) or
1, 14, 19, 22, 24, 29, 38,
55, 176 — to
Cambridge Circus

TOTTENHAM COURT ROAD
Tube: Tottenham Court
Road, Goodge Street
or Warren Street
Buses: 14, 24, 29, 73, 134, 176, N90

KHAN5

Marylebone and Bayswater is an area of contrasts. It is characterised, to the west of the Edgware Rd, by its tall, stuccoed Regency terraces and older style apartment blocks. Bedsits and cheap tourist hotels are interspersed with expensive service flats for the wealthier of London's populace, and the polyglot mixture of inhabitants range from long-standing residents to foreign students and tourists. Westbourne Grove and Queensway, the two main areas of activity, offer a variety of eating places; fast-food establishments in the form of fish and chip bars and pizzerias, and the ubiquitous hamburger houses vie for trade alongside restaurants and cafes sporting ethnic cuisines. Indian, Chinese, Malay, Greek, Iranian, Italian, German and Czechoslavak food can all be found. The area to the east of the Edgware Rd is typified by the Georgian Squares and the private clinics: altogether more prosperous, it lacks the vitality of its left-hand flank. The restaurants are of a higher quality, catering less to passing trade — unless they be well-heeled tourists from the grander hotels — and more to local residents

35

and, at lunch times, to the businessman and his expense account.

LUXURY

Didier
5 Warwick Place, W9 (286 7484)
FRENCH
Mon-Fri 12.30-2.30, 7.30-10.30.
Food £25. Wine £3.95.
Tucked away in Warwick Place, between Warwick Avenue and the Canal, is Maison Didier — a small cosily-run restaurant, clearly dedicated to the provision of good French cooking and homespun atmosphere. There is an old pine dresser to house the desserts, flower print wallpaper, and a feeling of quiet welcome. The menu is varied: eight specialities du jour for starters, and five for the main course, as well as the standard menu. There is no hint of 'la nouvelle cuisine' here: most of the dishes are rich with delicious cream sauces, and the vegetables are cooked in butter — but the result is sometimes more than one can manage. The house wine is very good value at £3.95. Come here for lunch, and visit the bookstore next door.

Odin's Restaurant
27 Devonshire St, W1 (935 7296)
FRENCH
Mon-Sat 12.30-2.30, 7.00-11.15, closed Sat lunch.
Food £38. Wine £5.
Peter Langan's gallery-cum-restaurant, where the artists sit at the tables and the food reflects the talent, has a rich and creative menu which is frequently changed. Like their cousin next door, there is a Patrick Proctor painted menu, which will tempt you with feuillete of asparagus with chervil, seabass pate, duck breast with raspberry vinegar, mushroom pate en brioche, and crayfish fricassee with fresh chanterelles. Odin's is stylish, grand and obviously expensive: the ultimate restaurant in which to impress your companion.

MID-PRICE

Le Bistingo
117 Queensway, W2 (727 0743)
FRENCH
Mon-Sat 12 noon-3.00, 6.00-12 midnight; Sun 12 noon-2.30, 7.00-11.00.
The first of the great chain bistros, Bistingo now seems a little worn at the edges, and on a visit after a long gap, the coq au vin tasted as though it had been waiting for me all that time. In a narrow candle-flickering room, with a wooden floor, and the menu written on the blackboard, one can have rabbit, pepper steak, tuna and bean salad, and a vanilla ice, trickling dark and decadent with chocolate and nuts. There are other branches at: 5 Trebeck St, W1; 56 Old Brompton Rd, SW7; 65 Fleet St, EC4.

La Brasserie
68 Queensway, W2 (727 4037)
FRENCH
Mon-Sun 12 noon-3.00,
6.00-11.30.
Food £12.50. Wine £3.80.
*Of all the brasseries in
London, this probably least
deserves the label, since it
doesn't attempt to serve
breakfast and tea, even at
weekends, and is small and
quiet in a way no brasserie
should be. A green facade,
awning, mirrors, and an
intermingling of pasta on the
menu are not enough.
Nevertheless, the plain French
food is well-cooked, and
includes lemon sole and
calves' liver. The starters —
avocado, egg mayonnaise,
fried mushrooms with tartare
sauce — are good, if
predictable. Have the citron
sorbet for pudding, and avoid
'sweets from the trolley'.*

Bunga Raya
107 Westbourne Grove, W2
(229 6180)
MALAYSIAN
Mon-Sun 12 noon-3.00,
6.00-11.30.
Food £12. Wine £4.40.
*This is an immensely clean,
rather spartan restaurant,
reminiscent of a private
screening room — the screen
in this case showing the rush
of cars along Westbourne
Grove. Unobtrusive, recorded
music, and the most courteous
service make this a relaxing
place to come in the evening. I
would recommend starting
with a Satay and the delicious,
but small, Spring Rolls; there
is a wide selection of main
courses to choose from. There*

*are flowers on the table:
essentially though this is a
restaurant to which you should
bring your own colour.*

Canaletto
451 Edgware Rd, Little
Venice, W2 (262 7027)
ITALIAN
Mon-Sat 12.30-3.00, 7.00-11.00,
closed Sat lunch.
Food £19. Wine £3.95.
*At one corner of the canal is
this light and airy restaurant,
just the place to come at
lunchtime or on a balmy
summer evening. The
presentation of the food is a
delight; the service cheerful.
Begin with the Canelloni, filled
with a creamy cheese sauce,
and then select the pollo
sorpresa perhaps (breast of
chicken with butter and
garlic), or the scaloppina alla
valdostana. There is a very
tempting selection of sweets
from the trolley.*

Le Chef
41 Connaught St, W2 (262
5945)
FRENCH
Tue-Sat 12.30-2.30, 7.30-11.30;
closed Sat lunch.
Food £20. Wine £2.90.
*If you choose a restaurant by
appearance you might walk
straight by this one, though
regulars have been coming
here for years. In a friendly
and informal atmosphere,
savour the Soupe de Poisson
or Champignons a la Greque;
and follow with Poulet
Basquaise, Entrecote au
poivre, or Rognons Dijonnaise.
Proceed to Coupe de Peche,
sorbet or a glace, but leave
room for the impressive*

cheese board, the likes of which are seldom seen even in more expensive restaurants. The set menu on Saturday night is excellent value (even with VAT and service charge). It is advisable to book.

Chez Franco
3 Hereford Rd, W2 (229 5079)
ITALIAN
Mon-Sat 12.30-2.30, 7.00-11.00; closed Sat lunch.
Food £17. Wine £3.90.
Photographs of celebrities, many signed, hang from the walls of this cosy restaurant; smiling genially, they offer warm welcome to the diner turning in here from Westborne Grove, as do the hosts, Bruno and Carlo. The food is well-presented, and simple. One might start with Truite Marinee a L'Oignon, Sherry et Vin Blanc, or a pasta dish (served also as a main course), and follow with Supreme de Volaille a La Kiev, stuffed breast of chicken with butter, parsley and lashings of garlic. There is a good selection of puddings, and coffee to follow. Attentive service and soothing strains of piped Italian music encourage one to linger; although it is equally possible to eat here quickly before going on elsewhere.

Concordia Notte
29-31 Craven Rd, W2 (723 3725)
ITALIAN
Mon-Sat 12 noon-3.00, 6.00-11.45.
Food £17. Wine £2.70.
The outside is rough white plastering and spiralling yellow panes of glass, that were once the sign of all Italian restaurants, before Apicella and his dentist-style caught on. The inside is ironed primrose tableclothes, darkened paintings, stiff-backed chairs, and careful service. The menu is just as classic: saltimbocca al romana osso buco, fegato veneziana, gnocchi, tagliatelli and zabaglione. I recommend ordering something quite simple — clams or fritto misto, to start, then river trout grilled with butter and sage. Finish the meal with a perfect creme caramel.

Le Dodo Gourmand
30 Connaught St, W2 (258 3947)
MAURITIAN
Mon-Sat 12.15-2.30, 7.15-10.30; closed Sat lunch.
Food £22. Wine £4.50 (Set lunch £9.50 inc per person).
They advertise the cuisine as Franco-Creole, and serve typical island dishes, as well as less spicy ones. The service is attentive and unobtrusively efficient, the surroundings pleasant if uninspired. The Bouillabaisse, well-flavoured with fennel, is recommended as a starter, though we were disappointed by the muted flavours in some of the other Creole dishes. We had Carri de Porc and Pot-au-Feu de Volaille, and the same brown, floury sauce appeared on both. Complimentary pineapple cocktails are provided on arrival, but this did not make up for the poor and unimaginative meal that followed.

MARYLEBONE & BAYSWATER

Green Jade
29-31 Porchester Rd, W2 (229 7221)
CHINESE
Mon-Sun 12 noon-11.30.
Food £15. Wine £3.85.
A neat Chinese restaurant with a very large menu of some two hundred Peking (Northern) and Canton (Southern) dishes. The service (10%) is friendly and efficient, but uninformative. Inexperienced patrons confused by the multiplicity of choice are likely to be directed to the set menus (£6.95 and £7.95). Some preliminary research in Kenneth Lo's excellent Chinese Provincial Cooking *is therefore recommended. For example, if you like garlic, duck or lamb, choose a Pekinese dish; if you prefer ginger, dogs (not available here!) or fish, choose one of the many Canton dishes offered. I particularly enjoyed the whole crab (£4) with black bean sauce and fried rice.*

The Hellenic
30 Thayer St, W1 (935 1257)
GREEK
Mon-Sat 12.30-2.30, 6.30-10.30.
Food £15. Wine £4.
This is a two-tiered restaurant with a clattering, noisy, bistro feel about it, but thankfully no do-you-remember-last-summer folksy music. Apart from the usual hoummus, taramasalata, moussaka and avgolemono try their fish kebabs, afelia, and sweet lamb dishes. Those diners with a sweet tooth should leave enough room for baclava.

Kalamaras
76-78 Inverness Mews, W2 (727 9122)
GREEK
Mon-Sat 7.00-12 midnight.
Food £17. Wine £4.50.
Hidden away just off Queensway is this charming, low-ceilinged restaurant where the food is excellent and bazooki plays when it feels like it, and not when the tourist demands. The menu is in Greek — though ever-patient waitresses will interpret — and includes the traditional taramasolata, and spanakotyropites (spinach and cream cheese in layers of flaky, hot pastry), keftides (fragrant, herby meatballs), crunchy kalamares (squid), and the best dolmades in the city, served with yoghurt and raw tomato. If you are still hungry have the melt-in-the-mouth lamb or fresh sea bass; then baclava oozing with honey, nuts and calories; bitter coffee and loukoum. If you want a romantic evening, or a fun evening with a group of friends, in a truly Greek ambience, come here. At No 66 Inverness Mews (727 9122) is another Kalamaras, run by the same family, and with similar food, but cheaper, rougher and unlicensed.

Khyber
56 Westbourne Grove, W2 (727 4385)
INDIAN
Mon-Sun 12 noon-3.00, 6.00-12 midnight.
Food £12. Wine £4.75.
For those people who have only a nodding acquaintance with Indian food, the Khyber

39

makes a very good spring board for a closer look; the menu is quite short and informative, the service charming. Try the Lamb Pasanda Nawabi, a mild lamb curry cooked in cream, or the Chingiri Jhol, king prawns in a delicious sauce. There is a selection of pulses and beans, or rice, to choose from; and the usual array of Indian desserts. There are flowers on the tables, and candles in the evening.

Langan's Bistro
26 Devonshire Place, W1 (935 4531)
FRENCH
Mon-Sat 12.30-2.15, 7.00-11.00; closed Sat lunch.
Food £16. Wine £4.
Probably one of the most intelligent places to have a civilised lunch, Langan's Bistro is quietly Parisian with faded nostalgic photographs upon the wall. From a painted menu (Paul Kasmin eating pea soup by Patrick Proctor) choose sweet pasta with tiny shrimps, soft and fluffy lemon sole quenelles with hollandaise sauce, sliced fillet with green peppercorns, crunchy vegetables, and if there is room enough and time, the legendary Mrs Langan's Chocolate Pudding.

Mandarin Kitchen
14 Queensway, W2 (727 9012)
CHINESE
Mon-Sun 12 noon-1.30am.
Food £11. Wine £4.80.
At the greener end of Queensway is this large Cantonese restaurant, with bubbling tanks of greeny-mauve live lobsters, spinning transparent shrimps, and fat fish ready for the steaming cauldrons. The interior is in a duller vein: it has a sleek, airport style. As the tanks would suggest, the fish is best - steamed bass, baked crab with ginger and spring onion, fried squid in black bean sauce. The carnivore should have the hot and sour soup, fried chicken with Chinese mushrooms, and sliced beef with bitter melon. The true adventurer is the one who embarks on the lonely voyage of braised duck's web with fish's lip. And the best of luck to him.

Le Mange Tout
34 Sussex Place, W2 (723 1199)
FRENCH
Mon-Sat 12.30-2.30, 6.30-10.30; closed Mon lunch.
Food £18. Wine £4.25.
Le Mange Tout is a small light green space in a corner of the quiet grand part of Bayswater. Since they buy and choose the fish themselves each morning at the market, fish is the main song. Try the melting crepe de crabe in a light sauce, ragout de poissons (a small bouillabaisse) and grilled monkfish. Hot avocado is quite the thing to start meals with; here it is en papilotte with cheese and prawns. There are set menus (£7.95 for dinner, £6.50 for lunch) where you can eat very well on langoustine soup, merlot dori (whiting with prawns and clams), puddings such as profiteroles, fresh pineapple, or lemon brulee, and then coffee. There are

alcoves downstairs for those who want to keep business to themselves.

New Lee Ho Fook
48 Queensway, W2 (229 8624)
CANTONESE
Mon-Sat 12 noon-11.15.
Food £15. Wine £5.
The Cantonese were ever a fractious and turbulent people: no better is this trait demonstrated than by the crisp and immediate management of this restaurant, contrasted with the subtle and satisfying result from the menu. Enjoyed properly, a Cantonese meal resembles a medieval siege; first the solid ordinance of Crab and Sweetcorn Soup *were advanced to undermine the foundations of any acute hunger; then the precision implements of* Sliced Beef with Scallions, Diced Chicken with Cashew Nuts *and* Braised Duck *are employed to rout any remaining cravings; lastly, the senses lie supine before the consolidation of victory:* Green Tea, Mai Toy *and* Lychees. *The meal was accompanied by hot 'Shogun' Sake and highly attentive service, with a cost of around £7 per head.*

Le P'tit Montmartre
15-17 Marylebone Lane,
Wigmore St, W1 (935 9226)
FRENCH
Mon-Sat 12 noon-2.30,
6.00-11.00; closed Sat lunch.
Food £18. Wine £4.90.
Business men come here for lunch; families for dinner. I come as a treat after visiting my dentist. Choose from Pate

de Volaille, Oeufs Benedictine, and then perhaps the Truite aux Amandes, Filet de Boeuf Oriental, two fillets (one covered in a delicious spicy sauce, the other in a Madeira sauce), or the Steak Tartare. The vegetables are crisp and fresh; the puddings tempting. Have the Crepes Suzette (for two). There is also a short menu that changes weekly. This is a restaurant for the well-heeled lover of first-rate French food.

Semiramis Restaurant
4 Hereford Rd, W2 (727 4272)
GREEK
Mon-Fri 12 noon-3.00, 7.00-12 midnight; Sat-Sun 7.00-12 midnight.
Food £15. Wine £4.50.
An unqualified 'yes' to this small, cheerful Greek restaurant just off Westbourne Grove, much favoured by regulars, who are perfectly happy to sit at tables packed closely together. I would suggest starting with Halloumi, a grilled cheese dish, or the Taramosalata and hot pitta bread. To follow there is Moussaka; they call it 'the best in town', and it may well be. The Kleftiko (tender lamb cooked in wine and spices) — 'the food of thieves — so delicious it's worth stealing for' — and the Dolmades are also excellent. Delicious Greek salads are served with the meals; the very hungry and adventurous should order the Greek Meze (£5.90) and sample a broad range of dishes. There are not many desserts; but I can firmly recommend the Baklava. At lunchtimes there

41

are numerous non-Greek 'specials' in accordance with some chosen theme. A take-away service is available, as is catering for parties (for which they like advance warning).

BUDGET

Al Khayam
27/29 Westbourne Grove, W2 (727 5154)
INDIAN
Mon-Fri 12 noon-3.00, 6.00-12 midnight; Sat-Sun 12 noon-12 midnight.
Food £10. Wine £3.90.
Al Khayam lies on the same stretch of Westbourne Grove as Khan's, is less crowded and less smoky. Unhurried, courteous service, and beautifully prepared food, kept warm at the table on small burners, more than compensate for what it lacks in atmosphere. Begin with Onion Bhajee and Keema Nan, filled with cooked mince meat. For those who like mild curries, Chicken Korma and Lamb Pasanda are both very good, as is the Chicken Muglai, listed as a Chef's Suggestion, and cooked with spices and topped with nuts; for those who like their curry hot there are Vindaloos aplenty. (Fortunately the restaurant is licensed). There is a broad selection of vegetables, and the usual Indian sweets; have the Kulfi and then coffee. There is also a take-away service.

Baba Bhelpoori House
118 Westbourne Grove, W2 (221 7502)
INDIAN
Tue-Fri 12 noon-3.00, 6.00-10.30, Sat, Sun 12 noon-10.00.
Food £6. Unlicensed.
Conveniently placed next to the Westbourne Odeon, this is a good place to come for a snack before or after the cinema. It is clean and spartan, serving vegetarian food to 'regulars'. The food is tasty and professionally put together: have bhajias, an onion and potato fritter, and a dosa, a stuffed pancake, with a choice of accompaniments. There is a set meal — the Gujrati Style Thali (£2.60) — which is excellent value; and a take-away service. The vegetables tend to be over-cooked; but the sauces are light; the service helpful. Try it.

Diwana Bhel Poori House
50 Westbourne Grove, W2 (221 0721)
INDIAN
Tue-Sun 12 noon-3.00, 6.00-11.00.
Food £5.50. Unlicensed.
This is probably the neatest, cheapest and most delicious place to find vegetarian Eastern food, and where one comes to prove to people that there is more to vegetables and curry than just a cinema snack, and that lassi is no dog. Dip beyond the darkened window to a fairly stark interior, and feast on a richly tempting mixture of chick pea, black pea fritter, mango, saffron, rice pancake, sour

sauce, lentil soup and strange breads. Lazybone choosers should have the Thali, a set menu for £2.75. Then simmer down with kulfi — Indian frozen milk, studded with nuts, chopped fruit and spices. Take-aways are also provided for the quick at heel.

Khan's
13-15 Westbourne Grove, W2
(727 5420)
INDIAN
Mon-Sun 12 noon-3.00, 6.00-12 midnight.
Food £8.50. Wine £3.25.
Hot and speedy curries are served here in cracked Empire glory — pillars, dark wood, white tablecloths, huge palms and a turning ceiling fan. When John Mortimer praised its food and charms in the Sunday Times, the cool crowd crushed in, and arriving late will almost certainly involve queuing for a table. The food, however, can be delicious, especially the tandooris. It is advisable to take a seat as early as possible in the curving window at the front — the back room is rather dull and claustrophobic — where one can watch the seedy drift of Westbourne Grove. Keep an eye open for the waiters with trolleys, for they can be lethally quick. Khan's is not the place it used to be.

Mehran Indian Restaurant
115 Westbourne Grove, W2
(727 8938)
INDIAN
Mon-Sun 12 noon-2.00am.
Set lunch: £1.25; set dinner £2.10 & £2.70. Wine £3.50.

A restaurant caught in the poverty trap, recommended for anyone similarly trapped who enjoys a quiet lunch on his own. The atmosphere of westernized oriental vagueness and decay vividly evokes some of the Pakistani chapters of Naipaul's Among The Believers. The set lunch offers a choice of soup or popadum, followed by meat, chicken or vegetable curry or pillau. My chicken pillau was well cooked and very good value at £1.25.

The Standard
23 Westbourne Grove, W2
(727 4818)
INDIAN
Mon-Sun 12 noon-3.00, 6.00-12 midnight.
Food £10. Wine £3.99.
In a street alive with Indian restaurants, this is the oldest and the most traditional. Inside darkness prevails and the waiters are famous for their insolence (my knives and forks were flung down with a dismissiveness that was almost charming). It is best to restrain the temper and concentrate on the food which is often excellent — mutton tikka, spicy sagwala chicken (with spinach), and melting butter chicken. Round off the meal with fresh mango or rasmalai.

Pizza Express
The Colonnades, Bishops Bridge Rd, W2 (229 7784)
ITALIAN
Mon-Sun 12 noon-12 midnight.
Food £6.50. Wine £3.20.
This is a largish branch of the acclaimed pizza chain, recognised by the circular

marble tables, cheese plants and bright red wooden chairs. As the pizzas are cooked open-plan the sweet smell of tomato and oregano may well entice more than the edible result; though the dough is usually crisp. Have a capricchiosa with extra pepperoni and chillis, and several glasses of Peroni beer (the wine can be very rough). Remember the name for a hungry gap just before midnight. There are other branches at: 30 Coptic St WC1;

Satay House
13 Sale Place, W2 (723 6763).
MALAYSIAN
Mon-Sun 12 noon-3.00,
6.00-11.00.
Food £10. Wine £3.80.
Satay House combines log cabin with roadside caff (though a face-lift is underway) — a curious blend for a Malaysian restaurant, serving Tiger Beer from glasses inscribed with RAF Alconbury Suggestion Program. The food is absolutely authentic. Begin with Satay, the traditional Malay kebab, served with a peanut sauce; then try Dending, beef marinated with spices, or Ayam Percik, chicken cooked in coconut cream, and Pajri Nanas, sweet and mild pineapple curry. Finish with an interesting sweet — particularly recommended are Ice Kacang, Rambutan and Sagu Gula Melaka. Two, or more, people can order the formidably extensive set menu (£5.50 a head). Friendly service and piped Malaysian music add a final touch.

Sea Shell Fish Bar
33-35 Lisson Grove, NW1 (723 8703)
FISH
Tue-Sat 12 noon-2.00;
5.30-10.30.
Food £6 (restaurant); £3.50 (take-away). Unlicensed.
Fish restaurant and separate take-away just off the west end of the Marylebone Rd, and opposite the Labour Exchange, deservedly popular both with lovers of really good well-cooked fresh fish and connoisseurs of fish-and-chips. The two very respectable married ladies at my lunch table had come from some distance, seemed to do this regularly, and ended up by taking home fish-and-chips for their husbands' dinner. The restaurant has recently been redecorated with unexpectedly successful rustic cork walls. Quick, friendly service; tips appreciated but not expected. A wide choice of fish in season, including Dover Sole (£4.10) and Halibut (£3.70) is available if you arrive early. By 1.30 the special dish of the day — Cornish Hake Cutlets — was 'off', but I can recommend the Skate (£2.40). Chips are included. Mediocre coffee. The fresh cream gateau (60p) looked delicious; only those with gargantuan appetites will have room for it.

TRANSPORT

Tube:	Bayswater, Queensway, Paddington, Marylebone, Edgware Rd, Baker St
Buses:	1 (Mon-Fri only), 2, 2b, 3, 13, 27, 30, 53, 74

CHRISSEW SUNKISSED RESTAURANT

Notting Hill Gate is a curious area, a mixture of high chic at the Holland Park end and low tat up past the Westway (although strictly speaking this part is dismissed as North Kensington). Its restaurants reflect these social niceties; there are a few that are expensive and lush, a few real cheapies and plenty of mid-range bistros/trattorias which span the rent-a-flat land in between. As far as food is concerned, it's certainly not the culinary centre of London. It does boast some gems which are worth travelling across London for; but there are several in the OK-to-eat-there-for-a-quick-and-cheap-meal category which is exactly what you want from a neighbourhood restaurant.

LUXURY

L'Artiste Assoiffe
112 Kensington Park Rd, W11
(727 4714)
FRENCH
Sat 12 noon-2.30, Mon-Sat
6.30-11.00
Food £27. Wine £4.40.
*Like most people you'll
probably think you've walked
into the wrong place — but it is
a restaurant not an antique
shop, although that's a very
understandable mistake!
Everywhere you look there are
cunningly arrranged
collections. Victorian ewers
and kitchen utensils balance
precariously and fairground
horses prance around the
tables. L'Artiste Assoiffe
certainly wins hands down on
the clutter. The food, in
comparision, is not nearly as
imaginative and is cooked with
a somewhat heavy hand. But if
you're after a jolly rather than a
culinary evening — I would
certainly try it.*

Leith's Restaurant
92 Kensington Park Rd, W11
(229 4481)
INTERNATIONAL
Mon-Sun 7.30-12 midnight.
Food £42. Wine £6.80.
*As the flag ship of Prue Leith's
fleet (there's a cookery school,
catering company, numerous
books etc) the restaurant
reflects her imaginative style of
cooking — not that the admiral
has time to cook anymore. The
set menu is quite short — five
starters, eight main courses -
but it's nicely balanced and
well cooked and presented.
There's a heavily laden hors
d'oeuvre trolley with a rich
ballotine of duck, a smooth
lemony avocado mousse and
apples bulging with dressed
crab meat. The chicken breasts
stuffed with pistachio mousse
are light and delicately spiced
and the breast of pheasant
moist and most flavoursome.
Puddings are described as
'dorm feast' but obviously we
never went to the same school:
plenty of creamy syllabubs, hot
orange and lemon souffle, and
for those of fainter appetite a
passion fruit sorbet. The wine
list is comprehensive with some
good value full-bodied red
Rhones, the service is attentive
and the decor everything you
would expect from an
'international' restaurant. Try it
for a special occasion or when
you can wangle an expense
account.*

MID-PRICE

Chez Moi
3 Addison Ave, W11 (603 8267)
FRENCH
Mon-Sat 12.30-2.30, 7.00-11.30
(not Sat lunch)
Food £24. Wine £4.85.
*A classic French restaurant
with no nonsense or frills but
with plenty of emphasis on
good food. As the chef/part-
owner told me with
disingenuous honesty, 'We
have been criticised for not
changing our approach but I
don't believe in this nouvelle
cuisine'. The result is that some
of the dishes may be a little
rich and heavy on the cream
and butter for some people's
taste but if you order carefully*

you will have an excellent meal. Carre d'Agneau (rack of lamb stuffed with garlic and mint) is to be recommended and you can order it pink, very pink or very, very pink!

Franco Ovest
3 Russell Gdns, W14 (602 1242)
ITALIAN
Mon-Sat 12 noon-2.30, 7.00-11.30 (not Sat lunch)
Food £22. Wine £3.75.
*Peppered at lunchtime with BBC executives, this must be a good place to eat if you're an aspiring TV star. Actually it's worth going anyway as it is a pleasant restaurant with enjoyable food. There's a wide selection of fresh fish — sardines, sea bass, squid, pacific prawns, scallops — both as a starter and a main course. Try Calamari Luciana (squid with a **very** garlicky tomato, olive and wine sauce) or Trotella Spaccata (trout with prawns and clams in white wine). Stick to the house wine, it's estate bottled and cheap at the price.*

Jonathan's
71 Blythe Rd, W14 (602 2758)
FRENCH
Mon-Sat 12 noon-2.30, 7.00-11.00 (not Sat lunch) Sun 12 noon-3.00.
Food £22. Wine £3.75.
Jonathan's is a very relaxing restaurant. Upstairs is the bar (note the early pair of Pears prints by W Coleman; most covetable); downstairs is a subdued brown and cream colour scheme, candles and soothing songs by Neil Diamond and others of his ilk. For total tranquillity book one of the alcoves, but wherever you sit you'll have a calm quiet evening — it's that sort of place. Specialities include Rognons Henri IV (kidneys filled with bearnaise sauce) and Poulet au Scampi (Chicken sauteed with Scampi and lobster sauce). The wine list is quite special — they buy their clarets from Christies and have obviously struck lucky. Jonathan's also serve lunches (£4.95 plus service daily or a Sunday special for £5.95 plus service).

Julie's
135 Portland Rd, W11 (229 8331)
ENGLISH/FRENCH
Mon-Sat 12.30-2.30, 7.45-11.15 (not Sat lunch) Sun 12.45-2.15, 7.45-10.15
Food £21. Wine £4.85.
If ever I had to write about the social colonisation of a restaurant, Julie's would make a perfect case history. In the 70s it was the place for the smart-art set (rub shoulders any night with PM, David Hockney et al); when they moved on the Hooray Henrys adopted it as one of their hang-outs. Nonetheless Julie's has withstood the changes; it's still the prettiest restaurant in London and the creme brulee is still the best ever. You can also hire their private room. Bookings are for a minimum of 16 and a maximum of 24. They insist on a deposit of £3.50 a head; allow plenty of notice as they get quite busy.

Le Detour
5 Campden Hill Rd, W8 (937 9602)

FRENCH
Brasserie: Mon-Sun
10.00am-11.30;
Restaurant: Mon-Sat 7.30-11.00.
Food £22. Wine £5.85.
I advise you to take a detour and come here — there's excellent food to be had. It's divided into two parts with one side a brasserie and the other an adjoining restaurant. The former opens at 10.00am with fresh coffee and the best croissants in town (from Pechon in Kensington Church St). Lunch is served from 12.30 and you can eat either all three courses on the set menu (£8.95) or choose what you want (two starters etc) and pay accordingly. Tea is to be had in the afternoon with delicious French cakes and tartes; then at 7.30 dinner is served. The set menu (and it changes from lunch) at £12.80 for three courses and a half litre of wine offers a variety of dishes but you could also eat a la carte. The restaurant which is quieter and more formal only serves the a la carte menu and although it's a much lusher place (carpets, soft seats) it doesn't cost any extra to eat there. Explaining the logistics has left me with no space to eulogise about the food. Suffice it to say I ate a truly memorable salad of green beans and fresh walnuts doused in walnut oil. So why not try it for yourself?

Mama San
11 Russell Gdns, W14 (602 0312)
CHINESE
Mon-Sun 12.30-2.30, 7.00-11.30
(not Sat lunch)
Food £17.25. Wine £4.50.
Don't eat upstairs unless you enjoy an unimpeded view of wall-to-wall traffic hurtling down Holland Road. Insist on the basement, it's far more relaxing and most un-Chinesey — white-washed walls, cane chairs, palms etc. There's a prix-fixe menu (£7.50 a head plus service) with a rather uninspired choice of the usual favourites — chicken and cashews, roast barbecue pork; but try the toffee apples; groaning in caramel with sesame seeds they're every dentist's dream but your fillings' nightmare.

Monsieur Thompson
29 Kensington Park Rd, W11
(727 9957)
FRENCH
Mon-Sat 12.30-2.30, 7.30-10.30.
Food £24. Wine £4.50.
Monsieur Thompson's is for lovers of good food. The menu — although not large — is full of delicious treats and everything is prepared with immense care and concern. I tried Steamed Spinach and Slices of Smoked Chicken and although both ingredients were of the best quality, together they did not make a successful marriage. My partner in indulgence had Chicken Liver Pate with Truffles which we both rated the best in London. For a main course I chose Sliced Breast of Duckling with Green Peppercorn Sauce, served slightly pink with a delicate creamy sauce a la cuisine nouvelle. My friend opted out and ate a light M Thompson Winter Salad, a colourful plate of crisp winter vegetables and leaves dressed in a strong olive

oil dressing. For pudding there are splendid home-made tartes, Alsacienne Apple Tarte with Calvados or a caramelly (which is exactly how it should be) Tarte Tatin; or there is a groaning cheese board with over 15 French cheeses including several goat cheeses, a creamy Brillat-Savarin and Epoisse Attine from Michel our waiter's village in Burgundy. There's nothing pretentious or stuffy about Monsieur Thompson's. The food is neither too nouvelle or too bourgeoise and it has a standard of excellence which many restaurants should aspire to.

Pomme D'Amour
128 Holland Park Ave, W11 (229 8532)
FRENCH
Mon-Sat 12.30-2.00, 7.00-10.30 (not Sat lunch)
Food £23.50. Wine £4.80.
The manager oozes Gallic charm the minute you walk in the door and from then on, you just know you're going to be cosseted. It's 'veery romantique' candles, soft lights, open fire and a stunning courtyard out at the back which used to be their garden, but British summers are what they are, so they covered it over. There's a seasonal menu which changes three times a year and daily specialities. I enjoyed a smoked trout mousse with a light watercress sauce and a crisply cooked duckling with a fresh sweet/savoury pineapple sauce. The vegetables are all cooked 'al dente' and there's a good choice. For pudding I

recommend the Raspberry and Cassis sorbet — it's so refreshing that you almost feel you could start your meal all over again.

Rama Sita
6 Clarendon Rd, W11 (727 9359)
INDIAN
Mon-Sat 12 noon-2.30, 6.00-11.00.
Food £18. Wine £3.99 (Carafe)
It is immediately apparent that this is an unusual Indian restaurant. The walls are hand-painted with the legend of Rama and Sita; the menu tells not only their story, but also informs one of the very special style of cooking of the chef and patron Monsieur Ali Ashraf. The various dishes are taken from different periods of history and regions of India, and are quite different to the standard Indian style of cooking. Sharp spices, such as chilli and curry power, have here been replaced with more delicate and light imported herbs. We chose a set menu, which came with the SAS (Speciale Aphrodisiaque Sauce), and a fascinating briefing from Monsieur Ashraf. Opinions will vary as to his success; we were all agreed that it had been a gratifying and interesting meal out. I would prescribe that everyone tries it once — some will want to return.

Topo D'Oro
39 Uxbridge St, W8 (727 5813)
ITALIAN
Mon-Sat 12 noon-3.00, 6.00-11.30, Sun 12 noon-3.00, 6.00-11.00.
Food £16. Wine £3.60.

Tucked away in a basement, at least this is one Italian restaurant without white-washed walls, tiled floors and harsh spotlights; although there isn't an awful lot more to say in its favour. Everything was mediocre; the tortellini in brodo was heavy and dull, the stuffed aubergines rather dry. I perked up for the Scaloppine Pizzaiola as the sauce was quite rich and tomatoey but the Petti di Pollo Topo D'Oro (breast of chicken in breadcrumbs deep fried and stuffed with butter, ham, parsley and garlic) was minus its ham. The sweet trolley looked as tired as the waiter pushing it, the cheeses were most ordinary and the biscuits stale. What more can I say?

BUDGET

Balzac Bistro
4, Wood Lane, W12 (743 6787)
FRENCH
Mon-Sat 12 noon-2.30,
7.00-10.45, closed Sat lunch.
Food £9.80. Wine £3.75.
With three set menus to choose from (£6.25, £8.25 and £9.75) Balzac's certainly packs them in. It's a hive of activity, waiters whisk around narrowly averting dreadful damage to the parasols which crowd the place. The food is good for the price (that's not meant to be as damning as it sounds) and I plumped for the middle-priced menu as the most tempting. Stuffed mushrooms swimming in a sea of garlic butter were just the right texture (it's so easy to overcook them and

reduce them to rubber), the Rib of Beef was a little overcooked but then I like it dripping in blood. The puddings are adequate although the much vaunted Profiteroles Stuffed with Icecream were a disappointment. They do change one or two dishes a week — so it's worth trusting your luck.

Bistro Valerio
10 Phillimore Gardens, W8
(937 4542)
FRENCH/ITALIAN
Mon-Sat 12 noon-3.00,
6.00-11.00 Sun 12 noon-2.30,
7.00-11.00.
Food £12. Wine £4.65.
This must be the only restaurant to boast a 'pipi room', it's writ large on the door for all to see. Apart from that I couldn't find a lot to recommend it; the menu is French/Italian and not very exciting at that although I was amused by the topical Escaloppe a la Prince Charles (veal with mushrooms and tinned asparagus in a white wine sauce with not a hint of cherry brandy £3.55). The set lunch is cheap — pate or soup, a choice of roasts and two vegetables or lasagne and salad and coffee £3.80 — stop there on a Sunday after a walk in Holland Park!

The Caribbean Sunkissed Restaurant
49 Chippenham Rd, W9 (286 3741)
CARIBBEAN
Mon-Sat 12 noon-3.00,
6.00-11.00
Food £13. Wine £2.85.

It's a real gem. Decorwise, there's kitsch clutter everywhere (view the outrageous twirl carpets and the basement murals) but it's very clean and neat. The food is sensational, with stunning soups – velvety pumpkin, fiery pepperpot and sharp spinach calalou. There's a good choice of fish — Calypso Mullet was very tasty with the fish cooked to perfection and Hurricane Chicken which had certainly got wind of the rum. The vegetables were unusual — dasheen, breadfruit, cho-cho — but were excellently cooked and very fresh. The waitresses could be more helpful, everything was described as 'in a sort of sauce', curried goat as 'actually lamb', and coats were brought when they wanted to leave! Hurry along, it's newly opened and deserves support.

Cassidy's
6 Holland St, W8 (937 3367)
AMERICAN
Mon-Sun 11.00am- 12.30am
Food £8. Wine £3.90.
This is one hamburger joint where the music is not too loud and they don't try to hustle you out. The hamburgers are 'great' according to my young 'companion' who reckons to be an expert in such matters and he enjoyed his sophisticated 'Burgundy', topped with mushrooms, tomatoes, herbs and red wine. They also serve specials — steak sandwiches, quiche and a selection of salads. I tried cottage cheese and it was a generous portion and terribly healthy. The ice-cream was 'OK', but I noticed that the plate was wiped clean and seconds were asked for. What's worth remembering is that you can drop in anytime and provided it's not too busy, they're perfectly happy to serve you with just a cup of tea.

Costas Grill
14 Hillgate St, W8 (229 3794)
GREEK
Mon-Sat 12 noon-10.30
Food £7.00. Wine £3.20.
Costas scores heavily in the summer as there's a garden out in the back where, under a jasmine tree, you can tuck into Sheftalia to your heart's delight dreaming of balmier nights on the Greek Islands. In winter, it's a little drab, formica tabletops and wooden benches inside; but the food is very good value. You'll find all the old favourites — humous and taramasalata with hot pitta bread, keftedes (meatballs), kleftico (lamb), moussake and a rather tough sikotakia (slivers of liver in wine). It's not worth upsetting Costas so order his excellent greek coffee and greek delight to go with it — Costas is very patriotic! He has recently opened **Costas Fish Restaurant**, a couple of doors up; it is clean and inviting and one can either order a take away, or eat there in a light and airy room at the back.

Geales Fish Restaurant
2 Farmer St, W8 (727 7969)
ENGLISH
Tue-Fri, 12 noon-3.00, 6.00-12 midnight, Sat 12 noon-3.00, 6.00-11.00.
Food £7.00. Wine £2.80.
Be prepared to queue to share a table, but it's worth it as

Geales serves excellent fish 'n' chips in old world surroundings. The fish, coated in a crisp, crunchy batter, is very fresh and the chips — although cut a little thick for my taste — are still diet defyingly delicious. Puddings are of the boarding school variety but the apple crumble is made with cinnamon and comes covered with a cloud of cream. Watch out for the specials — they're written on the wall — as they sometimes serve shark!

Globe Restaurant
103 Talbot Rd, W2 (794 4832)
ENGLISH/WEST INDIAN
Mon-Sun 8.00-5.00am.
Food £6. Unlicensed.
The Globe restaurant is to be found in the nether regions of Notting Hill Gate. Roy Stewart, a former Mr Universe, is the proud owner; with all that body building he is — no doubt — up to coping with any neighbourly aggro. Once safely inside you'll find walls emblazoned with his former triumphs (there's a particularly arch pose hanging above the juke box), a fine example of 'plastic art' surrounded with flashing lights and a collection of homilies painted merrily around. With such visual treats, it's hard to comment on the food (and I defy anyone to go for a serious eat) but there's a choice of pleb English or West Indian.

Holland Street Restaurant
33c Holland St, W8 (937 3224)
ENGLISH
Mon-Fri 12 noon-2.30,
7.00-10.30.
Food £4.40 lunch, £6 dinner.

Wine £4.
A small place with the emphasis on home cooking and a friendly atmosphere. There's a set menu both for lunch and dinner with a choice of two dishes for each course. Everything is fresh, cooked to order and patriotically English. I ate a perfectly pleasant smoked haddock pate and a Veal with Caper Sauce which did more to mask than enhance the flavour of the meat. It's not the most inspired of restaurants but their local customers always seem to come back for more.

Holy Cow
38 Kensington Church St, W8 (937 2005)
INDIAN
Mon-Sun 12 noon-2.30, 6.00-11.45.
Food £12. Wine £4.
Holy Cow is new wave Indian or to quote Kenny Everett, 'Look folks, no flock wallpaper'. Upstairs they have a cocktail bar where, with typical Indian insouciance, the bartender claims to have up to 2,000 cocktails at his fingertips — some lush ought to put him to the test. After that, weave your way down to the restaurant; Tandoori is the speciality — chicken, lam, prawns and more chicken or there's a mix with a selecton of the above. It's good if not rivetingly original.

Mildred's
135 Kensington Church St, W8 (727 5452)
ENGLISH/FRENCH
Mon-Sat 12 noon-3.00,
7.00-10.30 (not Sat lunch)
Food £12. Wine £3.75.

When I noticed the micro-wave nestling behind the bar, my heart sank; but I was somewhat reassured when informed that 'It's only used to heat up the apple pie, everything else is freshly cooked.' Actually the food is perfectly competent bistro, with daily specialities added to a moderate sized menu. There's nothing unusual (steak and kidney pie, sweet and sour pork, marinated mushrooms, chicken liver pate etc) but the meat is fresh from the country where the owner has a tame butcher and the quality for the price is above average.

Obelix
294 Westbourne Grove, W11 (229 1877)
FRENCH
Mon-Sun 12 noon-11.00.
Food £9.50. Wine £3.45.
Obelix is working hard at changing its image from a creperie to 'more of a bistro which happens to serve crepes'. What that means is that now they have a selection of daily dishes (casseroles, pasta, barbecue spare ribs) as well as plenty of galettes (buckwheat pancakes) and straight crepes. The former have savoury fillings ranging from the luxurious smoked salmon, caviar and sour cream to plain cheese, whereas the latter are sweet with such delights as black cherries and ice-cream or stewed apple with calvados. It's very handy if you're in the Portobello Road.

Olivers
10 Russell Gardens, W14 (603 7645)
INTERNATIONAL
Mon-Sun 12 noon-10.00.
Food £13. Unlicensed.
Olivers is a good place to go if you want to linger over the meal. In fact they seem to encourage it! It's relaxed and very friendly, with everyone, waiters and customers alike, on first name terms. The menu is bog standard bistro — soups, pates, boeuf strogonoff, steaks — but everything is freshly cooked and all the main courses are served with two vegetables. Lunchtime lingerers can stay on for tea (served between 2.30-6.00) and indulge in the delicious homemade chocolate and creme de menthe cake. There's no license, so don't forget to take your bottle, corkage charge is only 30p.

Savvas Kebab House
7 Ladbroke Rd, W11 (727 9720)
GREEK
Mon-Sat 12 noon-3.00, 6.00-11.30.
Food £7. Wine £3.30.
A family concern run by Savvas, whose twirling moustache merits more than a second glance, and his wife. There's dolmades (stuffed vine leaves), avgolemono (chicken and lemon soup) and taramasalata for starters and almost all the main courses are cooked on the charcoal grill. The chicken is particularly succulent and you can order a generous portion of Horiatiki (greek salad with feta cheese) to accompany it. Puddings comprise the usual unpronounceable cakes on sale at most of the supermarkets in

53

London which is probably where the ones I tasted came from ie they're no better or worse than most. In summer — weather willing — the tables spill out onto the pavement but on winter nights Savvas does his utmost to transform the not terribly salubrious surroundings by the cunning use of candlelight.

Tootsies
120 Holland Park, W14 (229 8567)
AMERICAN
Mon-Sun 12 noon-12 midnight.
Food £8. Wine £3.25.
Tootsies is an up-market hamburger joint, frequented by a young and lively crowd, and decorated with old posters, even a moose head or two. The food is very American, and very good: meaty hamburgers (particularly delicious is the Blue Cheese Sauce); thick milkshakes; and generous desserts (have the Hot Chocolate Fudge Cake). Or try a Tootsies Special Salad; a BLT; Quiche; or perhaps a steak. And for the under-10s there is a small hamburger, with small accompaniments, at a tiny price. The service is efficient and friendly, which makes it possible to either grab a quick bite to eat, or to linger. There are other branches at: 115 Notting Hill Gate; 48 High Street, Wimbledon Village; and 117 New King's Road, Parsons Green. They all provide a take away service; the Holland Park Tootsies caters for breakfasters, with The Eye Opener — orange juice shake with raw egg, 'for those who did and wish they hadn't' — and fried eggs, bacon, toast etc, 'for those who didn't and wish they had!'

TRANSPORT

(All details subject to change. Phone 01-222 1234 at anytime, day or night to check details. Some routes shown do not operate every day of the week.)

Tube: Notting Hill Gate, Holland Park, Ladbroke Grove

Buses: 7, 12, 15, 23, 27, 28, 31, 52, 52a, 88 **Night:** N89

THE ARK

Central Kensington has always been a strange area for restaurants (I leave out West Kensington which, unfortunately, seems to be a culinary desert). General inaccessibility (bottle-necks at Knightsbridge and at the Royal Garden Hotel, busy traffic at Hammersmith, complicated one-way systems) and the fact that it is not really 'a night out in the West End', have meant that it is an area which is patronised mainly by locals. And, as the old Colonels' pensions have dwindled, and more and more houses have been converted into bed-sits,

restaurants have been forced to keep up with the 'restricted' times. So High St Kensington, for instance, is now a row of fast food joints. There is clearly little room for a really First Class restaurant such as the admirable Le Bressan (which closed last December). As Alex Grant of this once highly fashionable restaurant has commented: 'The clients make grand promises to return, and then they forget their dinner as soon as they go to the lavatory'. It seems extra concessions do have to be made to attract the ephemeral customer if you

55

are not part of an established chain (from the generous Bistro Vino *and* Bistingo *to the more up-market* Wheeler's *and* Mario and Franco's).

So we find the recently-opened Quai St Pierre *has a downstairs oyster bar,* L'Estanquet *has an upstairs cocktails and appetizers bar and a disco. People are more and more in search of fun as well as food, so they go to restaurants like those above or, perhaps, to the* Texas Lone Star Saloon, *where they can listen to Country and Western music and thus 'escape'. The next most popular alternative seems to be a visit to one of the new Chinese restaurants that have sprung up recently:* I Ching, Crystal Palace, *and* Tiger Lee, *to name but three. These have a different atmosphere altogether, one that has much to do with 'formal informality'.*

However, with all this, the battered facades of the old Eastern restaurants (The Curry House *and the* Kuo Yuan *in the Earl's Court Rd) still stand. Alongside the long-established French and Italian restaurants — from* La Toque Blanche *and* Chanterelle *to* Gondoliere *and* Casa Porrelli — *one wonders how they survive in the face of 'modernity'.*

LUXURY

Alcove
17 Kensington High St, W8
(937 1443)
FISH
Mon-Sat 12.30-2.30, 6.30-10.30.
Closed Sun.
Food £27. Wine £3.95.
Wheeler's is a well-established and deservedly successful chain of restaurants. These always stick to their proven standards of comfort, culinary reliability, and efficiency of service. However, they rarely surprise favourably on any of these three counts either. The Alcove has a green and white facade and plushy red dining-room that characterise the chain. Here M Rene Guano (no relation to the 'Dr Strangelove' figure) will guide you through, for example, 10 varieties of lobster and 23 of sole, including the 'unique' Sole Alcove (with a filling of prawns, mushrooms, smoked salmon, and white wine sauce). Have the Meuniere version of any of the fish (it will be the simplest and the best) don't expect to rave about the vegetables or puddings; drink the good house white; and impress the visitor from abroad (from the Royal Garden Hotel oppsite) who is bound to be at the adjoining table.

Al Gallo d'Oro
353 Kensington High St, W8
(603 6951)
ITALIAN
Mon-Sun 12 noon-3.00, 7.00-12 midnight.
Food £21. Wine £3.75.

You can rely on an enthusiastic welcome from Renato and Marcello and their staff and a generally sympathetic atmosphere at this most attractive of Apicella-designed Italian restaurants. The service can occasionally be affected adversely by a 'full house', but will remain enthusiastic and cheerful as you order excellent Antipasto (Hors d'Oeuvre) from the trolley, 'dream' Pagilia e Dieno alla Crema (home-made green and white pasta) perfect calves' liver alla Veneziana, or select from the dishes of the week. These can surprise both ways: very well-prepared Agnolotti with butter and sage, and delicious sweetbreads, and then very disappointing Scallops Bercy. If you want a relaxed and smart Italian dinner out and want to spot the occasional 'face', come here. You won't be sorry.

Chanterelle
119 Old Brompton Rd, SW7
(373 5522)
FRENCH
Mon-Sun 12 noon-2.30, (Sun 12.30-3.00),7.00-12 midnight.
Food £21. Wine £3.95.
The old disused library next door has been closed for years. Chanterelle has been here for much longer. But a change of owner has ensured that it has kept pace, and is deservedly still very popular. Loyal regulars return to this attractive wood-panelled and green-carpeted restaurant that is always busy, serving often delicious but perhaps sometimes over-elaborate dishes from a frequently changing menu, such as pheasant's chestnut broth, celeriac's scallop soup, roasted pidgeon with orange and cinnamon, sweetbreads, and rack of lamb. There are set lunches at £4.50 every day (£6.50 on Sun).

I Ching
40 Earls Court Rd, W8 (937 0409)
CHINESE (all areas)
Mon-Sun 12 noon-11.30.
Food £21. Wine £4.50.
'Every aspect of the food has been analysed from its palatableness to its texture, from its value to its effectiveness, and from its fragrance to its colourfulness, until as in other works of art proportion and balance are instilled in every dish'. This may sound like a tall order, but the experienced manager (from 'Tai-Pan') and chef (from Hong Kong) of this relatively new restaurant have set themselves very high standards which, in almost all cases, they have achieved. The atmosphere is elegant, with grey carpet and pink tablecloths; upstairs was more rough and ready on my last visit. The menu promises much, with dishes with names such as 'Ants Climbing Up Tree', and, although gluttons might find the helpings rather small, the food is often simply perfect. Try starters such as sliced pork with garlic and chilli sauce Szechuan-style or minced quail wrapped with lettuce; then have the Nam King Duck served in two stages and a variety of main

KENSINGTON

courses: delicious noodles;
wonderful sea-bass; incredibly
tender beef fillet sauteed with
fruity sauce (unbeatable!).
Even that normally 'tired old
favourite', sweet and sour
crispy pork, is given a brilliant
new lease of life. Service is
very good, although wine
glasses can be refilled with
over-bearing haste. If you want
an expensive and smart, but
totally delicious, Chinese night
out, look no further.

Le Quai St Pierre
7 Stratford Rd, W8 (937 6388)
FISH
Wed-Sun 12.30-2.30. Mon-Sun
7.30-11.30 (Sun 7.30-11.30)
Closed Mon, Tue lunch.
Food £24.Wine £5.50. No
credit cards.
*The perfect place to imagine
you are no longer in grimy
London. Like its sister
restaurants, La Croisette and
Le Suquet, you immediately
feel it's really summer, as you
enter through the take-away
section of fresh fish and ready-
prepared dishes, and either sit
at the downstairs bar or in the
small upstairs dining-room
(thoughtfully enlarged by a
vast mirror along one wall).
Friendly service from T-shirted
waiters and jazzy recorded
music encourage one to feel
expansive and wade through
the gigantic Plateau de Fruit
de Mer and any number of
fish specialities: excellent
mussels and scallops prepared
in various ways; all sorts of
very fresh fish (turbot, skate,
brill etc) crayfish tails or crab
in flaky light pastry
(occasionally perhaps not
shelled carefully enough) and*

finally the wonderful 'Quai St
Pierre Special' — a fresh fruit
and raspberry sorbet, and
then framboise poured on top.
Save yourself the exorbitant
airfare to Cannes or Nice; and
come here a few times
instead.

Sailing Junk
59 Marloes Rd, W8 (937 2589)
CHINESE (Cantonese/Peking)
Mon-Sun 6.30-11.30
Food £21. Wine £4.25
*Walk down the leafy path that
leads into the Sailing Junk, and
you are suddenly a thousand
romantic miles away. This very
popular restaurant has
cornered the market in the set-
menu category: there is no
menu. Efficient, pretty,
friendly waitresses bring
course after delicious course
of the compulsory (£9.60)
Dragon Festival dinner; ten
courses in all, including spicy
meatballs and sesame prawn
toast as starters; then the
steamboat (chicken, lettuce,
chestnut and bamboo shoot)
soup cooked over sizzling
water at your table; noodles;
spare ribs; various well-
prepared 'standard Chinese'
main courses; toffee bananas;
and orange sorbet presented
in a pineapple case. Candles,
warm flannels, Eastern music:
all these little attentions make
for a memorable evening for
two (or four...or six...)*

Tiger Lee
251 Old Brompton Rd, SW5
(370 2323)
CHINESE
Mon-Sun 6.00-11.30.
Food £25. Wine £5.60.
This is probably the most

formal and luxuriously smart Chinese restaurant in London, and the prices correspond. However, as you admire the spotlit pictures on the relaxing pale walls and the first-class service, you will not be disappointed by the many original dishes, such as roast duck fillet with lychee and beef fillets with mango. The seafood, though, is the highlight; follow your 'Rainbow Beancurd Chowder' with the wonderful sea-bass or sweet-and-sour deep-fried fish, accompanied by any of the perfectly-cooked vegetables. The dinner, like many of the dishes' names ('Shadow of Butterfly') will be spectacular.

La Toque Blanche
21 Abingdon Rd, W8 (937 5832)
FRENCH
Mon-Fri 12.30-1.45, 7.00-10.45.
Food £26, Wine £4.40.
The menu never changes and the fanatical regulars always pack it out. La Toque Blanche has a long-established loyal following, and this is not surprising from the moment one enters M Giovagnoli's informal, warm, relaxed restaurant. Start with the Fish Soup or the deservedly popular Seafood Pancakes; follow with Breast of Duck with grapes, crayfish tails with herbs and cream, or Stuffed Chicken; finish with the famous cheeseboard or puddings like the Mont Blanc. As the wine-list is also much to be admired, you can be sure of a successful lunch or dinner out.

Ark
35 Kensington High St, W8 (937 4294)
FRENCH
Mon-Sun 12 noon-3.00, 7.00-11.30. Closed Sun lunch.
Food £16. Wine £2.95.
While the restaurant premises next door change hands with alarming rapidity, the Ark remains constant. Perhaps Noah ate here. If he did, he would have undoubtedly enjoyed the same classy French Bistro atmosphere upstairs that makes this restaurant such a perennial favourite. (Downstairs is more 'universal' in feel). While you admire the French prints and the dark wood panelling, order dishes from the short menu such as Quenelles Saunce Nantua and Oeufs en Cocotte, followed by the Supreme de Volaille Gastronome (!) or the excellent Rack of Lamb with herbs. After eating here, if you're not feeling 'bourgeois', you probably are.

L'Artiste Affame
243 Old Brompton Road, SW5 (373 1659)
FRENCH
Mon-Sat 12.30-2.15, 6.30-11.15.
Food £19. Wine £4.40.
There is a welcoming rustic atmosphere in this attractive, busily-decorated restaurant. Suspended rocking horses, antiques, a log fire in winter, and, above all, friendly service help you to relax and enjoy provincial French cooking of some style, such as the famous

spinach, almond and cheese pancakes, the charcoal-grilled beef fillet glazed with Dijon mustard and brown sugar, and the roast duck with black cherry sauce.

Casa Porrelli
1a Launceston Place, W8 (937 6912)
ITALIAN
Mon-Sat 12 noon-12.30, 6.00-10.30.
Food £18. Wine £3.90.
This is one of Kensington's well-established favourites. Recently expanded, it is comfortable and pleasant, the service is good, and the menu offers few surprises. But the pasta, insalata tricolore, and 'standards' such as osso bucco alla milanese are more than adequately prepared, and make you want to return. There is a menu of the day at £5.55.

Company
242 Old Brompton Rd, SW5 (373 3730)
ANGLO/FRENCH
1.00-3.00 (Sun) 7.15-12.30am (Mon-Sun).
Food £18.50. Wine £4.50.
Definitely not the place for tweed jacketed young men to bring their 'Lady Di' lookalikes from the opposite Coleherne Court, Company begs an alternatively 'single-minded' type of male customer. At the same time, it is unique in this area (if not in most of London) in possessing a surprisingly mellowed and relaxed feel. Upstairs, Mike Riser sings and plays songs by Manilow, while you relax at the Piano Bar, drinking Brandy Alexanders

or whatever takes your fancy. Downstairs there is a smart soft-grey coloured room, where a short menu offers soup and salad starters, followed by well-presented 'standards' such as Blanquette de Veau and Grilled Salmon Trout. On Sundays, there is a £12.50 set-price dinner that also includes cabaret from 'weighty' artistes such as Diana Dors and Dana Gillespie.

Crystal Palace
10 Hogarth Place, SW5 (373 0754)
CHINESE (Peking and Szechuan)
Mon-Sun 12 noon-3.00, 7.00-12 midnight.
Food £17. Wine £4.50.
The Chelsea Rendezvous, Paper Tiger, and Tai Pan (three of London's more successful 'smarter' Chinese restaurants) are the background for the chef of the Crystal Palace — a fine pedigree and a very fine restaurant. You are immediately struck by the friendly, helpful service and the delicacy of the decor, polished wooden floor, pink rose tablecloths. Indeed, everything on the Peking and Szechuan (hot) menu that you have seen in other restaurants seems to have been improved upon here. The Griddle Fried Pork Dumplings and (very hot) Crispy Beef Shreds with Chillies and Carrots are miraculous, the Szechuan Duck, and Prawns in Garlicky Black Bean Sauce are excellent, and even standard dishes such as the fried

'Seaweed', and the toffee bananas seem to taste better than ever. Go immediately; this restaurant cares.

L'Estanquet
158 Old Brompton Rd, SW5 (373 9918)
FRENCH (Gascon)
Mon-Sat, (Upstairs) 12 noon-3.00, 6.00-2.00 (cocktails and appetisers);
(Downstairs) 7.30-2.00am.
Food £18. Wine £4.20.
M Fernand Casteras (formerly of the Brompton Rd Brasserie) has taken over these seemingly ill-fated premises and has opened this proudly 'Gascon' restaurant. It deserves to be a great success. Upstairs, there is a snack-bar open all day, where one can pass the time in a convincingly 'Gallic' atmosphere. Downstairs, a spacious restaurant is divided into various sections: a cocktail bar; hidden corners for discreet tete a tetes; and rooms of candlelit tables, where one of the most varied, interesting, and sensibly priced French menus in London tempts one to sample the excellent Moules Farcies; Ragout of snails, ham and mushroom in red wine, Endive salad and goose fillets as starters; then Eye Rib of Beef in Green Peppercorn Sauce (once returned by the waiter even before asking because it was not quite 'rare' as ordered), Breast of Duck (excellent), or French regional specialities such as Cassoulet and Tripe Sausage. Also, leave room for the Izarra liqueur pancakes — a treat not to be missed. Vivent les Gascons!

Gatamelata
343 Kensington High St, W8 (603 3613)
ITALIAN
Mon-Sat 12 noon-2.45, 7.00-11.30, closed Sat lunch.
Food £18. Wine £3.75.
This is a small and always busy restaurant that contrasts well with Al Gallo d'Oro a few doors away, in its unassuming and simple, yet equally pleasant, decor. It can also get quite noisy with its local clientele as they enthusiastically launch into the excellent home-made pasta and hors d'oeuvre and many well-prepared Italian specialities, such as a Calves' Liver with sage and butter, and Italian Sausages with Beans. The latter dish features in a £3.95 daily set-price three course menu that is remarkably good value for the care that goes into it.

Gondoliere
3 Gloucester Rd, SW7 (584 8062)
ITALIAN
Mon-Sat 12 noon-2.00, 6.00-11.00, closed Sat lunch.
Food £15. Wine £3.90.
Remind yourself of your Italian holiday by coming to this old Kensington favourite, and admire the use of murals, dark wood, red carpet, and lattice-work to create a relaxing Venetian feel. Mrs Moulton and her staff are welcoming and attentive in their service, and you will find that many of the standard Italian dishes, such as Spaghetti with Clams, and Saltimbocca alla Romana,

are better cooked here than in other 'local' Italian restaurants. There are daily specialities and a dinner set-menu at £7.85.

Majlis
32 Gloucester Rd, SW7 (584 3476)
INDIAN
Mon-Sun 12 noon-3.00, 6.00-11.30.
Food £15. Wine £5.20 (litre)
The most recently opened Indian restaurant in this area, Majlis comprises a long thin, smart and modern room that is sympathetically lit in the evening. The excellent Meat Tikka arrives sizzling, and popular dishes such as Chicken Bhuna and Lamb Pasanda have been cooked to a higher standard than usual. Takeaway service is available, although they have charged VAT for this, claiming that 'the containers are free'!

Mandarin
197c Kensington High St, W8 (937 1551)
CHINESE (Singapore and Peking)
Mon-Sun 12 noon-3.00, 6.00-12 midnight.
Food £16. Wine £3.50.
If you happen to like the colour of light brown, you will be pleased by the colour scheme of this large low-ceilinged dining-room below High St Kensington. The colour is enlivened by Chinese prints, red lanterns, and crabs that cling precariously to the wall. There is a large wood-panelled bar. If this review doesn't seem over-enthusiastic, nor do the staff. Efficient they are

certainly but not over-enthusiastic. No smiles allowed. However, the food is good. Excellent tender beef satay, followed by dishes such as Kungpo Hot Chilli Prawns and Chicken, Singapore Fried Mee Hoon, and 'Mother Ma's' Hot Chilli Beef Mince and Beancurd. There are set menus at £8 and £9.

Noorjahan
2a Bina Gardens, SW5 (373 6522)
INDIAN
Mon-Sun 12 noon-2.30, 6.00-11.30 .
Food £15. Wine £3.50.
The Noorjahan always seems to be the most attractive of the cluster of Indian restaurants near this junction in Old Brompton Rd. The often ambitious curries are always very good, as are dishes such as the tandoori chicken with almonds, and the mushroom bhaji, and they are served in a pleasant, relaxed atmosphere.

Phoenicia
11 Abingdon Rd, W8 (937 0120)
LEBANESE
Mon-Sun 12 noon-12 midnight.
Food £16. Wine £4.90.
This restaurant proudly announces 'Three Thousand Years of Lebanese Culinary Art' and then offers you a 'JR Style' set 'Meze Menu' at £4.60 per person. Enough said? No. Ignore the photograph of the beaming Texan in the window and enter a pleasantly smart restaurant, where the food is good, and, if you cannily go for the aforesaid 'Oilman's Feast', you will sample

national dishes such as hommos, tabouleh, falafei, samboussek, arayen, and chicken wings. 'Steer' your way here, it's worth it.

Pontevecchio
256 Old Brompton Rd, SW5
(337 9082)
ITALIAN
Mon-Sun 12.30-3.00, 7.00-12 midnight.
Food £18. Wine £3.50.
A large-roomed busy trattoria that has long been a well-known 'favourite'. You can eat inside in the lively 'standard Trat' atmosphere, or outside on tables protected from the passing cars by thick box hedges. All dishes on the Tuscan menu are to be recommended, from a very fine selection of pastas to delicious charcoal-grilled specialities.

Siam
12 St Alban's Grove, W8 (937 8765)
THAI
Tue-Fri 12.30-2.30, Mon-Sat 6.15-11.15, Sun 12 noon-2.30, 6.00-10.30.
Food £15. Wine £3.90.
This charming restaurant is divided into two floors. Downstairs, you can sit on cushions and watch Thai Classical Dance Shows seven nights a week, with a set menu of £7.50 that changes daily. Upstairs is less 'exotic' but the unhurried and sympathetic service ensures an equally enjoyable visit while one savours the subtle delights of Thai dishes such as Spicy Soup, Sateh, Dim Sim Minced Pork Dumplings,

various noodles, and countless beef, chicken, and prawn dishes, with intriguing names such as 'Neau Tod Kratiem Pick Thai'. This may sound like an exhortation to 'choose Thai', but in fact means 'Fried Beef with Pepper and Garlic'. Now you know.

Star Of India
154 Old Brompton Rd, SW5
(337 2901)
INDIAN
Mon-Sun 12 noon-3.00, 6.00-12 midnight.
Food £16. Wine £7 (litre)
A local institution. Big Burmese Mr Kim has run this unpretentious, cheerful restaurant for years, and he offers a menu that has all the favourites: bhaji, biryani and mughlai dishes etc. Some specialities have to be ordered a day in advance (with a deposit).

Trattoo
2 Abingdon Rd, W8 (937 4448)
ITALIAN
Mon-Sun 12 noon-3.00, 7.00-1.00am
Food £18. Wine £3.95.
Like Wheeler's, Mario & Franco's are a very reliable and deservedly successful London (and provincial) chain. Here, it is advisable to book for downstairs so as to be able to admire the clever use of mirrors and plants which give an elegant impression of space. Then, if you can put up with the idea of salads named after 'Francis Albert Sinatra' and 'Sammy Davis Jnr', you can eat reliably good food, that can occasionally scale greater heights, as in the

Linguine alla Luciana, and the astonishingly good Fegato di Vitello Bacchus (sliced calves' liver saute with sage, wine and grapes). The atmosphere is always busy, yet service from the waiters in white tunics is above average, and little attentions to detail like sweetmeats with the excellent coffee ensure you feel well looked after.

Witchity
253 Kensington High St, W8 (937 2654)
INTERNATIONAL
Mon-Sun 11.00am-2.00am. Disco 10.00-3.00am. Breakfast 2.00am-7.00am.
Food £18. Wine £3.50.
Who would have thought the old Lyons Corner House would end up looking like this? At night, behind the sinuous figures on the blinds that spell out the restaurant's name enter to discover a spacious though usually packed room, with tables arranged round a central small waterfall, Erte prints on the bright walls, and people drinking cocktails at the long bar, while the thump of bass and bass drum comes through from the excellent disco below. If you eat, dancing is free, and it is worth eating, as the 'Continental' menu contains many surprises: very good onion soup, delicious Coronation Chicken, quite excellent sweetbread in turnips, carrots, onions and cream, and even the charcoal-grilled beefburgers leave most competitors standing. The wines are good, and so they should be as the Managing Director is the astutely-nosed

Michel Gautier of the Froggies Wine Business. For a treat, try the Armagnac '41 (one of the very best drinks in the world!) and then destroy the other dancers downstairs. Of course, you could always look in during the day and have lunch or tea...but it won't be the same.

BUDGET

Bitter Lemons
98, Lillie Rd, SW6 (371 1069)
GREEK
Mon-Sun 12 noon-3.00, 6.00-12 midnight.
Food £11. Wine £3.85.
This used to be a purely take-away service, and now half has been turned into a restaurant. All the standard popular Greek dishes are here, and, although no great heights in comfort or culinary art are reached, the friendliness of the Cypriot owner and staff and a general cosy feeling more than make up for this, if you are looking for an unpretentious night out.

Byblos
262 Kensington High St, W8 (603 4422)
LEBANESE
Mon-Sun 11.45am-11.45.
Food £11. Wine £3.85.
An unimpressive exterior houses a charming room, with a 'tent' roof, mosaics and mirrors, blue tablecloths, and a good selection of Lebanese national dishes, some from the charcoal grill. There is a good value three course menu for £4.35, which consists of Mezzeh

(mixed hors d'oeuvres) then a main course, such as molouhieh or 'double' or even 'triple' kebabs, that changes daily, and then choice of pudding. Lebanese wine and music complete the 'national' picture. There is a take-away service.

Hamburger Heaven
159 Old Brompton Rd, SW5 (373 1926)
AMERICAN
Mon-Sun 12 noon-12 midnight.
Food £9. Wine £3.20.
A pleasant alternative to the usual dark and crowded burger restaurant, Hamburger Heaven hits you with its relaxed and bright atmosphere. Friendly staff offer the standard burgers, BLTs etc, and on Wed nights you can listen to live jazz music.

Mario's Pizza Express
15 Gloucester Rd, SW7 (584 9078)
ITALIAN
Mon-Sun 12 noon-12 midnight.
Disco to 1.00am.
Food £7. Wine £3.50.
Another deservedly successful chain. Upstairs, this Pizza Express is similar to the others in decor — plenty of pictures on the walls, bright lighting, and open kitchen. However, downstairs, there is the added attraction of a free mini-disco, which plays good current music to the young foreign students and parties of short-on-dough (geddit?) Londoners who regularly flock there. The pizzas are reliably good; try the American Hot with added garlic (best in London!) or the

unique Pizza Mario. There is a take-away service, as always.

Paulo's
30 Greyhound Rd, W6 (385 9264)
BRAZILIAN
Mon-Sat 5.00-11.00.
Food £12. Unlicensed.
Bring your own wine to this Brazilian restaurant, that is full of South American expatriots as well as local Londoners. Very much a cottage industry-type place; the service is cheerful, and the authentic food is based on a cheap limited-price menu (£5.25) of a Help Yourself variety: starters such as Crab Paulo's, followed by a buffet of hot and cold dishes (on Saturday this is replaced by the national dish, Feijoada), good interesting salads, and ethnic puddings. There is a new branch in Wellington St, WC2.

Pot
5a Hogarth Place, SW5 (370 4371)
INTERNATIONAL
Mon-Sat 12 noon-1.00am, Sun 12 noon-12 midnight
Food £10. Wine £3.50.
Legendary cheap and cheerful restaurant that has been a haven for young impecunious students and locals for years. Down its own charming little alley, this small, unassuming restaurant has now added more interesting 'Continental' dishes ('Eggs Flamenca', 'Zarzuela' — mixed seafood) to the ever-present pasta and risotto fare.

Texas Lone Star Saloon
154 Gloucester Rd, SW7 (370 5625)
TEX-MEX
Mon-Sun 12 noon-12 midnight
Food £12. Wine £3.80.
Go West, young man, in Gloucester Rd, and find yourself surrounded by fun-seeking locals in this unique restaurant. Vast open room, divided into cubicles; live and recorded (occasionally over-loud?) country music, where you can all clap and join in; Buffalo Bill and Old Moosehead's relics on the walls; Clint Eastwood on the silent TV; eager young waitresses, most of whom seem to be 'out-of-work' actresses or models; cocktails and Schaefer Specials (imported US beer) to get you going; and surprisingly good food. Start with Spicy Avocado Guacemole or any number of Corn Tortilla variations, like the Texas Pup (Frankfurter in Corn Tortilla). Move on to the Best Chilli in Town (it is!) with Real Chunks of Meat in it, or the equally delicious Hickory-smoked BBQ Ribs with salad, or, if you're really feeling hunky, the 11/4lb T-bone Steak. There is even pecan pie to follow!

Toddies
241 Old Brompton Rd, SW5 (373 8217)
ENGLISH/AFRICAN
Sun 12 noon-4.00, 6.00-12 midnight, Mon 6.00-12 midnight, Tue-Thu 6.00-2.00am, Fri-Sat 6.00-6.00am
Food £11. Wine £4.10.
Come and drink at the cocktail bar until 12 and then move on to English or hot and occasionally over-salty African specialities, such as 'Black-eyed beans with plantain and sweet potato with beef or chicken pieces' or 'Skewered beef Freetown style'.

The Yodelling Sausage
159 Earl's Court Rd, SW5 (370 5107)
INTERNATIONAL
Mon-Sun 6.00-2.00am.
Food £11. Wine £6 (litre)
If you are a bockwurst, bratwurst or Knackwurst freak, here is your Valhalla! Slip on your lederhosen, and come and swill back your Lowenbrau and yodel along with the sausages. Come to think of it, how on earth does a sausage yodel? The 'Wurst' person to send me the correct answer will win...

TRANSPORT

(All details subject to change. Phone 01-222 1234 at anytime, day or night to check details. Some routes shown do not operate every day of the week.)

Tube:	High Street Kensington, South Kensington, Notting Hill Gate
Buses:	9, 27, 28, 31, 33 (Mon-Sat only, but not evening), 49, 52, 52a — to Kensington High St
Or:	14, 30, 45, 49, 74 — to South Kensington

FULHAM

LE CARAIBE

Fashionable Fulham, as it's fast becoming, has some very good restaurants and the range is enormous — from Russian sepcialities at Nikita's in Ifield Rd to Creole cuisine at elegant Le Caraibe in Wandsworth Bridge Rd to some unusual English finds. In fact, if you are looking for a certain English decor and adventurous dishes steeped in the best of traditional cooking, Fulham is one of the best areas in London. Try September, Wags and Fingal's, all on Fulham Rd, go to King's Rd and Worlds End which spills over from Chelsea into Fulham and make for Langton St with trendy, trattoria-style Italian restaurants and the star-studded French Bagatelle. For variety and value though, a short stretch of the old Brompton Rd merits special mention. From the Canadian restaurant Adam's at the junction with Earls Court Rd look along and see the discreet, attractive, French L'Artiste Affame and the equally attractive but showier, Italian Pontevecchio. In between are two wonderful Chinese finds: Tiger Lee, where you will find luxury-style food at appropriate prices, and the beautiful black and pink Lotus Garden which offers a superb selection of food at unbeatable budget prices.

LUXURY

Bagatelle
5 Langton St, SW10 (351 4185)
FRENCH
Mon-Sat 12 noon-2.30, 7.00
11.30.
Food £28. Wine £5.
Often described as 'a pretty place for pretty people'. Flourishing menu of a few well-chosen items. I can enthuse wildly over the fish soup and a favourite hors d'oeuvres is marinade de fillet de boeuf. Have tasted marvellous duck in this Worlds End haunt: paupiettes de canard aux prunneaux, aiguillette de canard poivre vert. Assorted vegetables and salads are well up to scratch. Crepes and mousses for dessert.

Barbarella
428 Fulham Rd, SW10 (385 9434)
ITALIAN
Mon-Sat 8.00-1.00am (2.00am Sat)
Food £27. Wine £4.30.
*Restaurant disco dive of the reputable kind with canopied entrance. Extensive menu, reliable if uninspiring food. The most appetising of the antipasti are twists of salmon filled with scrambled eggs, and baked avocado with crab, prawns and lobster sauce. The pick of the pasta is fresh fettucine 'alla Raffaele' — noodles with peas and Parma ham tossed in cream. Scampi and mozzarella grilled over charcoal might well appeal or one of the usual chicken and veal dishes.
Also at 43 Thurloe St, SW7 (584 2000).*

La Croisette
168 Ifield Rd, SW10 (373 3694)
FRENCH/FISH
Tue-Sun 1.00-2.30, 8.00-11.15
(no lunch on Tue).
Food £30. Wine £5.
Uninspiring entrance but brightens up considerably once you spiral downwards to the small light basement restaurant, which has its own garden area. Executives with generous expense accounts order the excellent seafood. Daily menu changes, inventive and zesty sauces, crisp salads and competently cooked vegetables. Moody French waiters negotiate the none-too-generous space between tables. Meat dishes also available but as this is one of the best fish restaurants in town it would be foolish to try otherwise. Try especially the seafood platter which has to be seen to be believed.

Mio Sogno
871-873 Fulham Rd, SW6 (736 3910)
ITALIAN
Sun-Fri 12 noon-3.00; Mon-Sun
6.30-12 midnight.
Food £28. Wine £3.65.
A typically designed Italian restaurant. Service is good, the menu inventive, and standard of cooking high, but the prices a bit much. You'll love fettucine Bell'Antonio (a sauce of cream, mushrooms, tomatoes and herbs) and Crespolini of fresh spinach and cheese covered with Hollandaise sauce makes a stimulating starter. Chicken is always a good choice here — breast of chicken in pimento artichokes and sherry sauce or baby chicken cooked in brandy

and wine sauce with herbs.
Surprisingly cheap and good
house wine.

Nikita's
65 Ifield Rd, SW10 (352 6326)
RUSSIAN
Mon-Sat 7.30-11.30.
Food £26. Wine £4.20.
*Flattened onionesque domes
and geometric patterns give an
English folky interpretation of
old Russian. Make your way
inside where it's cosy, dark and
busy. Real Russian black or red
caviar, superb smoked
sturgeon or salmon. Egg caviar
mousse or, for a Russian
version of pasta try borscht and
piroshki. Steak Tartare is
excellent and there are some
ingeniously named dishes
including Pork Rasputin.*

September
457 Fulham Rd, SW10 (352
0206)
ENGLISH
Mon-Sun 12.30-2.30, 7.30-11.30.
Food £24. Wine £3.75.
*September is decorated in
green; from grassy carpets to
deeper drapes and woodwork
stained green. Friendly service
and many unusual dishes.
Delighted to see the wonderful
culinary combination of steak
and oysters — Carpetbag steak
— on the menu. Some inventive
vegetarian dishes as well as
good old roasts. Venison with
orange comes from 'The
Middle'. In 'The Beginnning'
you might've indulged in
grapefruit and orange salad or
Boasie's coarse pate. 'The End'
is more predictable with
sorbets and mousses.*

Wags
306b Fulham Rd, SW10 (352
7343)
ENGLISH
Mon-Sat 7.00-11.30.
Food £26. Wine £4.95.
*W.A.G. are the initials of
William Anthony Gaff, Rod
Stewart's manager, who took
over Provans. Now in this
attractive, shuttered, long and
narrow, first floor room make a
good start with stuffed
mushrooms. Red meat is a firm
favourite here and ranges from
steak tartare to chargrilled,
Australian-size sirloin. Fish pie
has proved popular but their
steak and kidney pie which
includes oysters and is cooked
in red wine and beer goes like
wildfire. For a riveting dessert
go for either coffee and rum
cake or hazelnut and almond.*

MID-PRICE

Adams
239 Old Brompton Rd, SW5
(373 3502)
CANADIAN
Mon-Sat 6.30-11.30; Sun
1.00-1.00am.
Food £12. Wine £5.
*Canadian lawyer Brian Morris
went into the restaurant
business because of the
unavailability of 'decent spare
ribs in London'. So a big
feature of the small menu is
their rib platter, or, appetite
permitting, giant rib platter.
Delicious thick Quebec pea
soup. Bread, really dripping in
garlic, is hard to resist. Good
sweets also. A side entrance
will take you upstairs to their
cosy wine bar. Remember*

'Canadian cooking is just a bit above American'.

All My Eye & Betty Martin
Chelsea Wharf, Lots Rd, SW10
(352 6015)
ANGLO/ITALIAN
Mon-Sun 7.30-11.30.
Food £15. Wine £3.85.
Part of the old Chelsea flour mill is taken by this imaginatively named, 'alternative' nightclub/restaurant on the ground floor with a couple of tables overlooking the Thames. Licensed to 1.00am and with entertainment as varied as possible: jazz, rock, satirical cabaret. Food is secondary to the entertainment but they serve good home-made soups and pates and good quality steak, pasta dishes, tasty desserts. Friendly service. By the way the first mention of 'all my eye and Betty Martin' appeared in the Dictionary of Vulgar Tongue, and the meaning? Eyewash.

Bagley's
New King's Rd, SW6 (736 7110)
ENGLISH
Mon-Sat 12.30-3.00, 7.00-11.45.
Food £15. Wine £3.75.
Pleasant feel to a good value English eating house. Painted green and red with unobtrusive wallpaper. Starched white tablecloths and dark wood chairs, short, imaginative menu with such starters as salad of smoked chicken, smoked quail and avocado, and pastry envelopes stuffed with stilton and spinach. Watercress and walnut salad too. Then braised pheasant with cream, white

wine and celery sauce or perhaps venison and chestnut pie. For dessert, fruit sorbet or cream brulee. Set menu lunch.

Blue Trattoria
Walham Green Court, Fulham Rd (near Fulham Broadway tube) (381 0735)
ITALIAN
Mon-Sat 7.30-11.30.
Food £18. Wine £3.40.
Squeezed into a monstrous tower block is this modest dolls' house-type trattoria with little blue curtains. The menu is a revelation in that it differs so radically from that favoured by the usual chic London Italian establishment. Particularly with their 'piatta di resistenza' which include sirlion cooked in white wine, tomato sauce, garlic and spiced with marjoram, and petti di pollo Casanova (pate is added to the usual Kiev stuffing). Black forest gateau is a treat to accompany strong coffee.

Carlo's Place
855 Fulham Rd, SW6 (736 4507)
FRENCH
Mon-Sat 7.00-11.30
Food £20. Wine £4.25.
Attractive, discreet exterior. Interior and staff warm and welcoming. Popular place with imaginative menu. Consistently high standard dishes. Enterprising entrees such as escargots cognac, pamplemousse cocktail, ham and asparagus mornay. The main course is equally good: sweetbreads meuniere, guinea fowl boussenay. Perfectly cooked vegetables, a relatively rare commodity in London restaurants. Mouth-watering

desserts include almond meringue, home-made cheesecake and crepe Grand Marnier.

Fingal's
690 Fulham Rd, SW6 (736 1195)
ENGLISH
Mon-Fri 12.30-3.00; Mon-Sat 8.00-11.30.
Food £20. Wine £3.50.
Richard Berry and Bremner Johnson run a charming wood-panelled restaurant with a glassed-in eating area at the back. Great atmosphere. Dip into the crudites or have appetising avocado filled with celery, apples, prawns and walnuts. Other good starters too; so much so that the menu carries a note: 'starters as main course £1 extra'. Interesting follow-ons in the form of marinade haunch of venison steak with chestnut and blackcurrant sauce, and roast wild duck with fresh fruit sauce.

Gastronome One
313 New King's Rd, SW6 (731 6381)
FRENCH
Mon-Fri 12 noon-2.30; Mon-Sat 7.00-11.00.
Food £14. Wine £3.95.
Pleasant, modern brasserie with authentic French menu. Amid plants and wood you can gaze upon paintings for sale at interesting prices. Cheese souffle and crudites merit mention. Main bites, and there are some good ones, include lamb chops in pastry with mushroom filling, veal kidneys in pernod, and a personal favourite, breast of chicken in roquefort sauce. Salads are

crisp and crunchy, vegetables al dente and addictive.

La Belle Epoque
45 Fulham High St, SW6 (736 4372)
ENGLISH
Mon-Thu, Sat 12 noon-11.00; Fri 5.00-11.00; Sun 12 noon-3.30.
Food £12. Wine £3.20.
Small, unpretentious place, easy to walk into at almost any time of day. Unpretentious menu too, and as such not the most exciting. However if you omit the prawn cocktail starter syndrome things pick up considerably. Some good chargrilled steaks and the barbecue spare ribs come in a zesty sauce. French fries, salads and garlic bread. For 'afters' why not try banana split or home-made apple pie.

La Famiglia
7 Langton St, SW10 (351 0761)
ITALIAN
Mon-Sat 12.30-2.30, 6.30-11.15.
Food £22. Wine £4.40.
Brick floor and Victorian group photographs of assorted shapes and sizes on white walls. A fair sprinkling of trend-setters in this lively meeting place. Comprehensive coverage of Italian dishes, from delicious home-made pasta to stupendous bone marrow and good seafood. Salads are crisp and inviting and there's usually a wide selection of cheeses. A leisurely cup of coffee followed by that aniseed liqueur wonder, Sambuca.

Le Caraibe
182 Wandsworth Bridge Rd, SW6 (731 0732)
CREOLE

71

Mon-Sun 7.30-11.30.
Food £19. Wine £4.40.
*Le Caraibe is beautiful.
Framed by plants, the
architecture is elegant, the
woodwork superb. Elsewhere
the colours are subdued ochres
and pinks. The food is Creole
as prepared in the Caribbean.
West Indian spices, rum, lime
juice and coconut cream give
distinctive flavours to such
starters as stuffed crab backs
and marinated port with
cucumber. From the French
isles stupendous sancoche:
chicken, saltfish, tomatoes,
coconut cream, onions,
pepper, herbs and spices. Also
curried goat, flying fish in
piquant sauce and pork Creole.
Good vegetables including
banana-like plantain and sweet
potatoes.*

The Filling Station Bistro
144 Wandsworth Bridge Rd,
SW6 (736 2418)
ENGLISH
Mon-Sat 7.30-11.00.
Food £11. Wine £3.40.
*Pine interior reflects an almost
equivalent food taste.
Generous-enough portions as
the name suggests, and
extremely good value. Short
menu featuring the English
passion for combining sweet
and savoury. Such a starter is
Camembert croquettes with
gooseberry preserve. Follow
on with grilled petit poussin
with banana and sherry filling
or roast lamb stuffed with
apple and onion. Adequate
vegetables. Sweets include
chocolate and orange mousse,
lemon syllabub and apple
crumble with custard.*

Othello Psarapoula
606 Fulham Rd, SW6 (736 0772)
GREEK
Mon-Sat 6.00-12 midnight.
Food £15. Wine £4.50.
*Rooms, alcoves and arches.
Patterns galore in carpet and
tablecloths. Mixed meze 'for
really hungry people' is filling
and delicious. Or go a la carte
and try stuffed vine leaves.
Lounza (smoked fillet of pork) is
also very good, and, of course,
there's humous and tarama.
Nice fish soup but better
avogolemono (chicken soup
with lemon). Recommended
main dishes: moussaka with
creamy topping, fish kebab,
and stifado — beef and onion in
thick, rich, red wine sauce.*

The Red Onion Bistro
636 Fulham Rd, SW6 (736 0920)
ENGLISH
Mon-Sat 7.00-11.15.
Food £13. Wine £3.30.
*Floor of quarry tiles, walls of
whitewashed brick and fringed
lamps hanging from the
ceiling. Considering the name
of the bistro French onion soup
should be, and is, good. Lots of
different fillings for the
pancakes; try the celery and
bacon with bechamel sauce or
deep fried mushrooms with
garlic and butter. Some
unusual main dishes — in
particular baked mackerel with
gooseberry sauce, and
vegetarian salad with honey
dressing. Chocolate mousse is
good, so too is the home-made
apple crumble.*

Ristorante La Barca
541 Kings Rd, SW6 (731 0039)
ITALIAN
Mon-Sat 12.30-2.00, 7.00-11.30.

Food £19. Wine £4.00.
The very successful team of Luciano Ferrari and chef Pasquale Fini recently opened this, their second restaurant. Superb marble floor, cool ambience, and caring service from the friendly staff. Wide selection of antipasti and mouth-watering pasta. Spaghetti la Barca with a seafood sauce that includes moules, octopus and squid, comes packaged in a brown paper bag, ritually opened before you. It is one of the best pasta dishes I've ever had. Papardelle alla Vera (wide strips of home-made pasta with kidney, onion and white wine) is indeed 'special'. Good main course dishes including some unusual ones, such as succulent fillet of pork with prawns, brandy and cream. Generally the vegetables are fresh and well prepared. Very good sweets, particularly zabaglione and banana flambee.

Zia Sophia
1a Langton St, SW10 (352 7517)
ITALIAN
Mon-Sat 12.00-2.45, 7.30-11.30.
Food £17. Wine £3.65.
Small window panes of tinted glass with woody surrounds under green canopy. Inside rough Italian walls with the odd Chianti flask providing the wall decoration. Zuppes and pasta very much what you would expect. Some good antipasti including fried whitebait and that delicious combination of tuna fish and beans. Usual range of Italian main course dishes with some nicely prepared veal and liver.

Annabelle's
356 Fulham Rd, SW10 (352 1295)
ENGLISH
Mon-Sat 7.00-11.30; Sun 1.00-3.00.
Food £9.00. Set lunch £3.95.
Unlicensed.
Atmospheric wax-dripping haunt popular with those seeking a budget night out. Sturdy as opposed to stupendous starters with filling gazpachio and well prepared dishes, complete with irresistible names: Zara's pepper chicken, Alic's spare ribs, and best of all Aunt Grace's steak and kidney pie. Vegetables are adequate, as are the sweets and cheeses. Bring your own wine (no corkage charge).

Carlette's
755 Fulham Rd, SW6 (736 8524)
AMERICAN
Mon-Sun 6.00-12 midnight.
Food £9.00. Wine £3.95.
1982 saw the opening of this brasserie-type restaurant with cocktail and piano bar. Red and white exterior/interior. Savoury crepes, described as creplettes, are made with buckwheat flour and tempting fillings include mozzarella and tuna, spinach and sour cream. The cute naming policy continues with riblettes (of the spare variety) and burglettes — I suppose it gives a different ring to the old hamburgers. Saladbowl, apple pie and gateaux. Cocktails with local flavour from Fulham Funky to

FULHAM

Parsons Blue.

Lotus Garden
257 Old Brompton Rd, SW5
(370 4450)
CHINESE
Mon-Fri 1.00-3.00, 6.00-1.00am;
Sat-Sun 1.00-1.00am.
Food £10. Wine £3.85.
*Facade of black wood divides.
Inside is small and intimate
with low-slatted ceiling and
cane-potted pink flowers on
pink tablecloths. The bonus
comes in the form of great
food at budget prices. The
imperial mixed hors
d'oeuvres, including smoked
fish, boiled prawns, pork,
chicken, cabbage and
mushrooms, is, as claimed, 'a
delightful dish of cold
delicacies'. Continue with
chicken, crab, pungent
smoked fish and peppery
sweet vegetables.*

Staveley's
642 Kings Rd, SW6 (731 4248)
ENGLISH
Mon-Fri 12.00-3.00, 6.00-12.00;
Sat 12 noon-12 midnight; Sun
12.00-4.00.
Food £8. Wine £2.90.
*A colourful graphic fish to
grab you at the door of this
northern style fish and chip
joint. 'Nowt'll taste better'.
Kids' disco at weekends.
Written on the window: 'Home
made fish or steak and kidney
pie all at £2.50 with chips'.
Home made or not, the fish
tastes good — the usual plaice,
rock, cod, skate and haddock.
'Mushy' peas too. This could
have been preceded by jellied
eels or a prawn cocktail,
mackerel pate or soup. A good
time to be had by all for a*

minimum outlay.

Uddins Manzil
194 Wandsworth Bridge Rd,
SW6 (736 3584)
INDIAN
Mon-Sun 12.00-2.30, 6.00-11.30.
Food £10. Wine £3.25.
*A variety of colourful, exotic
fabrics line the walls. An older
sister restaurant in Oxford has
been extremely successful.
Service there and here is most
attentive. A spicy start with
prawn puree or samosa. Next
try tasty tandoori specialities
such as chicken marinated in
herbs and spices, and lamb
marsala. As a change from
budget fare there is 'Exotic
oriental cooking, favourite to
Indian aristocrats', culminating
in Kurzi chicken or lamb for
which 24 hours' notice is
required.*

TRANSPORT

**(All details subject to change.
Phone 01-222 1234 at anytime,
day or night to check details.
Some routes shown do not
operate every day of the
week.)**

Tube: Fulham Broadway,
Putney Bridge, West
Kensington, Parsons
Green
Buses: 11, 14, 22, 28, 30, 31,
74, 91 (Mon-Sat only),
220, 295
Night: N97

THE HUNGRY HORSE

Chelsea ranks as one of the restaurant areas. One can dine and wine in well-designed, often quirky, places, and usually at a price which will astonish you by its moderation. Most of the restaurants selected fall, rather surprisingly, into the medium price range. However, well worth visiting, if you can afford the mark-up, is La Tante Claire, one of the best restaurants in London, while at the other end of the market is La Bersagliera, a budget spectacular. For an area rife with Sloane Rangers, bijoux businessmen, itinerant workers and students, nightly diner imports, and the arty set, the range of food, not unnaturally, is vast. From up-market Chinese to easy Italian trattoria-style food, from Greek tavernas to Tandoori restaurants, and from French grandeur to English cosiness, Chelsea has something for everyone. The heart of Chelsea is King's Road, Old Brompton Road and Fulham Road, which are packed with restaurants, wine bars and pubs. The increasingly fashionable World's End is fast catching up; and a little further from the beaten track Hollywood Road, Draycott Avenue, Elystan Street, Royal Hospital Road and Park Walk, which boasts the trendy Number Eleven, are well worth a visit by the lover of good food.

LUXURY

Brinkley's
47 Hollywood Rd, SW10 (351 1683)
ANGLO/FRENCH
Mon-Sat 7.30-11.30.
Food £28. Wine £5.
John Brinkley's Hollywood Road restaurant is low key elegance. Surprisingly there is no cover charge and the service is friendly without being overwhelming. Stimulating starters such as fresh asparagus bound with scallop mousse and served with a butter sauce. Steak tartare is delectable too, gorge oneself on another appetising delicacy before opting for fillet en croute with perfectly cooked vegetables. Good selection of French cheeses. Sheltered courtyard at the back, ideal for summer dining.

Dan's
119 Sydney St, SW3 (352 2718)
ANGLO/FRENCH
Mon-Fri 12.30-3.00, 7.30-11.15, Sat 7.30-11.15.
Food £27. Wine £4.45.
A small, stylish, in vogue restaurant. Young up market appeal. The four day terrine — duck and wild birds marinated for four days in Armagnac with selected herbs and spices makes a tremendous starter. Or have quails' eggs on a bed of French beans. Chef Philip Britten does these and more; from the main course, rendezvous of turbot and lobster, coated with subtle lobster sauce and laced with Pernod. Or marinated loin of venison with fresh cranberries in a spicy mustard sauce. Sweets seem a bit superfluous at this stage.

Daphne's
112 Draycott Ave, SW3 (589 4257)
FRENCH
Mon-Sat 7.30-12 midnight.
Food £28. Wine £5.
Conservative restaurant and clientele. Short seasonal menu with immaculately prepared food. From poulet fume et avocado, house pate and potted shrimps through filet de boeuf au poivre vert, supreme de volaille a la kiev, grilled sole to orange and ginger salad, and lemon crepes. Supreme sauces such as the one which comes with the noisettes d'agneau beurre de menthe. Rare welcome words on the menu: 'Our chef would be pleased to show you around the kitchen and to discuss any special dish'.

Meridiana
169 Fulham Rd, SW3 (589 8825)
ITALIAN
Mon-Sun 12.30-2.45pm, 7.00-11.45pm.
Food £26. Wine £3.80.
A rare combination of fashionable restaurant and fantastic service. Have a drink in the cosy basement bar lined with Apicella drawings, then make your way upstairs to either of the cool, modern, white rooms or, in summer, dine in splendour on the roof balcony. Home made paglia e fieno crema e prosciutto is a popular starter, as is the seafood salad. Their carpaccio

must be among the best in London and the vegetables are always done to perfection. Delicious sweets as well.

Le Suquet
104 Draycott Ave, SW3 (581 1785)
FRENCH
Tue 7.30-11.00, Wed-Sun 12.30-2.30, 7.30-11.30.
Food £28. Wine £5.50.
A real sense of France. Fresh seafood prepared and cooked as you would wish. Specialities include plateau de fruits de mer, soupe de poisson and moules marinieres. The merits of the langoustines and coquille St Jacques deserve special mention. The accompanying vegetables and salads are difficult to fault. Limited number of meat dishes as well. Attached to the restaurant is the best up-market take-away seafood in London.

La Tante Claire
68 Royal Hospital Rd, SW3 (352 6045)
FRENCH
Mon-Fri 12.30-2.00pm. 7.00-11.00.
Food £40. Wine £5.
One of the top restaurants in London, a fact, naturally enough, reflected in the prices. Narrow room with disappointing decor but distinguished dishes more than make up for this. Extraordinary seafood as in Pierre Koffmann's andouillette de la mer au vinaigrette Cassis, turbot in a subtle yet tangy sauce. Vegetables surpass platitudes. Presentation is perfect. Superb

duck and pigeon, excellent cheeses, good sweets. Coffee with petits fours to conclude a gastronomic extravaganza. Book a month ahead.

Thierry's
342 Kings Rd, SW3 (352 3365)
FRENCH
12.30-2.30pm, 7.30-11.30pm.
Food £30. Wine £4.95.
Discreet, dim, 'English' decor with walls covered in framed prints of angelic subjects and tasteful flowers. A couple of imposing mirrors as well. A short, inventive, seasonal menu. The moules and escargots are to be recommended and the vegetables are extremely good. A meal here is incomplete without the superb souffle Grand Marnier. Excellent wine and good coffee.

MID-PRICE

Au Bon Accueil
27 Elystan St, SW3 (589 3718)
FRENCH
Mon-Fri 12.30-2.30, 7.00-11.30, Sun 7.00-11.30.
Food £16. Wine £3.85.
Casual, unobstrusive restaurant patronised by a very mixed crowd. A perfect filler/warmer is their soupe a l'oignon gratinee with wholesome bread. The Fillet mignon is good, the sauce Bearnaise even better. Coq au vin is a house speciality and well worth trying. Lots of imaginatively prepared vegetables to choose from. A wide selection of delicious

sweets among which are chestnuts and Jersey cream. Small outdoor street area for summer eating.

Beccofino
100 Draycott Ave, SW3 (584 3600)
ITALIAN
Mon-Sun 12.30-2.30, 7.30-11.30.
Food £20. Wine £3.80.
Bland interior but far from bland food. 'Fresh home-made pasta to choose from the basket', as the menu informs, will draw you back again and again. Make it spaghettini al marinara, another time order penne all'arrabbiata or spaghettini al zucchini. Enjoy the combination of smoked salmon and scrambled eggs, also their trout and almonds. Poultry and meat dishes too, but not so enticing. A sweet tooth is satisfied by a smooth zabaglione. Pleasant pavement summer dining in quiet street.

Bones
Chelsea Cloisters, Sloane Ave, SW3 (584 6532/581 4215)
AMERICAN
Mon-Sat 12.30-2.30, 7.00-11.30.
Food £19. Wine £3.75.
Recently opened, Bones is an up-market hamburger joint — so up-market in fact that Spare Ribs, Smoked Poussin, Lemon Sole, Skewered Monkfish, Fillet Steak replace more traditional fare. We started our meal with a very tasty and filling smoked Turkey and Almond Salad, and the Salmon Mousse, which was disappointing (as was the Chocolate Mousse). The Beef Spare Ribs, covered in a barbecue sauce, were

generous and spicy (vultures dotted about the room made me a little nervous at this point); the frighteningly large skewered prawns, rather dull. Country and Western music, and very courteous service add a soothing touch to this spacious, possibly kitsch, certainly expensive restaurant.

Busabong
329 Fulham Rd, SW10 (351 4238)
THAI
Mon-Sat 12.30-3.00, 6.30-11.20.
Food £24. Wine £4.60.
Delicate, subtle cuisine too little known in Britain. Three dining rooms; to be authentic book a table in the Thai style room, with low tables and cushions. Timeless Thai dancing. Vast menu. The piquant fisherman's soup is a delight, the prawn salad divine, The hot sweetish beef curry is interesting and the fiery chicken with chilli is very popular. An evening out with a difference.

Chelsea Kitchen
98 King's Rd, SW3 (589 1330)
INTERNATIONAL
Mon-Sat 11.30-11.45 (Sun closing 11.30)
Food £10. Wine £2.95.
This is an attractive and extremely popular restaurant — so be prepared to share your table. Excellent lunchtime place for the tired shopper. Alcoves downstairs offer a little more privacy. Efficient and very speedy service. Interesting soups; casseroles; spaghetti; and well-cooked vegetables, which

arrive automatically with the meals. Apple or rhubarb pie, ice cream, fruit salad. Conclude the scenario with coffee. Take-away service provided.

Chelsea Rendezvous
4 Sydney St, SW3 (351 3605)
CHINESE
Mon-Sun 12.30-2.30, 7.00-11.30.
Food £21. Wine £4.50.
Contemporary Chinese chic with strong Italian overtones. Sophisticated setting, sane service. Arouse the appetite with spring rolls, dried scallops and greens and/or egg drop soup with tomato. Heavenly seafood, comprising prawns, lemon sole, abalone and Chinese mushrooms and bamboo shoots or steamed whole fish continue the process. Aromatic crispy duck is another favourite but hotter still, deep fried shredded beef and chilli referred to as sexy beef. As an alternative to toffee apples and bananas try orange tamarindo.

Choy's
172 King's Rd, SW3 (352 9085)
CHINESE
Mon-Sun 12 noon-12 midnight.
Food £16. Wine £4.60.
Cantonese specialities in green canopied surrounds. Various set menus but well worth your while making a close study of the a la carte listings for therein lie some little gems. Minced prawns wrapped in rice paper immediately spring to mind, as do fried sliced bamboo shoot and celery with shredded ham and pork. Choose at least one crispy

concoction: ever popular duck with pancakes, crispy meatballs and crunchy pancake rolls. Reliable service.

Le Cliche
206 Fulham Rd, SW10 (352 3700)
FRENCH
Mon-Sat 7.30-12 midnight.
Food £18. Wine £3.95.
A French restaurant which deserves to be much better known. Great care is taken over the preparation and presentation of the food: the 'cuisine nouvelle' menu changes weekly. Excellent home-made bread and some interesting starters; we particularly enjoyed the fish soup and the stuffed clams. The main course, included salmon, duck and lamb, accompanied by some delicious vegetables. This basement restaurant is pleasant and unpretentious; the food quite excellent.

Clives India
62 Lower Sloane St, SW1 (730 1110)
INDIAN
Mon-Sat 12 noon-2.30, 6.00-11.30.
Food £24. Wine £4.85.
Sophisticated Indian cuisine. Elegant decor; pink marble on two floors. Gentle service and feel to pleasant place. Senvesticks, a mini masterpiece and ideal hors d'oeuvres is macaroni cooked with capsicums, tomatoes, cheese and lightly flavoured with massalas. Mild and creamy pasanda is always good, prawn patia too. The chef's speciality, navratan

kofta, is scrumptious (grated marrow with batter, deep fried and served in a cream, tomato and onion sauce). Vegetables are equally good. Usual sweets.

La Corse
362 King's Rd, SW3 (352 0071)
FRENCH
Mon-Sat 12 noon-2.30, 6.30-11.30.
Food £16. Wine £4.85.
Well run, unpretentious restaurant with carefully chosen set menu. The crudites are excellent, sardines imaginatively combined with garlic sauce, and there is always a good selection of French salamis, pates and hams. Compliments all round for the grilled charcoal dishes: les escalopines de porc aux champignons, le poulet aux herbes du 'Maquis'. At £4.50 the set lunch is perhaps even better value than dinner.

Costa del Sol
224 Fulham Rd, SW10 (352 5675)
SPANISH
Mon-Sun 12 noon-3.00, 7.00-1.45am.
Food £18. Wine £4.
Not quite transported to Spain but vicarious pleasure from langostinos ajillo o plancha (king prawns grilled or fried in garlic) or their mixed fish soup, Bouillabaisse style. Move on and savour the carre Segovia, lamb with rosemary, garlic and vinegar. Better still, allow 20 min for paella Velecia — and if you prefer it with extra fish and minus the chicken, go for paella marinera. Also set menus at

around £4.50 per person. Soothing sweets and good strong coffee.

Dominic's
259 King's Rd, SW3 (352 1918)
FRENCH
Mon-Sun 12.30-2.30, 6.30-11.30.
Food £20. Wine £3.95.
Pass by the antique bust on Baroque pillar into atmospheric white-washed brick walled room. Assorted prints, brass plates, wheels, old lights and other paraphernalia surround you. Imaginative menu featuring both traditional starters such as French onion soup and the more unusual garlic snails in pastry case. Likewise with the tasty follow-ons. Worthy of note: boned chicken with fish mousse in poultry sauce, lamb cubes in wine in a pastry envelope.

Don Luigi
33c King's Rd, SW3 (730 3023)
ITALIAN
Mon-Sun 12 noon-3.00, 6.00-12 midnight.
Food £16. Wine £3.95.
An ex-Mario and Franco restaurant, it remains very much in that mould. Simple, functional interior. Appealing appetisers such as baked eggs with mushrooms and oregano, and rich creamy mozzarella in carozza. For piquant presentation, insalata tricolore: cream mozzarella, red tomatoes and green avocado. Popular chicken Kiev and spareribs but better antipasta and pasta: rigatoni alla Siciliana (aubergines and tomatoes), tagliatelle alla Romagna (a sauce of cream

and tomato fondue). Good
trolley sweets.

Drakes
2a Pond Place, SW3 (629 9933)
ENGLISH
Mon-Sun 12.30-2.15, 7.30-11.00.
Food £22. Wine £3.98.
*A Sloane Ranger haunt.
Bar/basement restaurant.
Young, friendly staff enthuse
over the game pate with
Cumberland sauce. In fact, a
good variety of game is
normally available. Some
unusual dishes including
breast of chicken with cream
and saffron sauce and there
are the traditional all-time
favourites such as steak,
kidney and mushroom pie.
Some tempting English
desserts on offer: hot treacle
and orange tart, mincemeat
pie with brandy butter.*

Eleven Park Walk
11 Park Walk, SW10 (352 3449)
ITALIAN
Mon-Sat 12.30-3.00, 7.00-12
midnight.
Food £20. Wine £4.
*Trendy, convivial, cool Italian
restaurant. A place to see and
be seen in. Have a long cool
drink at the bar, take in who's
around, and descend by spiral
staircase to the dining room.
Weekly menu changes but by
popular demand several true
and trusted dishes remain.
Such specialities include home
made fettucine with Scotch
salmon, rosette al pomodoro.
One of the most clamoured-
after main dishes is their
succulent duck in black
cherries. Perhaps meringues
with Grand Marnier to finish
off with?*

Foxtrot Oscar
79 Royal Hospital Rd, SW3
(352 7179)
ANGLO/FRENCH
Mon-Sun 12.30-2.30, 7.30-11.45.
Food £16. Wine £3.75.
*Just down the road from
exclusive Tante Claire is
exclusive (in the trendy set
sense) Foxtrot Oscar,
discreetly venetianed in wood
with blackboard announcing
such starters as avocado, sour
cream and caviar. The house
pate is excellent. Good
seafood pancake. Reasonable
chicken and veal dishes
usually on. A place favoured
by the rich young
Chelsea/Knightsbridge set*

Foxtrot Qango
14 Hollywood Rd, SW10 (352
8692)
ANGLO/AMERICAN
Mon-Sun 12.30-2.30, 7.00-11.45
(Sun closing 10.45).
Food £17. Wine £4.15.
*Sister restaurant to Foxtrot
Oscar, formerly Jake's, now
revamped, and with the
addition of an upstairs cocktail
bar. Same ownership and
management as previously,
and the most popular dishes
remain. Open seven days for
lunch and dinner.*

Le Francais
259 Fulham Rd, SW3 (352
4748)
FRENCH
Mon-Sat 12.45-2.00, 7.15-11.00.
Food £18. Wine £3.80.
*Supreme cuisine regionale
from owner/chef Jean Jacques
Figeac and service at its best
from owner/manager Bernard
Caen and his friendly staff.
Weekly regional listings*

(Bretagne, Provence, Normandie, Paris etc). You can choose from one of two set menus, which, at £9 and £10 per head, are tremendous value. Carefully selected and wonderfully co-ordinated provincial dishes. Superb setting. Get a copy of the yearly schedule of French provincial feasts and treat yourself periodically.

La Fringale
4 Hollywood Rd, SW10 (351 1011)
FRENCH
Mon-Sat 7.00-11.30.
Food £14. Wine £4.10.
Warm welcome, subdued lighting and acquiescent atmosphere as a prelude to crab mousse or crepe a la Levroux, a pancake filled (stuffed is a more apt word) with cheese, spinach, tomato and bechamel sauce. Such creations are the work of French Moroccan chef Azizi, ensconced here ever since his arrival from France five years ago. The limited number of dishes and seasonal menu ensures everything is absolutely fresh and the vegetables exquisite. Smooth house wine and the sweets to applaud are chocolate mousse and creme brulee.

Golden Duck
6 Hollywood Rd, SW10 (352 3500)
CHINESE
Mon-Sat 12 noon-2.30, 6.30-11.30.
Food £16. Wine £4.85.
Long established restaurant with devotees from afar. Bright graphic window, unpretentious interior. Lots of

choice but the seafood is irresistible. Nor should you resist one of their namesake dishes: roast Peking duck (a few hours advance order for not less than four), crispy aromatic Szechuan duck, and crispy fried duck with green ginger and scallions. Or there's the flawless flavour of Mongolian Hot Pot, a feast rounded off with the aromatic soup you've made yourself. The usual Chinese sweeties.

Il Girasole
126 Fulham Rd, SW3 (370 6656)
ITALIAN
Mon-Sun 12 noon-2.45, 7.30-11.15.
Food £18. Wine £3.95.
Pleasant place with an amazing array of hors d'oeuvres to choose from, including well prepared aubergines and mouth-watering squid. Generous portions of pasta are as popular as a main course as a starter. Note the tortelloni with butter and sage, and fresh basil trenette al pesto fresco. Nice to see the still little known osso bucco Milanese on the menu. Reasonable sweets, better cheese and summer outdoor eating if you can cope with Fulham Road noise and fumes.

Good Earth
91 King's Rd, SW3 (352 9231)
CHINESE
Mon-Sun 12.30-11.30.
Food £24. Wine £4.
Crisp and pretty as is their presentation of Pekinese and Cantonese food. An a la carte selection is considerably

cheaper but the Good Earth Gourmet is not to be missed. After the impressive imperial hors d'oeuvres enjoy the shark's fin soup which comes with crab meat and shredded chicken. Duck for the pancake treat is crisp and fragrant. I also liked the shredded pork and Chinese mushrooms and the prawns in spiced salt.

The Hungry Horse
196 Fulham Rd, SW10 (352 7757)
ENGLISH
Mon-Sun 12.30-2.30, 7.00-11.30.
Food £16. Wine £3.85.
Evocative name and beckoning entrance to attractive underground restaurant with a myriad of small rooms and private corners. Ironically this most English of places is owned by an Australian. Have the English smoked eel and horseradish. Or perhaps the Yorkshire pudding and gravy followed by one of their traditional pies. Hungry as the proverbial horse, then have jugged hare in a first rate rich sauce. Save room for their steamed spotted Dick, Dorothy's glorious pudding and many others.

Monkeys
1 Cale St, SW3 (352 4711)
ANGLO/FRENCH
Mon-Fri 12.30-2.30, 7.30-11.30.
Food £20. Wine £3.85.
The three monkeys are Jamie Robertson, Thomas Benham and Brigitte Russell-Smith, who have owned and greatly cared for this restaurant for five years. Small tables, wall banquette seating in pleasant

spacious interior. Extremely short menu; great food. Weekly changes with customers apt to go berserk if at least one of the dynamic terrines is not included. A similar reaction assured if the steak and kidney pie isn't on. Scampi, often a dubious choice elsewhere, is combined with Pernod and is a most delicious surprise.

La Nassa
438 King's Rd, SW10 (351 4118)
ITALIAN
Mon-Sun 12 noon-3.00, 7.00-11.45.
Food £20. Wine £3.95.
Cottage-like green facade opening into casual restaurant with friendly service. Meat and poultry dishes served but it's the seafood that will draw you back here. Couple that with the pasta and you're away: vongole, marinara, and the rarer fusilli frutte di mare (twisted pasta with seafood and cream sauce) and the linguine puttanesca (a sauce of tuna, olives, garlic and tomato sauce). Stay in a fishy frame of mind for the succulent sword fish grilled and served with fresh mint sauce. Plenty of good desserts.

New York Cafe
50 Old Brompton Rd, SW7 (584 4028)
AMERICAN
Mon-Sun 12 noon-2.30am.
Food £13. Wine £3.95.
'Cafe' as used in a certain American sense, qualifies as a proper restaurant here. Clean, modern design that literally stops people in the street.

Sterling starters such as New York Reuben, salt beef tossed with melting Swiss cheese. Steak features prominently among the main course dishes: filet mignon, T-bone special. Also Surf 'n' Turf, 'juicy steak and prime grilled lobster', as the blurb goes. Reduced prices and portions for children. Cocktails and Californian wines too.

Poissonnerie de l'Avenue
82 Sloane Ave, SW3 (589 2457)
FRENCH
Mon-Sat 12.30-2.30, 7.30-11.15.
Food £24. Wine £6.50.
Oak-panelled walls, low ceiling, traditional restaurant. Smart, conservative clientele. Service: brisk at its best, brusque more the norm. Fish soup a la Nicoise is usually good, so too is the crab cocktail. A speciality is the Coquille St Jacques and the turbot, poached or grilled, is a sensation. Vegetables are a little disappointing. But the sweets are good, so indulge in profiteroles au chocolat a la creme.

Reflections
85 King's Rd, SW3 (352 1008)
ENGLISH
Mon-Fri 12.15-2.30, 7.00-11.30,
Sat 7.00-11.30.
Food £16. Wine £3.65.
Once you've located the name on the canopy make your way through a narrow hall — mirrored on one side, curtained on the other — down to a cosy basement restaurant that seats 30. Much care has gone into all aspects of catering and the service is charming. The freshest of

English products are used for the seasonal dishes. To start: deep fried Camembert with gooseberry sauce, delectable Stilton and onion soup served with croutons, prawns and mushrooms flamed in brandy, and other equally good but less adventurous dishes. To follow, there's always a good seasonal pie such as lamb and apricot in summer, steak and kidney in winter. Other appealing dishes include sweetbreads with chestnuts in wine, and Halibut with prawn sauce. Good vegetables. Fresh, tasty sweets.

Salamis
204 Fulham Rd, SW10 (352 9827)
INTERNATIONAL
Mon-Sat 12 noon-2.30, 6.30-11.45.
Food £16. Wine £4.80.
Still the same old place, and good that it is too. Old fashioned, quieter restaurant with pink and blue tablecloths reminiscent of Greece. Gold wallpaper and an eclectic if dubious selection of naive paintings by customers. The decor is as delicious as the food. Start with the hors d'oeuvres, ample for two and good value at £2.95. It includes tarama, humous, squid, sardines, vine leaves and meat balls. A vast menu with lots to tempt but who could resist filet de boeuf 'Latin Lover' in a brandy sauce?

San Frediano
62 Fulham Rd, SW3 (584 8375)
ITALIAN
Mon-Sat 12.30-2.30, 7.30-11.30.
Food £16. Wine £3.65.

Crowded, friendly restaurant popular for family get-togethers. Flexible menu that changes weekly; some excellent pasta dishes appear and disappear. Amongst the starters I can recommend the crema San Frediano (cream soup of tomatoes, leeks and potatoes) and lumache provinciale, otherwise known as snails. Liver aficionados will appreciate the fegato alla salvia (calves' liver with sage). There are delicious veal dishes one's come to associate with Italian cuisine. Good strong coffee.

Selamat Datang
234 Old Brompton Rd, SW5 (370 2421)
SOUTH EAST ASIAN
Mon-Sat 6.00-11.30.
Food £13. Wine £3.80.
For that evening when you're tired of the old faithfuls and want something different. Entertaining menu with good soups, from the well known wan tun to Singapore laska, thick noodles cooked in coconut milk. From the noodles section try Penang oyster mee. Various chicken dishes to tempt, particularly the five spices version. Lychees are ideal after all these distinctive tastes. For a special occasion there is a traditional 10 course Malaysian meal from a satay start to a coffee finish with lots in between from £7.85.

Shu Shan II
265 Old Brompton Rd, SW7 (589 3149)
CHINESE
Mon-Sat 12 noon-11.00.

Food £26. Wine £4.10.
Austere, elegant restaurant featuring Sichuan cuisine. The hors d'oeuvres — sliced pork, sliced beef, shredded chicken and smoked fish with trimmings — are special. So too, but perhaps an acquired taste, is the jellyfish blubber with sesame oil. Nuts and chilli occur in many dishes: king pao pork is with cashew nuts and fried with chilli, deep braised shredded beef with celery and carrots is also fried with chilli. An unexpected but quite delicious sweet: red bean pancake.

Tandoori Ashoka
181 Fulham Rd, SW3 (352 3301)
INDIAN
Mon-Sun 12 noon-2.45, 6.00-11.45.
Food £17. Wine £4.10.
Particularly well prepared tandoori specialities partaken in rather dreary surroundings. Amusing little lines of explanation on the menu: from 'the tastefulness is terrific' to 'a hot favourite with the Anglo Indians'. The latter refers to mulligatawny soup, literal meaning, pepper water, and made with meat and chicken flour. Chicken chaat, hot and sour, 'you have been warned', so says the menu. Seriously though, the food is imaginatively and immaculately prepared. Good set menus include a vegetarian for £4.75.

William F
140 Fulham Rd, SW10 (373 5534)
ANGLO/FRENCH

Mon-Sat 7.00-12 midnight.
Food £20. Wine £3.96.
Pinepanelled carriage-like restaurant. The menu changes from time to time but many favourites remain. So starters should include croustades de volaille with sherry and cream sauce, and flavoured with pimentoes and mustard. On to the main course and you can't go wrong with the stuffed trout. Delicious vegetables; all the while sipping away at the good quality house wine. Well organised, popular restaurant.

BUDGET

Bistro Vino
2 Hollywood Rd, SW10 (352 6439)
ANGLO/FRENCH
Mon-Sun 6.00-12 midnight.
Food £9.00. Wine £3.40.
Cheap and cheerful, more so if you're a student. Bench-like wooden tables and dim lighting. Predictable starters featuring avocado and prawns, and some quite nice soups: vegetable, onion, chilled vichyssoise. From fillet steak and steak Diane at extremely accessible prices to fried plaice and tartare sauce to chicken kiev. Good apple pie and creme caramel.
Also at 1 Old Brompton Rd, SW7 (589 3888), 5 Clareville St, SW7 (373 3903) and 303 Old Brompton Rd, SW3 (589 7898).

Ho Lee Fook
368-370 King's Rd, SW3 (353 6797)
CHINESE
Mon-Sun 12 noon-11.30.

Food £8.00. Wine £3.30.
Convenience dining from midday to midnight (almost) in this Chinese eatery with the curved glass facade. Extremely friendly service and excellent economical concoctions, including some good fondue pot dishes: abalone, chicken and Chinese mushrooms, braised fish head and bean curd. If you are daunted by the extensive lists then go for one of the set menus from £3.50. Finish off with addictive toffee bananas. Excellent take away service as well.

La Bersagliera
372 King's Rd, SW3 (353 5993)
ITALIAN
Mon-Sat 12.30-3.00, 6.30-11.30.
Food £9.00. Wine £3.20.
A large boxed sign proclaiming 'pizzeria' is most misleading. They certainly serve pizzas, and good ones at that, but it's their delicious fresh pasta and moules you'll be queuing up for. A mish mash of design, including Italian rural scene painted on one wall, helps the ambience. You will find lots of trendies coming here and loving the somewhat slapdash service. Great al dente tagliatelle and tagliarini with mouth watering Bolognese and tomato sauces. London needs more places like this.

Pizza Vino
205 King's Rd, SW3 (352 2134)
ITALIAN
Mon-Sat 11.00am-12.30.
Food £8.00. Wine £3.70.
Brisk, friendly service from the jaunty waiters. If you are

*afraid of aging, then this isn't
for you because so often Pizza
Vino seems to be full of all the
beautiful young boys and girls
from miles around. Good
range of pizzas, some unusual
ones too: pizza caviale, Danish
caviare and mozzarella, as you
might've guessed. Prefer
something more substantial?
Perhaps saltimbocca alla
Romana or roast beef with
roast potatoes, tomato salad
and pizza bread. The
homemade ice cream at 70p a
pop is quite a treat.*

TRANSPORT

**(All details subject to change.
Phone 01-222 1234 at anytime,
day or night to check details.
Some routes shown do not
operate every day of the
week.)**

Tube: Sloane Square, South
Kensington
Buses: 11, 14, 19, 22, 31, 39
(Mon-Sat only, except
evenings), 45, 49, 137
Night: N97

MR CHOW

Knightsbridge is glittering shop facade, rich red brick square, small manicured dogs, screeching taxis, Harrods like a flagship. Unreal streets. In Knightsbridge, one lives in an apartment, not a flat, and then only between business and the country. Restaurants reflect this shifting crowd, tourists and shoppers, the shrill upper voices, the low muttering deals, everyone waving their clear plastic wallet of cards (American Express, Diner's Club in alphabetical order). Veering towards a more human, shabby-bright Chelsea, the pastel-faced houses confront smaller, sweeter, more self-conscious gourmandize.

LUXURY

Brasserie St Quentin
243 Brompton Rd, SW3 (589 8005)
FRENCH
Mon-Fri 12 noon-2.30; Sat & Sun 12 noon-4.00; Mon-Sun 7.00-11.30.
Food £30. Wine £4.70.
Awash with glass and glitterati, this designer brasserie only echoes its roots at weekends when you can read the papers at breakfast and have sweet pastisserie and lemon tea in the afternoon. The sharp cut waiters have an irritating Gallic superiority and spend more time cultivating a disdainful glance in the mirror than delivering on time. The food however is good, quenelles (of course), paupiette de turbot, chiffonade de boeuf au paprika vacherin, assiete de sorbets. The lunch menu changes every day. Avoid being condemned with the noise and the headscarves and sneak downstairs.

Menage a Trois
14/15 Beauchamp Pl, SW3 (589 4252)
FRENCH (nouvelle)
Mon-Sat 11.30-2.30, 5.30-12.30; cocktail happy hour 5.30-8.00.
Food £24. Wine £3.95. 'Just starters + puddings no intercourse'.
The mirror on the stairway is a bad start but prepares you for the welter of self-consciousness inside. Kaffe Fassettish upholstery, a square of pink neon, tasty modern prints, waitresses in comic bandellero knickerbockers, some idle rich playing with taffeta balldress cocktails. The menu was written by a frustrated poet 'a terrine of many days and many birds' and is highly confusing since each dish has at least six separate ingredients — 'Whole peach (white of course) stuffed with pistachio ice cream, topped with honey and champagne sauce and toasted almonds'. 'The orgy of warm French salad leaves' was a minor affair, the terrines were pretty but bland and generally the throwing in of tiny truffles, quails eggs, sorrel and rocquefort is not worth the large price. If good taste has got more to do with the eye than the mouth, you'll love it. Service good, puddings better than starters, cheeseboard excellent.*

Mes Amis
31 Basil St, SW3 (584 4484/9099)
FRENCH
Mon-Sun 12.15-3.00, 7.15-11.00.
Food £26. Wine £5.25.
Ex-steak house now a corner awash with rough plaster and beams and pale green napkins. Bland French menu with a seemingly interesting fish list (baked brill to river trout with hazelnut butter) but the pink trout with capers was overcooked. Starters include les soupes pistou et poisson, plus some grillades, fresh free range chicken for the purists, puddings of the sorbet and cream variety. Alarmingly expensive wine list. Service good, discreet but a little turgid. Terrible boulevard musak.

Mr Chow
151 Knightsbridge, SW7 (589 7347)
CHINESE (Pekinese)
Mon-Sat 12.30-2.45, 7.00-11.45;
Sun 12.30-2.30, 7.00-11.45.
Food £30. Wine £5.00.
So you always thought Chinese food was taken downtown, red coloured ducks in the window, steel chairs and hot cheap jasmin tea at the table? Michael Chow has a great mahogany and glass facade, white tablecloth service and conscientiously delicious Pekinese food. Everyone will be discreetly rubbernecking like mad but if you feel a little lost in the media sea, console yourself with a glance between courses at the Dine and Caulfield on the walls. The bill will be fiendish.

Walton's
121 Walton St, SW3 (584 0204)
ENGLISH.
Mon-Sat 12.30-2.30, 7.30-11.30.
Food £35. Wine £5.00.
Rich, sumptuous, self-conscious interior where traditional English fare is served grandly, sometimes in a far too frilly dress. Calves Liver does not need mango and avocado to make it interesting. Smoked eel pate, vegetable terrine with fresh tomato sauce, breast of venison with port and redcurrant sauce and poached pears, water ices. Take a smaller cheaper meal at set lunch and after 10.30. The wine list is excellent.

MID-PRICE

Basil Street Hotel Restaurant
Basil St, SW1 (581 3311)
INTERNATIONAL
Mon-Sun 7.45am-10.00, 12.30-2.15, 6.30pm-9.45; closed Sat lunch.
Food £15. Wine £4.10.
Low-ceilinged pale green drawing room with quiet carpet and chintz curtains. The sort of place where well-dressed chidren stick out their tongue at you. The lunch menu varies its two or three course sets each day. The general fare will flourish the redoubtable avocado, lobster bisque, lemon sole, devilled whitebait, trolley puddings. Children's menus (spaghetti and ice cream with chocolate sauce for instance, £2.95) plus a tinkling classical piano of an evening. The menu kindly and wisely points out that roast rib, their speciality, can only be cut as it comes from the silver belly of its cave.

Bewicks
87/89 Walton St, SW3 (584 6711)
FRENCH
Mon-Fri 12.30-2.30, 7.30-11.30;
Sat 7.00-11.30.
Food £20. Wine £5.25.
Modernish space warmed by green and gold. The menu changes monthly but you may expect creme de huitres natures, artichokes hearts filled with smoked salmon mousse, carre d'agneau roti persille, sweetbreads, finely cooked vegetables, poisson et patisserie du jour, rich chocolate mousse, torte

marron. Those who partake luncheon with a sharp eye, come here for two course (£6.25), three course (£8) or four course (£9.75).

Bill Bentleys
31 Beauchamp Pl, SW3 (589 5080)
ENGLISH
Mon-Sat 11.00-2.30, 5.30-10.30.
Food £17. Wine £3.60.

You can take Bill Bentley's on three floors, basement and bistro, a glass of madeira on ground level and seafood upstairs, (cool and clever lunchies take all theirs in the summer garden). Luxury sea-people eat giant plates of oysters, timider fish gnaw at fried crab claw, fresh sardines, coquille St Jacques, plaice, and just have room for a dark little chocolate mousse. Wide wine list with many labels by the glass.

Borshtch N'Tears
45 Beauchamp Pl, SW3 (589 5003)
RUSSIAN
Mon-Sun 7.30-1.30.
Food £15. Wine £4.10 (litre)

Where the bass guitar meets the ukelele over that famous beetroot soup. This stroganoff bistro is crammed with noisy people eating Golubtsky (stuffed cabbage leaves) and Chicken Dragomir (white wine, cream and gherkin sauce). The tears must be tears of exasperation trying to get yourself heard. Forget that music and chew a sweet blinis.

Brasserie Des Amis
27 Basil St, SW3 (584 9012)
FRENCH
Mon-Sun 11.30-3.00, 6.30-11.00.
Food £14. Wine £4.95.

As you may perceive from the opening times, another of the city's faux brasserie. Trendy little sister of Mes Amis the food is plainer, and less expensive; (the trout with capers, albeit a non pink variety, was over one pound cheaper). Brochettes, tarte a l'oignon, a totally non-visual salade nicoise, terrines etc. surrounded by self-conscious black and white tiled floor, space-deceiving mirrors and green bamboo.

Chicago Rib Shack
1 Raphael St, SW7 (581 5595)
AMERICAN
Mon-Sat 11.45-11.30.
Food £13. Wine £4.25.

The Rib Shack is sister to the deep-fish phenomenon at the Chicago Pizza Factory in Hanover Square. As most things American, this lickerty spit eaterie sure knows how to sell itself. The concept is grabbed from Victorian ruins (a Glasgow mahogany bar, Lancashire stained glass) with a dash of Cocktail Hour, bibs with 'Bone Appetit' and a lunchtime/drinks harpist. Hungry meat eaters take large bites of juicy rib, barbequed chicken, potato skins stuffed with cheese and crunchy bacon, onion bread and piles of quick-chop salad. Little pigs carry on with cheese cake, carrot cake, pecan pie and ice cream washed with a plentiful river of Californian wines.

Drones
1 Pont St, SW1 (235 9638)
AMERICAN
Mon-Sun 12.30-3.00, 7.30-11.00.
Food £17. Wine £4.50.
Perhaps the nearest you can go to eating indoor al fresco. This chic greenhouse serves the hamburger in the sleekest up-market state, plus other nouvelle Americana like the munchy potato skins and plain (but never drab) veal and trout. The salads are excellent (try prawns, crackling lettuce avocado and crispy chillis). The service is very soothing but the people crammed at the next table can be irritating. Remember the name for post-theatre and bright chatty lunches.

English House
3 Milner St, SW3 (584 3002)
ENGLISH
Mon-Sat 12.30-2.30, 7.30-11.30.
Food £19. Wine £5.50.
Nobly is England striving to sell itself over the table. This is one of the few restaurants which serves something more intelligent than meat and two veg, though it has had to cull the recipes from less puritan eighteenth century cookbooks. Combine nostalgia and English floral print and sally forth upon pease soup with garlic and mint, potted meats and fish, steak, kidney and mushroom pie, galantine of rabbit, punch jelly and walnut pie. Set lunches (eg brie tart, braised oxtail, coffee served with chocolate fudge) are for £5.75.

Luba's Bistro
6 Yeoman's Row, SW3 (589 2950)
RUSSIAN
Mon-Sat 12.00-3.00, 6.00-11.45.
Food £11. Unlicensed.
The title role can be a tricky patronne but she sure serves a mean golubstzy. Most food can be taken as a neat reflection of their nation's characteristics — solid German wurst, plain-speaking English roasts, visual Italian pizza etc. The Russian meal is a sharp fish, stern grainy, sour cream affair with an odd flash of genius. The names at least always sound like an adventure. Apart from the expected borschts and goulashes, fill up with buckwheat piroshki and sernic, a sweet pancake filled with cream cheese and raisins. A chattering, clattering (the kitchen is included in the open plan), check-clothed room where you will have to bring your own wine (but no corkage).

Massey's Chop House
38 Beauchamp Pl. SW3 (589 4856)
ENGLISH
Mon-Sat 12.30-2.30, 6.45-10.45.
Food £15. Wine £4.05.
There is something very charming and eighteenth century about the idea of a 'chop house'; the twentieth century reality however lacks Boswell's wit and argument. Still no-one could complain with a set menu of shrimps, lamb cutlets, apple pie and coffee for £6.95, in the otherwise cottage-chic of Beauchamp Place. A la Cartes take their (large) chop grilled

and veal surrounded with prawns in turtle aspic, and Black Forest gateau.

Ma Cuisine
113 Walton St, SW3 (584 7585)
FRENCH
Mon-Fri 12.30-2.00, 7.30-11.00
Food £21. Wine £5.50.
This tiny elegant space is one of the most fiendishly difficult to fight your way into. The praise of grand gourmets hangs proudly in the air. French food as it is so rarely found cooked with fine ingredients and much imagination. Taste delicate red mullet soup, pate d'anguilles a la mousse de cresson, ballotine de volaille with a rich lobster sauce, melting noissettes of lamb with onion and mint puree, fruity and cream extravaganzas du jour and the tiny tempting cheeses of France. Book at least two weeks ahead.

Montpeliano
13 Montepelier St, SW7 (589 0032)
ITALIAN
Mon-Sat 12.30-3.00, 7.00-12 midnight.
Food £17. Wine £4.40.
Where the crowd grab their calf brains milanese, talk at round clothed tables surrounded by white tile and thick green plants and guess the names of the zappy prints (Lichtenstein et al). Those who condemn Italian food with a dull-never-as-exciting-as-French-label should come here to change their mind with fettucine, pollo valdosiana, seafood salads, sweetbreads. Take a wine that is not Valpolicella and finish

with zabaglione (excellent, not stingy with the Marsala) and fresh fruit (mango, paw paw, pineapple, strawberries). Charming service.

Newports
Knightsbridge Green, 22 Brompton Rd, SW1 (589 8772)
FRENCH
Food £18. Wine £3.95.
Newports is soft brown carpet, calm house surrounds and crisp white tablecloths. Though you may eat as you wish a la carte, it is probably sharper to choose from the short but ever changing set menus (two course £6.50, lunch only, three course for £7.50, four course £9.50). Light meals can be taken between 2.30 and 7.00, likewise afternoon tea; post-theatre bites from 11.00-12.00 midnight. The specialities are fishy, varying caviars, seafood bisque, brochette of sea bass, Essex whitebait. Alternative temptations are healthy crudites, chicken en papillote, creme brulee (ALC); tomato and orange soup, chicken and leek pie and ice cream with hot crushed raspberries (fix).

Sale e Pepe
13 Pavilion Rd, SW1 (235 0098)
ITALIAN
Mon-sat 12 noon-3.00, 7.00-12 midnight. Food £19. Wine £4.50.
Tiny furious Italian restaurant awash with white tile and greenery where the Harrods shopping bags clash with the spinning waiters. If you can ignore the bustle of it all, take lunch here with bowls green and creamy pasta, delicate

garlicky scampi, winter-defying bean and pasta soup (extra thick green olive oil added at table) octopus salad and some excellent veal (give the lamb a miss, it never sits well on an Italian plate). The sharp smell of raddicchio will whisk you back into travel nostalgia but the pepperpot tradition could be left out.

Shangri La
233 Brompton Rd, SW3 (584 3658)
CHINESE
Mon-Sun 12 noon-11.30.
Food £12. Wine £3.90.
Come here for quick Chinese snack in true Caulfield setting. As in many Chinese restaurants there are varied set meals (£5.35-£8.45). Explorers take an oriental drink (Mon Tai, Saki) before a speedy crisp plate of prawns; lingerers take a calmer candle-flickering step downstairs and play chopsticks on green jade soup, sate, duck with almonds, beef with oyster sauce and pimento, some stem ginger with cream, lychees and a pot of fragrant tea. Special dishes can be arranged with the management, ordinary ones can be taken away.

Shezan
16 Cheval Pl, SW7 (589 7918)
PAKISTANI
Mon-Sat 12 noon-2.30, 7.00-11.30.
Food £18. Wine £5.00.
The place to catch brilliant Pakistani cooking. A complete switch from the normal rich interiors of Eastern restaurants, Shezan is calm, cool tile, vanilla wall, fish behind glass.

Everyone behaves very politely. The menu reflects this, being deceptively simple. Take first the tandoori speciality, murgh tikka lahori, spicy soups (including mulligatawny), kebabs, lentils and the delicious basmati rice. Even the curries here are courteous and do not hit you in the mouth. Finish with an Indian pudding swimming in sweet milk, flourishing a silver leaf.

Sloane's
Knightsbridge, SW1 (589 6520)
AMERICAN
Mon-Sun 11.30am-1.30am.
Food £12. Wine £4.50.
Brownish checquerclothed burger hideout where you can deviate into other relish-hot, quick-fry, tv dinner Americana. Serious people go down the long cocktail list (Gloom Chasers to Zombies), sweet teeth take the cola floats. Not as slick as some of the harsher rock and steak palaces downtown but the helpings are large and there's a television if you're afflicted with kids. Take fried chicken, spare ribs, corn on the cob, chilli with crackers, BLTS and rabbit food salads. Live music downstairs at night. Plus take away.

Les Trois Canards
14 Knightsbridge Green, SW1 (589 0509)
FRENCH
Mon-Sat 12 noon-2.30, 7.00-10.15.
Food £17.30. Wine 3.90.
Pretty pink Provencal restaurant with much uncluttered charm and stripey wallpaper, on the corner of Knightsbridge Green. It is

without surprise that the speciality of the house is that rich bird the duck (take its breast with a green peppercorn sauce). Otherwise, feast upon Mediterranean sea food, light spinach mousse, lamb with mustard, turbot and delicious tarte tartin. Then a digestif — marc, calvados, poire william.

BUDGET

Bendicks
195 Sloane St, SW1 (235 4749)
ANGLO/FRENCH
Mon-Fri 9.00-5.30; Sat 9.00-3.30.
Food £6. Wine £2.45.
Bendicks is of course, home of the imperial bittermint. Have it boxed here with a sumptuous cream cake or two to take away or sit amongst les grandes dames du shopping and wait for croque monsieur, scones and butter, quiches, hot chocolate, ham salads or trout, depending upon mood or time. Much red plush and conversational hush will not appeal to those who prefer a muscular meal. Hangovers do not take kindly to the rattle of saucer and the genteely gilted mirrors.

Bistro Vino
303 Brompton Rd, SW3 (589 7898)
FRENCH
Mon-Sun 12 noon-3.00, 6.00-12.00 midnight.
Food £8. Wine £3.20.
Bistro Vinos lightly sprinkle this end of town, you can recognise them by their sombre reddish darkness inside and navy paint outside. In an area thick with poseurs, these are thankfully unpretentious, (certainly the menu would be cheeky to attempt such status). Expect a youngish, merry crowd, and friendly, if rather hurried service. Food is of the very bistro sort, pates, onion soup, pepper steaks, scampi provencale, chicken veronique, chocolate mousse and sorbets. Plainsong wines. A good place to go for a meal and argument, rather than social drama and gourmandise.
Also at 1 Old Brompton Rd, SW1; 5 Clareville St, SW7; 2 Hollywood Rd, SW10.

Pizza On The Park
Hyde Park Corner, SW1 (235 5550)
AMERICAN.
Mon-Sun 10.00-12 midnight.
Food £8. Wine £3.50.
Where the pizza and the burger jive hand in hand. Unlike their loud squabbling neighbour on the other side of the corner you won't get the queues, the dark thumping rock, the cram or the atmosphere but you will find a large, clean tiled space set about with mirrors and palms and palatable fast food with every relish. Quick, cheap, predictable. Regular live jazz downstairs in a smaller, smokier setting.

Spaghetti House
77 Knightsbridge, SW1 (235 8141)
ITALIAN
Mon-Sat 12 noon-3.00, 5.30-10.30; closed Mon evening.

Food £10. Wine £4.15 (litre).
More famous for its dramatic photo finish siege than for its pasta, Spaghetti House nevertheless serves a good honest plate. Life amongst the swinging chianti bottles can get a little hectic at lunch times but service rarely fails. A large menu declares Italianate favourites, tuna and butter beans, raw palma ham and prawns, veal milanese, lemon sole, cassata, zuppa inglese. Plus pasta e pizza in variegated forms for a snappier bite. See also Zia Theresa 4 Hans Rd, SW3.

Stockpot
6 Basil St, SW3 (589 8627)
INTERNATIONAL
Mon-Fri 11.30-10.30; Sat 10.30-9.30.
Food £4.30 (lunch), £6 (dinner). Wine £2.85.
Bleakish white wall and pine bench, loud with shoppers dropping in for bites. Worthy tea-room menu, very cold salad and cheese and biscuits, changes every day, becoming more sophisticated/expensive at night. All the food is home-made and veers from smoked mackerel to cannelloni, curried eggs to banana split. Certainly not innovative but you won't quarrel with the price.

Wolfe's
25 Basil St, SW3 (589 8444/7217)
AMERICAN.
Mon-Sun 11.30-12 midnight.
Food £9.50. Wine £5.
Do not be surprised if you fall over on entering, this place is extremely dark and brown carpeted (though not, it transpired, to hide something nasty on the plate). Those who like light, air and a witty buzz will not take kindly to its panelled brown mood, taped slick Americana or its weighty pecan pie. The Wolfburger has an up-market swing (Charcoal grill, sesame bun) and can be surrounded with sauerkraut, Rocquefort, chillis etc. Alternatives include chargrilled Pacific Prawns, huge but slimming salads and the variegated waffle. Also at 34 Park Lane, W1.

(All details subject to change. Phone 01-222 1234 at anytime, day or night to check details. Some routes shown do not operate every day of the week.)

KNIGHTSBRIDGE
Tube: Knightsbridge, Sloane Square
Buses: 9. 14, 22, 30, 52, 52a, 73, 74, 137
Night: N97

VICTORIA
Tube: Victoria, Sloane Square
Buses: 2, 2b, 10, 11, 16, 24, 25, 29, 36, 36b, 38, 39, 52, 52a, 55, 70, 76 (Mon-Fri only), 149 (Mon-Fri except evenings), 185, 500 (daily, but not evenings or Sun), 507
Night: N84, N90, N93, N95, N98 — to Victoria
Or: 137 — to Sloane Square
Or: 77a, 88 — to Pimlico

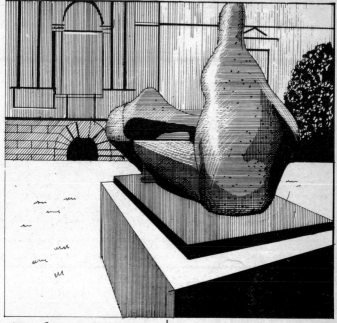

TATE GALLERY RESTAURANT

Victoria is first the station —
vast sooty arches over a
hurrying crowd, pigeons,
buses — a restless, ugly
place. Victoria Street, thick
with hamburger joint and
office block, is probably most
people's first glimpse of the
city. Cause enough to
despair. There are a few
travelling restaurants here
but a more civilised bite may
be found among the quiet
creamy squares and mews of
Belgravia — land of the
embassy and sharp accent.
Towards Westminster and the
river they become sturdy
masculine lunch spots for
MP's between debates.
Pimlico, immortalised by the
film, is a monotonous sparse
residential area relieved
suddenly by the cultural
portals of the Tate Gallery
and the grey stretch of the
Thames.

LUXURY

Capital Hotel Restaurant
22 Basil St, SW1 (589 5171)
FRENCH
Mon-Sat 12.30-2.15, 6.30-10.30;
Sun 12.30-1.45, 7.00-9.45.
Food £35. Wine £5.50.
There can be something daunting and isolated about eating in an hotel restaurant, especially if you're not a resident. However some of the city's best food is cooked in their kitchens, so if you are more interested in the gourmandise than the snappy, chic atmosphere, try them out. The Capital has a bright modern interior and a great reputation. Try mousseline of scallops, a la creme d'oursins, terrine de pigeons, carre d'agneau persille, fine breast of duck, quenelles and the notoriously delicious champagne sorbet.

Carlton Tower Rib Room
Cadogan Place, SW1 (235 5411)
INTERNATIONAL
Mon-Sun 12.30-2.45, 7.00-10.45.
Food £32. Wine £7 (litre).
Everything an old-fashioned rib room should be, quiet, carpeted, heavy cutlery, thick white tablecloths, bulky chairs although some of the prices might only entice those with a wallet of credit cards. Fine Aberdeen beef in enormous chunks, plus other meaty grills and calves' liver. The sort of place that usually has smoked salmon or caviar to begin with, or an excellently stirred martini. Good wine list. See also the brilliantly acclaimed
Chelsea Room for their predominantly nouvelle cuisine.

Mijanou
143 Ebury St, SW1 (730 4099)
FRENCH
Mon-Thu 12.30-2.00, 7.30-10.00;
Fri 12.30-2.00, 7.30-11.00.
Food £28. Wine £3.75.
Rather serious, careful French restaurant with red tablecloths, impeccable manners but shortish on joie de vivre. If you come to enjoy the food rather than your companion relish quails stuffed with wild rice and pecan nuts, served with a bourbon and orange sauce, a carnivores gateau of veal fillet and brains, garnished with calves' liver and sweetbeads, fish soup with sweet mussels, a mousseline of quails' livers and port, as well as a flourish of ice cream sodden with prunes, cream and Armanac.

Parkes
5 Beauchamp Place, SW3 (589 1390)
INTERNATIONAL
Mon-Fri 12.30-2.45, 7.00-11.00.
Food £36 (set incl). Wine £5.
Successful restaurant ablaze with fresh flowers, cocktail bar on ground floor, fountain and modernist sophistication. If you want an intimate evening of it, beware of the closely clinging tables and sly lighting. Good often inventive menu, includes artichoke and spinach, mushrooms with pistachio nuts, haddock souffle, guinea fowl casserole with asparagus, fine sole en croute. Cheese addicts will be interested by their Roquefort pate, otherwise

try a bowl of pears with apple and Calvados.

L'Amico
Dean Bradley House, 44
Horseferry Rd, SW1 (222 4680)
ITALIAN
Mon-Sat 12 noon-2.45,
6.30-11.00; closed Sat lunch.
Food £16. Wine £3.95.
Basement Italy upon the desolate reaches of Horseferry Road. Good pasta (spaghetti vongole or carbonara) but if you're in an expansive frame of eating take the crab soup, lemon sole in butter, white wine and prawns, involtini stuffed with ham and cheese, beef in paprika and cream, and a truly surprising mouthful of sweet chicken, parsley, butter and garlic in pollo sorpresa. Trolley puds and the redoubtable zabaglione.

Bumbles
16 Buckingham Palace Rd,
SW1 (828 2903)
ENGLISH
Mon-Fri 12 noon-2.30,
6.00-10.30; Sat 6.30-10.30.
Food £14.50. Wine £3.75.
Next door to Mainly English, the shop statement to British wine and cheese, Bumbles shares an owner but not the same purity of materials. The traditional dishes exist of course, rough home-made soups, whitebait, steak and kidney pie, pork in cider, syllabubs etc, but the rest has a distinctly dinner party fussiness. Does the smoked trout really need to be wrapped in smoked salmon?. Does good English lamb have to be stuffed with onions and mushrooms, be cut into steaks and caramelised with mint and redcurrant? Fried brie with gooseberry needs careful consideration before embarkation. Nice staff, and good to see that service charges/tips go into their pockets instead of the managements's.

Le Carafe
15 Lowndes St, SW1 (235 2525)
FISH
Mon-Sat 12.30-2.30, 6.30-10.45;
Sun 12.30-2.15, 7.00-10.30.
Food £24. Wine £3.95.
One of the up-market chain restaurants, know it by the label of Wheelers and green facade. Expect the usual comfortable red plush and prints inside and freshly cooked fish and shellfish...oysters, of course, scallops, smoked salmon, smoked eel, turbot, plaice, lobster etc, with a variety of sauces but probably best plain grilled with a crisp bottle of Muscadet and a bite of sharp cheddar to follow.

Chanticleer
Roebuck House, Stag Place,
SW1 (834 5695)
ITALIAN
Mon-Sat 12 noon-3.00, 6.30-12
midnight; closed Sat lunch.
Food £19. Wine £5.25.
A certain determination is needed to find this place. Locate it amongst a grey modern block, downstairs embellished with plaster Romanesque statues. Large

hotel atmosphere where a pianist plays from Monday to Thursday giving way to a band and dancing on Fridays and Saturdays. Italian food of the cream rather than tomato kind: fillets of sole in cream and cinzano, home-made fettucini in cream fois gras and port jelly, shellfish risotto, calves' brains in black butter and capers, pepper steak, chicken fried in butter, aubergine and cheese. Long table splashed with antipastos.

Como Lario
22 Holbein Place, SW1 (730 2954)
ITALIAN
Mon-Sat 12.15-2.30, 6.30-11.30.
Food £12. Wine £3.60.
A simple no-fuss, no-frill, let's-get-down-to-the-pasta-and-talk lunch place. Sit in an airy corner, order a Campari Soda and choose betwixt the classics: tuna fish with beans, mozzarella salad, fresh crab mayonaise, steak with wine and black pepper, scampi and a little sole. Hungry Valpolicella people take a bowl of fresh pasta, especially the gnocci and tagliatelli and indulge in mela stregata for a sweet end.

Eatons
47 Elizabeth St, SW1 (730 0074)
FRENCH/RUSSIAN
Mon-Fri 12 noon-2.00, 7.00-11.15.
Food £18. Wine £4.95.
Small carpety restaurant where an argument would not go unheard. The reputation for the dishes however, could quell the ego. Try the popular blinis with smoked salmon and sour cream, chicken pancake with curry, fresh herring stuffed with pickled cucumber and apple and sour cream sauce, pork filled with cabbage and raisons, fresh hake with almonds. The puddings and cheese do not linger in the memory.

Ebury Wine Bar
139 Ebury St, SW1 (730 5447)
FRENCH
Mon-Sat 11.00am-3.00, 5.30-11.00; Sun 12 noon-2.00, 7.00-10.30.
Food £15. Wine £3.65.
A crowded, wooden tabled place, clamoured for by the Belgravia crowd (despite its lack of pretension, probably best to book). The menu changes each day and may imaginatively zoom from fresh oysters, smoked eel, king prawns with aioli, venison terrine, assiete de charcuterie, to Old English walnut pie and raspberry milles feuilles via a delicious dish of roulade of ham and corn gratinee. Wake up, ye 'wine bars' of quicher temperament. Sundays will supply you with copies of the newspapers from the bar.

La Fontana
101 Pimlico Rd, SW1 (730 6630)
FRENCH/ITALIAN
Mon-Fri 12 noon-2.30, 7.00-11.30; Sat 7.00-11.30.
Food £15. Wine £4.10.
Plain, wooden-backed seated place, probably more conducive to grabbing a lunch than lingering over a dinner. Start simply with a good soupe de poissons or crepe de fromage and diversify into gigot d'agneau aux flageolets,

scampis provencales ou frites, osso buco, veal marsala and sober up with a sharp sorbet au citron or crunchy meringues.

Gavvers
61 Lower Sloane St, SW1 (730 5983)
FRENCH
Mon-Sat 7.00-11.00.
Food £29.50 (set; inc wine).
Slick brasserie where once stood the multi-media starred, Le Gavroche. Forget the bleakness that faces you from outside and indulge in the rich provincial specialities that change every day on the small set menu inside. Find Boudin Noir, assiete de charcuterie, tubot au cerfeuil, fresh watercress soup, oyster and mussel salad, gigot, bouillabaisse and for those addicted to Gallic offal, tripes a la marseillaisse.

Gran Paradiso
52 Wilton Rd, SW1 (828 5818)
ITALIAN
Mon-Sat 12.30-2.30, 6.30-11.30, closed Sat lunch.
Food £16. Wine £4.
Largish space hung with dark painting and palms, only a quick decision away from Victoria Station. Mainly classic menu fegato alla veneziana, fresh chicken livers in madiera, loin of pork with sausages, eggs florentine, tagliatelle and crispy whitebait. Recognise it by the bay trees in tubs outside.

Jacaranda
Walton House, Walton St, SW3 (589 0075)
FRENCH

Mon-Sat 12.30-2.30, 7.00-11.30.
Food £12. Wine £3.75.
Once the house of Lord Walton, now a navy blue restaurant that opens its walled garden in the summertime to the al fresco hordes. Try the courgette a la Procencal (stuffed with minced veal, tomatoes and garlic) coquille de fruits de mer, veal arlesienne, supreme de volaille Jaracranda and poussin cocotte grand-mere. Desserters leap for their tarte aux fruits and the profiteroles.

Ken Lo's Memories Of China
67-69 Ebury St, SW1 (730 7734/4230)
CHINESE
Mon-Sat 12 noon-3.00, 7.00-1.00am.
Food £24. Wine £5.
Mr Lo is famous, of course, for his innovative paperbacks on Chinese cooking. Here you can try it all out without going wok-mad. The menu is large, wide, classical, regional in plainly elegant surroundings. Taste crispy seaweed, sliced fish pepperpot soup, hand-shredded cold chicken in garlic sauce, Cantonese onion and ginger crab/lobster, steamed whole trout and seabass, and grand Peking Duck (which must be ordered ahead of time). Excellent set menus, including 'Tour of China in 7 Dishes', family lunch and health food (take those iron-plate sizzled dishes).

Kundan
3 Horseferry Rd, SW1 (834 3434)
PAKISTANI
Mon-Sat 12 noon-3.00,

7.00-12.30am.
Food £20. Wine £5.50.
Sleek brown basement laden with officals (eating not serving). Tandoori are the mainstream (take the juicy chicken with lemon and spices). Otherwise Shami Kabab Awadhi (finely ground lamb with rice and 'Himalayan herbs'), excellent roghan josh (lamb with butter brown onions, ginger, garlic and yoghurt), sag gosht (lamb with spinach and coriander with buttery rich tandoori paratha). Starters of the avoidable avocado and mulligatawny brand, finish with the milk puddings flecked with nuts and saffron, fresh fruit and jasmin tea.

Lockets
Marsham Court, Marsham St, SW1 (834 9552)
ENGLISH
Mon-Fri 12.15-2.30, 6.30-11.00.
Food £20. Wine £4.
In that cold characterless area within the hearing of the division bell sit whiteclothed tables, panelled walls and hunting pictures, waiting for the politicos to wheel in. Doubtful if anyone is going to be fooled by the 'Olde Englishe' quotes on the menu (Pepys again, poor man), nostalgia/history will never make food taste better, only more pretentious. The staunch fayre is probably the best: lamb and leek pie, baked monkfish with fresh fennel, jugged hare in port, lamb shrewsbury, shell of baked seafood, soft herring roes with mustard sauce and puddings of the frothy, alcoholic fruity

kind.

Mimmo D'Ischia
61 Elizabeth St, SW1 (730 5406)
ITALIAN
Mon-Sat 12.30-3.00, 7.00- 11.30.
Food £20. Wine £3.50.
Sometimes it is difficult to perceive what is meant exactly by the word 'lively' when applied to restaurants. Is it the food, the customers, the bill? Here it is most definitely the waiters, a jovial crew bouncing about the mediterranean walls. Seemingly calm tables will suddenly take upon them plates of spare ribs, fish salads, grilled sardines and butterfly prawns, crespoline (crispy pancakes with ricotta and spinach), tender veal with courgettes, chicken breast in breadcrumbs and asparagus. The puddings are of the zabaglione/gelati kind.

Mimmo e Pasquale
64 Wilton Rd, SW1 (828 6908)
ITALIAN
Mon-Sat 12.15-2.45, 6.30-11.00; closed Sat lunch.
Food £15. Wine £3.80.
White-walled pink tableclothed modernism, with a covered terrace for summertime eating. Catch a plate of aubergine al siciliana, some fresh fish salad, skewered scampi grilled with mint, dover sole with lemon, gelati. Carnivores take calf's brains in marsala and mushrooms, calf's sweetbreads, lamb with garlic and rosemary or a spring devilled chicken.

Motcombs
26 Motcomb St, SW1 (235
6382)
INTERNATIONAL
Mon-Fri 12 noon-2.45,
7.00-11.00.
Food £17. Wine £5.
*Motcombs is probably better
known as a wine bar of the
sleeker sort, serving cold
daytime food (spinach quiche,
cheese) with several wines by
the glass. Try the alternative
downstairs — lentil soup with
sausage, fresh spinach salad
with crispy bacon, herring
fillets with sour cream and
obligatory gulp of vodka, wild
duck, wild rice, tame orange
sauce, grilled seabass and for
real rangers, Sloane Salad
(mozzarella, avocado, tomato
and tuna).*

Os Arcos
44 Hugh St, SW1 (828 1486)
PORTUGUESE
Mon-Sat 12.30-2.00, 7.30-11.30;
closed Sat lunch.
Food £21. Wine £3.80.
*In an area peppererd with
Italian restaurants, it is a
gastronomic delight to find
somewhere to satisfy a
Portuguese palate. A light,
Adriatic place with good
service. The main plate is of
course fish (clams to salt cod).
Amongst the expected squids
and sea bass, diversify with a
stuffed spider crab, grouper
and swordfish. Interesting
wine list.*

Overtons
4 Victoria Buildings, Terminus
Place, SW1 (834 3774)
ENGLISH
Mon-Sat 12 noon-3.00,
5.30-10.30.

Food £16. Wine £3.95.
*Fish restaurant of the
charming stiff-lipped sort. If
the timing is right, an
excellent idea to delight in an
unhurried meal, before/after a
gruesome train journey
departing/arriving on the
platforms over the road.
(Overton's also prepare theatre
suppers from 5.30). Oysters are
the main song (take them
differently fried with bacon),
plus iced jellied eels, lobster
bisque with brandy, turtle
soup, seafood pancakes, skate
with black butter and capers,
turbot and poached haddock
afterwards. Puddings of the
apple pie kind, or perhaps a
sweet pancake or more oysters
disguised as angels on
horseback.*

Pomegranates
94 Grosvenor Rd, SW1 (828
6560)
INTERNATIONAL
Mon-Sat 12.30-2.15, 7.30-11.15;
closed Sat lunch.
Food £16. Wine £5.
*Slip away downstairs to a
private space with large tables
and Tiffany lamps and a menu
that makes Around the World
in Eighty Days look like child's
play. Start the voyage with
turkish chicken and walnut
pate, mexican baked crab with
avocado and tequila, gravad
lax with a sweet mustard
sauce or if available, lime
pickled raw salmon with a
spring onion and parsley
dressing. Cross over to
Szechuan pork with rice, via
some enchilades or wild duck
with apple and calvados and
head home delighting in
Balinese chicken with coconut*

103

and rice. *True Esperantos will understand the tarte and honey and cognac ice cream.*

La Popote
3 Walton St, SW3 (589 9178)
INTERNATIONAL
Mon-Sat 12.30-3.00, 7.30-12
midnight; Sun 1.00-3.00,
8.00-11.30.
Food £18. Wine £4.70.
Self-conscious (if one were being unkind, chi-chi) inside, dark pink walls, statues, green plush carpets and many a prancing waiter. A la cartes take the excellent cheese souffle, butterfly prawns, casserole of pigeon, grilled lamb's kidneys, game in season and solidly wicked puddings such as rice pudding with strawberry sauce, and bread and butter pudding. La Popote is well known for its sharply priced set menus: three course late night supper (after 10.30) £7.50, lunch £5.

La Poule Au Pot
231 Ebury St, SW1 (730 7763)
FRENCH
Mon-Sat 12.30-2.30, 7.00-11.15;
closed Sat lunch.
Food £16. Wine £5.
Warm woody French place, where the chatter is bright, the windows steam up from the cold Belgravia street outside and the waiters open the door and smile bonjour. Neither smart nor bistro, most forget the labels and concentrate on les coquilles, les crudites, la mousse de poisson, le canard aux citrons verts, le gigot breton aux flageolets, le porc au vermouth (not forgetting la poule in her pot and le coq in his vin). Finish with les crepes and les tartes.

Salloos
62 Kinnerton St, SW1 (235 4444)
PAKISTANI
Mon-Sat 12 noon-3.00, 7.00-12
midnight.
Food £22. Wine £4.60.
Find the spice in this perfect Belgravia mews. Coachhouse into modern restaurant serves chana (chick peas cooked in onions and spices), batiare (marinated and charcoaled quails), velvety almond soup, and the chicken in various guises, cut and dried for Chicken Tikka, hot and melting in Chicken Cheese, mouth-burning in Chicken Ginger. You will need to give 24 hours warning if wishing to dine upon The Barra (whole young lamb stuffed with Basmati rice, among other things).

Scats
27 Motcomb St, SW1 (235
1668)
ENGLISH
Mon-Sun 12.15-2.45, 6.30-10.45;
closed Sun evening.
Food £12. Wine £4.
Opposite the rigid cream pillars of Sotheby's Belgravia. Forget all flourishes of the Victorian and Art Nouveau and fetch a simple plate of potted shrimps, lemon sole, rack of lamb, steak and kidney pie or even just some sausages and mash. Set meals available. Sparse interior of brown tiled floor, pale woody panelling.

Tate Gallery Restaurant

Tate Gallery, Millbank, SW1
(834 6754)
ENGLISH
Mon-Sat 12 noon-3.00.
Food £17. Wine £3.75.
Break mid-way through the Turner and exchange for Rex Whistler's mural and a meal culled from cookbooks of the British Museum. Sample Hindle Wakes 'a medieval chicken dish from the spinners of Lancashire' (who knew their stuff), Joan Cromwell's (wife of the warts-sprinkled Oliver) Grand Sallet, buttered crab, and finish with a generous slice of Stilton or the famous pye with fruyt ryfshews. Excellent pioneer wine list and good waitressing. This restaurant goes the way of aeroplanes and cinemas and divides the room into smoking and non smoking. Before you leave sober up in front of the vast canvasses of John Martin. This is what happens to those of weakened flesh.

BUDGET

Nineteen

19 Mossop St, SW3 (589 4971)
INTERNATIONAL
Mon-Fri 12 noon-3.00,
7.00-11.45.
Food £9. Wine £3.25.
Friendly bistro-place with well-scrubbed tables, candles, and dashing service. Plainish menu includes onion soup gratinee, stilton and egg mousse, whitebait, fillet stroganoff, halibut meurniere, tangerine fool, apple and almond crumble and ginger syllabub. Set menu for lunch, £3.50.

Le Steak Nicole

72-73 Wilton Rd, SW1 (834 7301)
FRENCH
Mon-Sat 12 noon-2.30,
6.45-11.00; closed Sat lunch.
Food £11. Wine £3.50
Is this the Gallic snook to the hamburger? Upstairs a bar menu with onion cream soup, baked potato filled with prawns, vegetarian salad, vol au vent etc, in a room awash with melamine and cane. Downstairs for the entrecote menu (£5.50 all inclusive) which includes french bread, mixed salad (vinaigrette or blue cheese) and le steak in a sharp butter sauce.

TRANSPORT

(All details subject to change. Phone 01-222 1234 at anytime, day or night to check details. Some routes shown do not operate every day of the week.)

Tube:	Victoria, Sloane Square
Buses:	2, 2b, 10, 11, 16, 24, 25, 29, 36, 36b, 38, 39, 52, 52a, 55, 70, 76 (Mon-Fri only), 149 (Mon-Fri except evenings), 185, 500 (daily, but not evenings or Sun), 507
Night:	N84, N90, N93, N95, N98 — to Victoria
Or:	137 — to Sloane Square
Or:	77a, 88 — to Pimlico

TUTTONS

While Bloomsbury slept, Covent Garden, since the market closed, has changed from being a trade and theatrical backwater into the shop window of hip capitalism. The increased demand caused by the resulting influx, consisting mainly of natives between 25 and 35 and tourists, has been catered for by a mushrooming of youth-orientated eating-places.

But the old established restaurants (such as Boulestin) remain, giving the area a range of choice from, say, the stuffiness of Simpsons to the latest in stripped pine, loud rock music and cocktails. Amidst all this change some restaurants still specialise in 'ethnic' English food (Porters, Rules) and carry it off. When you add to this the numerous and reliable French and Italian places, and a sprinkling of the best in exotic ethnic (Japanese, Chinese, Indian, Brazilian and American) and a few whole food and health food places, the result is an area rich in culinary variety and quality. Drinking here is also easy and pleasant, given the number of wine bars and, particularly, of *discreet, unspoiled little pubs that dot the area. Little happens north of the British Museum, but the concentrated colour and diversity of Covent Garden make up for it.*

LUXURY

Boulestin
25 Southampton St, WC2 (836 7061)
FRENCH
Mon-Sat 12.30-2.20, 7.30-11.15.
Food £35. Wine £10.
Standards are still high in this veteran place despite recent upheavals in management. The cooking is inventive and the menu holds many delights; crabe a l'artichaut, pave la villette au poivre rose, deep fried puree of Roquefort and mushrooms in puff pastry, and superb cheeses and sweets (tulipe des trois sorbets). The dining room is both attractive and sumptuous — dress to suit the sombre oils and glorious chandeliers.

La Bussola
42-49 St Martins Lane, WC2 (240 1148)
ITALIAN
Mon-Sat 12 noon-3.00.
Food £35. Wine £5.
An elegant, upmarket Italian place for dining and dancing right in the core of the theatre district. There are two different bands to dance to, playing disco and Latin music. Other cuisines are represented on the menu, but one is best advised to stick to the Italian. They have good soups and a deliciously oily and savoury antipasta. You will probably need to dance a little to work off all the food you've eaten.

Chez Solange
35 Cranbourn St, WC2 (836 5886)
FRENCH
Mon-Sat 12 noon-3.15, 5.30-12.15.
Food £28. Wine £4.45.
In a vivacious and distinctively French atmosphere, much valued by theatre-goers, the Rochons offer straightforward but interesting food from a menu that changes regularly. The vegetables are as good as the main dishes, often a sign of thought and thoroughness in a restaurant. You can rely on having a tasty and generally satisfying meal here, which you may need before some of the shows in the West End.

Hispaniola
Victoria Embankment, WC2 (839 3011)
SPANISH
Mon-Sat 12.30-2.30, 7.30-11.30.
Food £28. Wine £4.95.
Some gimmick, this; a restaurant in a boat floating on the Thames. Let's just hope they don't catch the fish over the side. In the evening, the combination of the gentle undulation of the boat and the diamante lights on the riverbank create a certain romance. Good orthodox Spanish food is available on a choice of two decks, with the emphasis on seafood, and the usual favourites such as paella and gazpacho. A set menu is available. Screen your date for seasickness before you book.

COVENT GARDEN & BLOOMSBURY

Inigo Jones
14 Garrick St, WC2 (836 6456)
FRENCH
Mon-Sat 12.30-2.30, 6.00-11.45.
Food £45. Wine £6-£10.
*Somewhere along the line
modernity has slipped its leash
here and created an interior
with a dazzling melee of
conflicting influences —
airport lounge furniture, back-
lit stained glass windows, a
harpsichordist plinking away,
and waiters in leather aprons!
The consolation is that the food
and wine are sober and
excellent and the service
attentive. I had herring fillets,
delicate sweetbreads and
refreshing china tea sorbet.
Here you need only a strong
stomach for decor.*

Neal Street Restaurant
26 Neal St, WC2 (836 8368)
FRENCH
Mon-Fri 12.30-2.00, 7.00-11.00.
Food £34. Wine £6.
*A spotlessly elegant restaurant
in the heart of warehouseland,
walls lined with Hockney
prints and a menu offering
both the orthodox (filet au
poivre) and the exotic ('parcels
of crab from Cornwall') all
immaculately cooked and
served. If you want to venture
past the better than adequate
house wines there is an
extensive wine list. A classical
approach to food and service
presented in crisp, modern
surroundings, attracting a mix
of middle-aged pinstripes and
young art world turks talking
five figures. There are
rumoured to be prints of
naked men in the ladies...*

Savoy Grill Room
Savoy Hotel, Strand, WC2 (836
4343)
INTERNATIONAL
Mon-Sat 12.30-3.00, 6.30-11.30.
Food £35. Wine £6.50.
*There is little new to be said
about the grill room. The room
itself is magnificent and the
service as near perfect as you
can get, and the wine list is
particularly impressive. An
ageless atmosphere of refined
elegance prevails, and one
simply wallows in the sheer
style of it all — and the food is
excellent too. The menu is
varied and equally reliable
whether you choose French or
English. The clientele consists
of the cream of a variety of
elites.*

Savoy Restaurant
Savoy Hotel, Strand, WC2 (836
4343)
FRENCH
Mon-Sun 12.30-3.00, 7.30-11.30.
Food £28. Wine £6.50.
*The Savoy is universally
renowned for its flawless
cooking and service, and the
reputation does not flatter
them. There is a resident band
that provides discreet music
for discreet dancing. The food
is classic French and is
presented with painstaking
attention to detail. Everybody
should go to the Savoy at least
once in their lives, because it
represents a fastidious
approach to style that is
becoming extinct.*

Thomas De Quincey
36 Tavistock St, WC2 (240
3773)
ENGLISH
Mon-Sat 12.30-3.00, 6.00-11.15.

Food £28. Wine £5.90.
Actually situated in de Quincey's house (no, he wasn't a pathologist), the place has a strongly Victorian feel, but the food is not as heavy as that might suggest, although they do tend to over-sauce things. There are delicately flavoured souffles and mousses, sometimes inserted into turbot fillets or crepes, obscure vegetables and a restrained selection of sweets on the trolley. You can freshen up with a sorbet between courses.

MID-PRICE

Ajimura
51-3 Shelton St, WC2 (240 0178)
JAPANESE
Mon-Sat 12 noon-3.00, 6.00-11.00.
Food £14. Wine £3.80.
A place with a well-deserved reputation for quality, value and a sense of homely simplicity in the surroundings and service. A friend rates the sashimi 'the best in town', and the tempura and many of the more obscure dishes are fine too. Watching the cooking in the open kitchen is entrancing, and what better accompaniment is there to a trance than numbing sake and filigreed Japanese music? As good a place as any to start an acquaintance with Japanese food — the waiters will explain all.

Alcove
12 Mays Court, St Martin's Lane, WC2 (836 6140)
ITALIAN
Mon-Sat 11.30am-7.30
Food £15. Wine £3.35.
Cramped, lightning fast place where the pasta is home-made and as substantial and delicious as that would imply. Very useful if you are in a hurry for the theatre — in fact most of the cast will be in there with you. They offer the usual range of pastas and sweets and good coffee to assist in breaking it all down.

Beoty's
79 St Martin's Lane, WC2 (836 8768)
GREEK
Mon-Sat 12 noon-2.45, 5.30-11.15.
Food £20. Wine £3.60.
The key here is to avoid the French half of the menu and stick to the Greek specialities. The excellent taramasalata is a respite from the usual pink foam, and the entrees are mainly lamb and chicken. The souvlakia are deliciously flavoured with coriander, and you can have a classic Greek salad of tomato, cucumber and feta to go with it. It is a sober, quiet place with flock wallpaper and middle-aged waiters, but it's nice to have Greek food in these kind of surroundings for a change.

Le Bistingo
43 New Oxford St, WC2 (836 1011)
ITALIAN
Mon-Sat 12 noon-3.00, 6.00-11.30.
Food £17. Wine £3.95 (litre)
One of a chain of Italian

places, this is a very pretty room in which to eat. Light comes from the front windows showing off the part panelled, part white plaster walls hung with lovely mirrors and some slightly dodgy modern art. There are three set menus at different prices; otherwise a range of dishes that holds few surprises and few duds — snails, ravioli, artichokes Bistingo for starters, trout, steak, deep fried squid (very good) and various escalopes of veal for main course. The odds are against a bad meal here.

Le Cafe Des Amis Du Vin
12-13 Hanover Place, WC2 (379 3444)
FRENCH
Mon-Sat 11.30am-12 midnight.
Food £16. Wine £4.15.
Tucked away down an alley off Long Acre, this place really fizzes at lunchtime. I dropped my fork and a waiter caught it before it hit the floor. In a large, airy room decorated with the inevitable antique Parisian theatre posters you can have simple, authentic French food (andouillette, boudin noir, exquisite braised fennel) and, of course, become acquainted with a wide selection of wines. The service and cloakroom are equally efficient, and there is a wine bar downstairs; recommended for an economical meal with a little class.

The Calabash
38 King St, WC2 (836 1976)
AFRICAN
Mon-Sat 12.30-3.00, 6.30-10.00.
Food £15. Wine £2.45.
It's a little bit hard to find —
you have to wander past the poster in the Africa Centre down to the basement — but worth it when you get there. The tribal artefacts on the walls clash slightly with the sophisticated ambience, which includes a bar, but no matter; the food is all technicolour, as you might expect from Africa. There is chicken and nut stew, beef with exotic fruits, blackeyed beans and fish. Worth trying if you ever want something completely different.

Connaught Rooms
Great Queen St, WC2 (405 7811)
ANGLO/FRENCH
Mon-Sat 12.30-3.30.
Food £20. Wine £5.75.
No doubt much Anglo-French business is transacted here over lunch because the menu is versatile enough for a complete meal to be enjoyed in either cuisine. There are roast joints on the trolley as well as an a la carte selection, and stout puddings to mop up the survivors. The wine list is distinguished, and the dignity of the service matches the grandeur of the surroundings.

Garfunkel's
162 Tottenham Court Rd, WC2 (380 1228)
AMERICAN
Mon-Sun 12 noon-12 midnight.
Food £12. Wine £3.50.
One of what is now quite a large chain, Garfunkel's aims to provide basic American food quickly and cheaply in crisp, unobtrusive surroundings. The salads in their help-yourself bar sit

impressively on beds of ice but are fairly limp and taste tinned. The hamburgers and milkshakes are competent, and you can escape without feeling either that you have been ripped off or that you have wasted too much time.

The Grange
39 King St, WC2 (240 2939)
ENGLISH
Mon-Sat 12.30-2.30, 7.30-11.30.
Food £16. Wine £5.40.
The interior, predominantly brown with cool mirrors, is as tasteful as the food, which is organised into carefully thought out two, three and four course set meals which include a half bottle of wine. It's mainly country English, and the menus change every month. Pigeon pie, venison, Dover sole, mussels in cream and curry sauce, Beef Wellington, lime syllabub, these give a general picture. A meal which flows coherently from dish to dish is always more satisfying, and this is what the set meals achieve.

Ivy
1 West St, WC2 (836 4751)
INTERNATIONAL
Mon-Sat 12.15-2.15, 6.15-11.00.
Food £18. Wine £4.50.
A long standing restaurant well known for its sedate and sumptuous atmosphere. The food is classic, simple and fresh and is predominantly continental. They have a set meal and a wine list that is worth exploring. The rich, velvety surroundings are suggestive of one of the West End's more ornate old theatres, which makes it a good place for pre-show dining.

Joe Allen
13 Exeter St, WC2 (836 0651)
AMERICAN
Mon-Sat 12 noon-1.00am. Sun 12 noon-12 midnight.
Food £14. Wine £3.90.
Very popular basement 'joint' incorporating a restaurant serving the best of American food (excellent spare ribs, hamburgers, salads, pecan pie) and a cocktail bar. The cod-speakeasy ambience is quite successful, with mostly plain wood surfaces, blackboard menus and low lighting achieving that slight hum of excitement that the British concept of 'evening' lacks. They have a nice line in New York-style exclusivity — anonymous exterior, no truck with food guides — which is worth the effort of penetrating.

Last Days Of The Raj
22 Drury Lane, WC2 (836 5705)
INDIAN
Mon-Sat 12 noon-2.30, 6.00-11.30; Sun 6.30-11.30.
Food £16. Wine £4.
This is a softly lit, modern Indian place with a sophisticated, glinting bar down one side of a predominantly dark green room. The menu is manageably short, and includes three house specialities — two kinds of thali, and Murgh Masallam, a succulent whole baby chicken delicately flavoured with herbs in cream. There is a selection of tandoori dishes (king prawns recommended) and chicken and lamb curries. It's

a slightly more expensive Indian meal than usual, but worth it for the care that has gone into the flavouring and cooking.

Luigis
15 Tavistock St, WC2 (240 1795)
ITALIAN
Mon-Sat 12.15-3.00, 5.45-11.30.
Food £15. Wine £3.80.
This is a lively Italian bistro that must be doing something right to be so popular in an area teeming with restaurants. The feel is part wicker encased wine bottles, part showbiz, with celebrity photographs on the walls. The food has a really Italian tang; the cannelloni is particularly good and there is a large selection of veal and chicken in tasty sauces. It is well placed for a whole range of theatres and opera.

Magno's Bistro
65a Long Acre (836 6007)
FRENCH
Mon-Sat 12.30-2.30, 6.00-11.15.
Food £20. Wine £3.80.
Magno's is another attempt at a simple French restaurant in London that achieves simplicity but is, inevitably, expensive for what it is. The cream and dark green room is spacious, softly lit, and lightly decorated with prints and posters. The food is not over elaborate (crevettes a l'aioli, feuillete au roquefort, champignons bressanes to start; then carre d'agneau, foie de veau with sage or bacon, supreme de volaille nordique) but nevertheless flawed by slightly less than expert

cooking. The waiters, too, have to be prodded to bring you anything. Altogether the nearby Cafe des Amis is a better bet.

Mon Plaisir
21 Monmouth St, WC2 (836 7243)
FRENCH
Mon-Sat 12.15-2.00, 6.00-11.00.
Food £20. Wine £4.50.
A French bistro with a very convivial feel, you may well end up drinking more wine than you bargained for. The regular menu is fleshed out with daily additions on the blackboard. They serve onion soup (rivalled only by Jeeve's restorative as a tonic) and the main dishes are all satisfying and accompanied by expertly cooked vegetables. For cheese fanatics, who so often get neglected in London restaurants, there is an excellent cheeseboard.

L'Opera
32 Great Queen St, WC2 (405 9020)
FRENCH
Mon-Sat 12.15-2.30, 6.00-12 midnight.
Food £18. Wine £4.
The food here is mainly (but not exclusively) French and can be very good, but any chef would have a hard time producing food to match the exotic and sumptuous decor. Mussels, bouillabaisse, steaks, all washed down with wine from their excellent and comprehensive wine list. A meal at L'Opera is a mixture of intimacy and splendour.

Paulo's

28 Wellington St, WC2 (240 1919)
BRAZILIAN
Mon-Sat 12.30-3.00, 6.30-11.30.
Food £16. Wine £4.20.

Of all things, a Brazilian restaurant. A mock-tropical feel is created by the jungle and sky colouring, rattling Latin soundtrack and the delicious fruit cocktail aperitifs constructed from such exotica as mango and passion fruit. After one of these you can tackle such spicy delicacies as crabmeat with grilled cheese, skewered prawns and vatapa, a sort of vegetarian stew of nuts with coconut sauce served with rice. Beware the chilli sauce, which resembles napalm.

Penny's Place

6 King St, WC2 (836 4553)
FRENCH
Mon-Sun 11.30am-3.00, 5.30-11.00.
Food £12. Wine £3.70.

A small, unpretentious bistro has been slotted harmoniously into an old pub and the result is a lived-in atmosphere that is passably French. There is a select, if vague, wine list, and the menu, consisting of a few starters (minestrone, marinaded mushrooms) and four or five main courses (saucisse de Toulouse, Coq au vin) changes every day. The meats are subtle and tender and come with simple vegetables. But the real speciality is the immaculate cheeseboard, with everything moist and pungent. Avoid the basement and go for the cheese.

Poons

41 King St, WC2 (240 1743)
CANTONESE
Mon-Sat 12 noon-11.15.
Food £24. Wine £5.50.

A quality Chinese restaurant specialising in Cantonese cooking, done in the open kitchen Keystone-cop style by Mr Poon and his chefs. The menu is longer than Proust, but you must try Poon's wind-dried meats, sausages made from duck, duck liver and pork. The closest analogy is sweet Chinese salami. The rest is excellent too, especially crispy wun-tun and anything with ginger. Basically an upmarket version of Poons in Lisle St.

Porter's

17 Henrietta St, WC2 (836 6466)
ENGLISH
Mon-Sat 12 noon-11.30; Sun 12 noon-11.00.
Food £14. Wine £4.90 (litre)

Porter's inhabits a large, colourful room decorated with some bizarre objects. When you wrench your eyes away from the sinister dummy in the model car hanging from the ceiling to the menu, you will find simple English dishes, including a range of individually cooked pies with delicious meaty fillings, and fresh salads. To finish there are solid puddings and Stilton. It seems popular with innocent-looking youth and is a good place to take children. You get a flavour of the weird but happy Englishness of 'Mr Kite', all crusty pies and summersets.

Rules
35 Maiden Lane, WC2 (836 5314)
ENGLISH
Mon-Sat 12.15-2.30, 6.00-11.15.
Food £20. Wine £4.85.
A very old and dignified place once graced by all sorts of 19th Century superstars. The decor is heavy on brocade and the walls are crammed with pictures, caricatures and suchlike. The menu includes all the classic British dishes like oxtail, boiled beef and carrots and jugged hare. The service is dignified and old-fashioned as befits the air of Edwardiana and cigar smoke. Popular with tourists imbibing the Englishness.

La Scala
35 Southampton St, WC2 (240 1030)
ITALIAN
Mon-Sat 12 noon-2.45, 5.30-11.00.
Food £17. Wine £3.50.
A friendly and relatively inexperienced Italian restaurant, well placed for pre-theatre dining. There is a range of pastas, all of which are home-made and have the taste of the real thing. The chicken Kiev is excellent (use goggles for that vital first incision) and all the vegetables are toothsome and fresh. The service is attentive and it is altogether good value; what more can you say?

Sharuna
107 Great Russell St, WC1 (636 5922)
INDIAN
Mon-Sat 12.00 noon-3.00, 6.00-11.00; Sun 1.00-10.30.

Food £12. Wine £4.50.
It is more expensive than vegetarian Indian tends to be, but you are paying for a plush, modern interior that shames most similar restaurants (also for some highly inappropriate muzak). The menu holds a selection of soups (delicious Mulligatawny) and there are a few each of breads, vegetables, and rices, dosai and masala dosai, and piquant Thali (rice, chappatis, and various vegetables in little bowls) as a main course, a house speciality. Try out a bizarre Indian sweet like kulfi, to finish with.

Sheeky's
28 St Martin's Court, WC2 (240 2565)
ENGLISH
Mon-Sat 12.30-3.00, 5.30-11.30.
Food £18. Wine £4.50.
This longstanding restaurant has been providing theatre-goers with some of the best seafood in London since well before the turn of the century. The location is delightful; it's tucked away in pedestrians-only St Martin's Court, and the exterior and bold, glossy Sheeky's signs are worth a look. The lobster, salmon and turbot are always immaculate, and they have delicious oysters when in season.

Simpson's In The Strand
100 The Strand, WC2 (836 9112)
ENGLISH
Mon-Sat 12 noon-3.00 and 6.00-10.00.
Food £20. Wine £4.95.
Still the carnivore's Mecca as it has been for generations. The

spectacle is remarkable; in a formal, high-ceilinged room huge and irresistibly succulent joints of beef, mutton and duck swoop on trolleys from table to table, each accompanied by a skilful, tail-coated carver. Afterwards there are real English puddings and Stilton. It is very popular with the Daily Telegraph gang, and a jacket and tie are compulsory.

Tudor Rooms
80 St Martin's Lane, WC2 (240 3978)
ENGLISH
Mon-Sun 7.30-2.00am.
Food £18. Wine £5.
Although it stays open until two, there is not much point in arriving later than 10 when the show starts — and no point in turning up at all unless you're into a 'Carry On' concept of Olde Englande and the chance of being put in the stocks. There is a five-course meal served by Nell Gwynne lookalikes, and international cabaret acts too! Remember to book. Best approached by the coachload, I suppose....

Tuttons
11-12 Russell St, WC2 (836 1167)
INTERNATIONAL
Upstairs
Mon-Sat 11.30am-11.30. Sunday 12noon-11.30.
Food £14. Wine £3.75.
A reasonably priced restaurant alongside The Market serving almost good food. The service is prompt and efficient and the place informal enough to allow you to guzzle two or three dishes simultaneously should

you wish, to the accompaniment of taped music interspersed with live hack piano. Fried clams, oeufs florentine, steaks, salads, quiches, or just tea and coffee. Lots of plate glass and bright lighting turn you into something of an exhibit, although downstairs is quieter.

BUDGET

Bar Creperie
21 The Market, WC2 (836 2137)
FRENCH
Mon-Fri 10.30am-12 midnight, Sun 10.00am-6.00.
Food £8. Wine £3.75.
Warm little creperie where you can have a continental breakfast before midday. Perm any number of fillings from the list for your savoury crepe (prawns, cheese, anchovies, ham, chicken etc) and then the same for a sweet one (peach, honey, ice cream, nuts). It's fun to construct bizarre combinations of flavours. Also soups, salads and coffee.

Bruno's All Day Diner
35 Store St, WC2 (580 4791)
AMERICAN
Mon-Sat 8.30am-11.00.
Food £8. Wine £3.40.
Check-cloth covered tables range down either side of a long railcar of a room leading to a small bar that serves cocktails. A few plants and framed 'art' photos complete the restrained interior. The menu offers an orthodox burger/pizza/steak selection, but there is enough originality in the choice of garnish and

115

general presentation to rekindle one's jaded interest in these now routine foods. The salads are crunchy and fresh, and there are five different dressings. Only the disco music could be thought intrusive in this otherwise pleasant and tasty place.

Cranks
11 The Market, WC2 (379 6508)
VEGETARIAN
Mon-Sat 10.00am-8.00.
Food £8. Unlicensed.
Upmarket vegetarian and health food in a room dominated by antiseptic wood. The food is very good, fresh and moist, but tends to be overpriced. Wholemeal quiches, every imaginable salad, filled buns, muesli, nuts, yoghurt, thick soups, fresh fruit juices, carrot cake. The tables and chairs are a bit cramped, but then you're slim, perfectly slim, from eating their food, aren't you?

Food For Thought
31 Neal St, WC2 (836 0239)
VEGETARIAN
Mon-Fri 12 noon-8.00.
Food £4. Unlicensed.
A pocket sized vegetarian and wholefood restaurant, it fills up very quickly but it's worth the wait to sample their home-made soups, lentil and mushroom bake, chickpea curry, and tasty yoghurt and fresh fruit. There is also an assortment of other puddings and cakes. Although they are unlicensed you are welcome to bring your own wine, and a corkscrew will be supplied. Best of all, they have managed elegantly to avoid that awful

dry brownness of most 'wholefood'.

LS (Grunt's)
12 Maiden Lane, WC2 (379 7722)
AMERICAN
Mon-Sat 12 noon-11.30.
Food £9. Wine £3.75.
Huge and garish pizza place housed in what used to be an electricity sub-station. They have a help yourself salad bar with five dressings. The deep-dish pizzas are gooey and very filling (one will easily feed two people), with cocktails, garlicky stuffed mushrooms and garlic bread. The sweets are flamboyant, and include their own chocolate cheesecake.

My Old Dutch
132 High Holborn, WC2 (404 5008)
FRENCH
Sun-Wed 12 noon-12 midnight, Thu-Sat 12 noon-1.00am.
Food £10. Wine £3.25.
Considerably more taste has gone into the decoration of this place than into the choice of its name. The room is packed with homely wooden tables and chairs and hung with drooping plants and attractive lanterns. The food is simply pancakes, savoury and sweet, which come with a bewildering array of filling combinations. There are about 200 on the menu, let alone what you can dream up. Full of gorging youth.

Oodles
42 New Oxford St, WC2 (580 3762)
ENGLISH
Mon-Sat 11.30am-9.00, Sun 12 noon-8.00.

Food £8. Wine £4.

They call themselves a country restaurant and that theme is certainly reflected in the profusion of carvings, antlers, rustic signs and brassware that fill every space not panelled with wood. Service is canteen style, and there is firstly a wide choice of stews, pasta and casseroles, then fresh salads and cottage cheese, and finally puddings (apple pie, cakes) and a selection of drinks. You stagger downstairs with your tray to the spacious basement dining room, where the relentlessly beige wood lends a sauna feel. Solid, satisfying food consumed smartly and cheaply.

Pizza Express
30 Coptic St, WC1 (636 2244)
ITALIAN
Mon-Sun 12 noon-12 midnight.
Food £8. Wine £3.

This is one of the few genuinely worthwhile pizza deals in London. So many pizzas are heavy on the dough (literally) and have a parched, microscopic topping resembling hundreds and thousands, but these are crusty and gooey. The authentic pizza oven is centrally placed, in a spacious tiled room so that you can oversee the whole process. There is an adequate range of puddings and plenty of cheap wine to slurp.

Rock Garden
6/7 The Piazza, WC2 (240 3961)
AMERICAN
Mon-Sat 12 noon-1.00am, Sun 12 noon-11.00
Food £8. Wine £3.75.

Veteran food and music venue that was here before tourists replaced vegetables. The food is typical of these kind of places: hamburgers, ribs, salads, cheesecake. There is a cocktail bar and you can sit outside under cover and examine the world between the impressive stone pillars. Downstairs there are bands playing every night, mostly post-punk pub rock and 60s and 70s relics. On Thursdays, Fridays and Saturdays they stay open all night until 6.00am.

Spaghetti House
24 Cranbourn St, WC2 (836 8168)
ITALIAN
Mon-Sat 12 noon-3.00, 5.30-11.00.
Food £10. Wine £4.05 (litre).

You know the deal — plain wooden tables, walls hung with chianti bottles in wicker baskets, brisk but unexceptional. The atmosphere is warm and the food is hot. Starters include ham and melon, and avocado vinaigrette, and then you can choose from all the usual pastas, gnocchi, chicken and veal, and steaks. Get good and sticky with pastries afterwards or, if gorged, lick at an ice cream. Being an Italian place, the coffee is as it should be everywhere else.

Tango
38 Long Acre, WC2 (836 7639)
N & S AMERICAN
Mon-Sun 11.00am-1.00am.
Food £8. Wine £3.95.

Cool, stroll-in joint that aspires to be the hippest in Long Acre, but doesn't quite cut it for various reasons. On some nights (unpredictable, you see) between 9.00 and 11.00 various hippies play piano and sing, and the customers hunker down over their chilli. You can have guacamole (avocado mashed with peppers, garlic etc) burgers with salsa, hot casseroles, tacos, burritos, stuffed peppers and cakes 'n' ice cream. The Mexican is better than some found in London though that's not much of a compliment in a city which does poor service to the true excitement of Mexican cuisine.

Trattoria Bernigra
69 Tottenham Court Rd, WC2
(580 0950)
ITALIAN
Mon-Sun 10.00am-11.30
Food £7. Wine £4.50.
At first glance this would seem to be a brash and unappetising Italian place catering to the impatient hunger of Tottenham Court Road's shoppers. The menu is standard: melon, antipasto to start with, a range of pizzas to continue (monte bianco, quattro stagione, peperoni) and then to end with — merely the best ice-cream in London. A huge selection of flavours including liqueurs (zabaglione, marsala) which are unusual and delicious. Luckily, it takes a few visits to sample all the flavours. The scientologists next door will want to test your personality, so watch out.

TRANSPORT

(All details subject to change. Phone 01-222 1234 at anytime, day or night to check details. Some routes shown do not operate every day of the week.)

COVENT GARDEN
Tube: Covent Garden (closed Sun), Leicester Sq, Charing Cross, Holborn
Buses: 1, 6, 9, 11, 13 (Mon-Fri only) 15, 23, 77 (Mon-Sat only), 77a, 170 (Mon-Fri only, but not evenings), 172 (Mon-Sat only), 176 (Mon-Fri only).
Night: N68, N83, N85, N86, N87, N88, N91, N92, N93, N94, N97 — to Strand
Or: 5, 68, 77a, 170 (Mon-Fri only, but not evenings), 172 (Mon-Sat only), 188, 239 (Mon-Fri only, but not evenings), 501 (Mon-Fri only, but not evenings)
Night: N92 — to Kingsway
Or: 1 (Mon-Fri only, also Sat shopping hours), 24, 29, 176 (Mon-Fri only)
Night: N90 — to Charing Cross Road
Or: 14, 19, 22, 38, 55
Night: N84, N95, N98 — to Cambridge Circus

BLOOMSBURY
Tube: Russell Sq, Goodge St, Tottenham Court Rd, Holborn
Buses: 7 (Mon-Fri only), 8, 14, 19, 22, 24, 25, 29, 38, 55, 68, 73, 77a, 134, 176, 188, 239 (Mon-Fri only, but not evenings)
Night: N84, N89, N95, N98

MASH POTATOES · PEAS
2 FRIED EGGS · CHIPS 85p
1 PORK SAUSAGE · EGG ·
CHIPS · 83p
2 PORK SAUSAGES · CHIPS
TOM·IT ★ 1·03?

QUALITY CHOP HOUSE

People in Holborn and the City are mostly eating out because they work here; there are not as many amusements or actual residents in these parts as you\will find, say, in Chelsea or the West End. Thus the majority of places listed here are strictly Monday to Friday, lunches only and, though none of them like to stress the fact, most of them are geared to male appetites (hence the preponderance of steak, chops and treacle puddings). An enormous number of lunches are eaten in pubs and wine bars, and even more (I suspect) in clubs or the offices' own boardrooms. This leaves the visitor unused to bar stools or crowded saloons with less to choose from in the way of eating places than he or she might like, particularly if you're looking for somewhere at night or have children in tow. Nevertheless the selection here ranges fairly wide, with something to suit most pockets.

119

MID-PRICE

The Baron Of Beef
Gutter Lane, Gresham St, EC2
(606 9415)
ENGLISH
Mon-Fri 12.30-3.00, 5.30-9.00.
Food £18 (fixed menu), £30 (a
la carte). Wine £6.50.
*Baronial surroundings, in the
basement of a fairly faceless
office block; mainly geared to
business luncheons where, if
the price and quality of the
house wine is taken as an
indication of the rest of the
meal, the business needs to be
decidedly big. Starters include
a few unusual items such as
clam and oyster chowder,
quail's eggs and paw-paw;
also Beluga caviar (at £19 the
ounce). Naturally the
showpiece of the main course
is the roast sirloin of beef;
Lancashire hot pot, steak and
kidney pie, roast game, roast
lamb and salmon in season are
also listed and the vegetables
and puddings include
schoolboy favourites such as
butter beans, bubble and
squeak and spotted dick (also
to be found for a fraction of
the price at the chop house in
Farringdon Rd). Ladies are
given an orchid with their
coffee.*

Bubbs
329 Central Market,
Smithfield, EC1 (236 2435)
FRENCH
Mon-Fri 12.15-3.30.
Food £20. Wine £3.50.
*Bubb's is in a tall, narrow
building that juts out into
Farringdon Rd as if trying to
peer into Fleet St, whence
many of its customers come.
With the exception of Mr Bubb
all the staff (wife included) are
French and the food is very
good indeed. As most of it is
cooked to order, there's only
one sitting and it's essential to
book. A favourite starter is a
Muscovite crepe, which
contains smoked salmon
spiked with a dash of vodka.
Pike is grilled and given a
white wine sauce, venison
escalopes have a port and red
wine sauce. The cheeses are
excellent, the wines
reasonably priced. You can eat
downstairs in the little flower-
filled bar, or up some very
steep stairs, in a larger, lighter
room.*

Le Gamin
32 Old Bailey, EC4 (236
4379/248 4026)
FRENCH
Mon-Fri 12 noon-3.00.
Set price menu to include an
aperitif and 1/2 bottle of wine
per person, £13.75 for one.
£9.65 with no drink for one.
*This restaurant, like the
Poulbot is part of the Roux
brothers' family of star-
spangled restaurants. Here,
although the prices are lower,
the quality of the food and
service have the same high
standards. All the staff are
French, and hardworking and
civil with it. The menu
changes daily, the only two
permanent dishes are the
steak and the real boudin noir,
which, with all the other
charcuterie, cheese, herbs and
some of the vegetables, comes
weekly from France. Your
aperitif (kir) is served with
pieces of radis rose and*

120

fromage blanc; starters may be soup, pates or tartelettes with oysters. Seven main dishes include delicately sauced fish, gigot, duck or chicken, mostly cooked to order. Three veg and a salad are always served. Superb desserts and cheeses follow, and coffee is served with petits fours.

NOTE: Really cheap snack bar by the entrance serves plain dishes from the same kitchens.

Leeks
2-4 Russia Row, EC2 (606 2339)
INTERNATIONAL
Mon-Fri 12 noon-3.00.
Food £16. Wine £3.70.
This is, by City standards a slightly unconventional establishment; for one thing the Leek here is a Mrs Leek and she has created an unusually pretty bar and restaurant; pretty bamboo chairs, flowers on the tables, good modern prints on the walls, cocktails and snacks available from five till eight, hamburgers and satay dishes in the basement, a courtyard for eating out in the summer and, as work in the kitchens starts early, a continental breakfast from eight till nine am. For lunch she offers fairly conventional starters — pates, soups, salads. Main courses are sturdy; beef braised with chestnuts, steak and kidney pie, game casserole. The desserts include treacle tart, bread and butter pudding and creme brulee.

The Lugger
147 Strand, WC2 (836 8282)
ITALIAN
Mon-Sat 12 noon-2.30, 5.30-11.30.
Food £19. Wine £3.75.
As the name suggests, the theme at The Lugger is marine; walls crawl with plastic fish and crustaceans, a decrepit graffiti-covered dinghy hangs from the ceiling with several strings of onions and chianti bottles in keeping with the other theme, which is Italian. Thus on the menu you will find 'with the tide', scampi spiedine, soglia all a grilla, and cozze Napolitana. Crab claws and Mediterranean prawns are served as hors d'oeuvres with mayonnaise. 'Against the tide' means meat — chicken breasts squirting garlic butter, saltimbocca and fine steaks. For desserts there is always zabaglione and, no matter what the time of year, strawberries. The wines are mainly Italian and reasonably priced.

Mr Garraways
46 Gresham St, EC2 (606 8209)
FRENCH
Mon-Fri 12 noon-3.00.
Food £20. Wine £3.75.
Like many another City restaurant, this one is in the basement and also like many another, has a blood-red and mahogany feel to it. However, unlike many, this one is decidedly unpretentious, relaxed and friendly. The menu is described (by them) as 'sort of French', by which they mean dishes like herring roes sauteed with capers, or deep fried brie with gooseberry sauce to start with; liver and avocado, venison escalopes and chicken stuffed

with crab for main courses and 'the best treacle tart (with walnuts) in the City' for pudding. All the puddings are rather tempting in fact. The wine list is very long, reasonably priced and comprehensive and similar to the choice in Mr Garraway's Wine Bar upstairs.

Oscar's Brasserie
5-8 Temple Chambers, Temple Avenue, EC4 (353 6272)
FRENCH
Mon-Fri 12 noon-3.00, 6.30-9.30.
Food £20. Wine £4.40.
The menu will appeal to anyone seeking avocados stuffed with something other than just prawns; Oscar's adds smoked salmon and home-made mayonnaise for good measure. Everything is cooked to order. Entrecote steaks and chicken breasts are stuffed too, with stilton and peppercorns and crabmeat and prawns, respectively. Scampi are served with garlic and chillies and the sweets are so tempting — mostly based on whipped cream, meringue, fresh fruit and caramel — that few people ever get as far as eating cheese, hence only stilton or brie to choose from. The place is crammed with regulars from the Temple or Fleet St at lunch, but being a bit off the beaten track, is much calmer in the evenings. The decor is dark, but warmly and cheerfully so.

Le Poulbot
45 Cheapside, EC2 (236 4379/248 4026)

FRENCH
Mon-Fri 12 noon-3.00.
Food £19 (set menu); £40 (a la carte). Wine £7.50.
Managed and owned (like the Gamin) by the Roux brothers, the prices and standards at this restaurant are almost on a par with its celebrated sister Gavroche; (only they have three Michelin stars and Poulbot, two). The menu is slightly more masculine, however, in keeping with a mainly male, lunch-only clientele; but this doesn't prevent the presentation from being really pretty. Plates arrive under silver cloches. The waiter lifts off the lid and voila! your dinner looks like an illustration from a very expensive cookery book. Tessellated terrines are enriched with foie gras; fillets of fish are poached in delicate fumets, noisettes are perfumed with herbs. All are garnished with neatly turned or julienned vegetables. The desserts are similarly ravishing to look at and to eat. Above, the Poulbot Pub does a roaring trade in cheaper lunches and a continental Breakfast from 8.00am-10.00am. The croissants and pain au chocolat are made in the Roux's own bakery.

Sweetings
39 Queen Victoria St, EC4 (248 3062)
FISH
Mon-Fri 11.45am-3.00.
Food £15. Wine £4.50.
There's tradition here, but little ceremony. Money men and fur traders start work early, and lunch early; by midday the place is packed.

Oysters and black velvets are wolfed down at such a pace, however, that there can be as many as three lunch-time sittings here, the white tablecloths being covered with clean paper ones, the bar trade ever moving, like seaweed in a rock pool. Three sisters cut fresh salmon and cue sarnies, (Mary has been here forty years), George, the barman, opens oysters and provides smoked salmon 'nibbles' while you wait. Other fish are poached, grilled or fried; beautiful sole, turbot, halibut, plaice, mackerel, herrings. Only tongue, ham or cold beef in the way of meat, and that mainly for sandwiches. Traditional savouries to finish with — rarebit, roe on toast — and steamed syrup pudding of course.

BUDGET

Cosmoba
9 Cosmo Place, WC1 (837 0904)
ITALIAN
Mon-Sun 11.30am-11.00.
Food £8. Wine £2.90.
Tucked away in an alley running between Queen Square and Southampton Row, this place is packed with regulars, especially in the evenings. However, since it serves meals continuously, from mid morning till almost midnight, seven days a week, you should find room there at off-peak hours. Chicken Kiev and Cosmoba's involtinis are the favourite dishes; the

Scotch beef steaks are, for the price and the quality, well worth having. The modestly priced menu is in fact unusually long, listing many different sorts of pizza, pasta, veal dishes, and chicken dishes, as well as the steaks. Hung with greenery and bedecked with bright tartan cloths, it's cheerful and friendly, one of the best of several local restaurants run by Italians.

The Crazy Crepe
107 Aldergate St, EC1 (253 2428)
FRENCH
Mon-Fri 7.00am-8.00; Sat 7.00am-4.00.
Food £5. Unlicensed.
The hotplates for the crepes lie behind a counterful of packeted potato crisps, and at first glance the whole place has such an English appearance that you might well pass it by as just another caff. However, it's manned by a French family, the tapes murmur French pop songs, and the menu is based on French crepes. The savoury ones are filled with a choice of egg, cheese, sausage, salami, ham, chicken, mushroom and ratatouille. The same ingredients form the basis of a remarkably long list of other dishes; the chips are wonderful, and note that the Frankfurter-like sausages come from Strasbourg. The sweet crepes have a choice of 18 unelaborate fillings and eight richer ones. They are topped with jam, fruit and light, whipped cream. The home-made, deep apple pie is

famous too.
Breakfast: *served until 12 noon; bacon, egg, sausages, safely English.*
Tea: *served from 2.00 onwards; crepes of course, and very tempting cakes.*

Ganpath
372 Gray's Inn Rd, WC1 (278 1938)
INDIAN
Mon-Sat 12 noon-3.00, 6.00-10.15.
Food £8. Wine £3.75.
The food here is South Indian; most of the dishes will be familiar to anyone from Madras or thereabouts. It's juicy, fruity (lots of lemon and coconut in the savoury dishes) and spicy. South Indian specials start with sambar; rasam, idlis, uppama, vadais and bhajias — what these are made of will all be patiently explained to the uninitiated by the waiters; mop up fragrant curries of meat, eggs, fish or vegetables with huge soft potato pancakes (dosais), dhal, and lemon or coconut rice and finish with almond cake. Wine and lager are available, but many prefer lassee, made from yoghurt and served here salted or sweet. This small, clean and civilised restaurant is one of the best of the many to be found between King's Cross and Paddington stations.

Gonbei
151 King's Cross Rd, WC1 (278 0619)
JAPANESE
Mon-Sat 6.00-10.30.
Food £11. Sake £1.10 (180cl) £2.20 (360cl)
A tiny (but not cramped)

authentic Japanese restaurant, popular with Japanese City men on their way home after work. There is a full sushi menu, complete with raw fish, pickles and vinegared rice, or you can eat traditional hot dishes such as tempura tonkatsu and tendon. The helpful, English speaking waitresses will initiate foreigners into the mysteries yakiniku and sukiyaki by cooking them for you at your table. The Japanese seem to like drinking whisky with their meal (note the regulars' labelled bottles behind the bar) lager or sake are possibly better alternatives, or stick to green tea, which is served automatically.

The India Club Restaurant
143 Strand, WC2 (836 0650)
INDIAN
Mon-Sun 12 noon-2.30, 6.00-10.15.
Food £5.50. Unlicensed.
Conveniently facing the back of India House, and full of Indians and students from the nearby Kings College and LSE, this restaurant is worth climbing two floors up. (The Strand International Hotel is below it). Don't be put off by the institutional decor; it looks like a really bleak staff canteen but the smell of freshly cooked curries is heavenly. A wide range of Indian dishes is offered at staggeringly low prices — there is a minimum charge of £1.50, but most dishes are around £2. There's tandoori food, bhunas, chilly bhajais and (on Fridays) dahi vada. Krishna Menon founded it.

Kolossi Grill

56-58 Rosebery Avenue, EC1
(278 5758)
GREEK
Mon-Fri 12 noon-3.00; Mon-Thu 5.30-11.00; Fri-Sat 5.30-12 midnight, (no lunch Sat).
Food £7. Wine £3.20.

The food is exclusively Greek here, with one or two specialities not normally found in other Greek restaurants in London such as spicy meatballs (lachmodo and youvarlakia) and marinated, grilled spare ribs (sirinjiahi). There is usually a meaty stew on the daily special list, otherwise the menu lists a good range of starters with kebabs, sheftalias (homemade), moussaka and kleftiko — all served with rice and salads and firm favourites with the clientele. The place is crowded at lunchtime so it's advisable to book. The wines are all Greek or Cypriot. The decor is Trad Kebab (peasant artefacts dangling from the pine-panelled walls) and the service is most friendly. Family run and here at least 15 years.

The Maypole

83 Leather Lane, EC1 (405 8277)
ENGLISH
Mon-Fri 12.30-2.45.
Food £7. Wine £3.

Anyone with a schoolboy (or schoolgirl) appetite and tastes to match will absolutely love the satisfying lunches served here. There are no first courses but the main course consists of beautiful, freshly roasted meat, generously carved at the counter for you by the owner-chef, Alfred May. He cooks two different roasts each day; if it's pork you'll know it's Wednesday. There is also a lavish choice of vegetables, of which you can have as much as you like. Leave room for the hot and cold puddings (all served with thick cream); these are as good (and as filling) as the roasts; again there are set days for each one — Thursday is Sussex pond pudding, Friday is bread and butter pudding or apple pie; there are steamed suet puddings too. Customers come more for the food than the decor (which is sparse, to put it mildly) but among their number you'll find lawyers, journalists and diamond merchants, all from offices nearby.

The Nosherie

12 Greville St, EC1 (242 1591)
JEWISH
Mon-Fri 8.00am-5.00.
Food £10. Wine £4.20.

You can sit by the bar at the entrance and from it eat possibly the best hot salt beef on rye to be had in London; (top it up with a freshly cooked, crisp latke and a sweet sour cue if you feel peckish, then wash it down with lemon tea) or you can sit at the tables, be waited on by kindly, motherly ladies, and indulge in authentic Jewish nosh from the kitchens. Chicken knadle soup, carrot tsimmes, boiled or fried gefilte fish, chopped herring, schnitzels, lockshen pudding and strudel is the sort of thing. At lunchtime it's crammed with jewellers and diamond merchants, Hatton Garden being round the corner. The plastic tables and walls, and the circular fluorescent lights are unappealing, but don't let this put you off.

Quality Chop House
94 Farringdon Rd, EC1 (no phone)
ENGLISH
Mon-Fri 6.30am-4.15.
Food £4.50. Unlicensed.
Patronised by Mount Pleasant's Post Office workers on the one hand and Guardian journalists on the other, both being but a short step away, this restaurant is one of the last remaining working men's dining rooms left in London and a classic example of its kind. Spotlessly clean, with mahogany pews either side of mahogany tables; wrought iron supports to both; mirrors on the walls; sauce bottles on plinths at each table's end and a huge kitchen on view. From it issue traditional dishes such as oxtail stew, 'roast beef and Yorkshire', toad in the hole, braised kidneys etc. Masses of fish and chips on Fridays and delicious cups of tea. On the windows the legends 'Quick service', 'Civility', 'London's noted cup of Tea' and 'Progressive Working Class Caterers'.

Salad Days
86-90 Lamb's Conduit St, WC1 (242 4119)
ENGLISH
Mon-Fri 12 noon-3.00, 5.00-10.00; Sat-Sun 12 noon-10.00.
Food £4 (lunch), £6 (dinner). Wine £2.50 ½litre.
Everything on the self-service counter is cold here at lunch, but in the evenings you will find a hot menu and waitresses. At weekends the place is open all day, so you can eat lunch, dinner or tea. It's in a basement, but light, bright and cheerful with it and the food is fresh, good and wholesome to match. There are vegetarian dishes, cold meats cooked here, game pies, beautiful seedy rolls and excellent cheeses. In the evenings you can have as much soup or salad as you like for a starter, with hot garlic bread; casseroles and curries (freshly cooked each day) and lovely, home-made creamy desserts, all for a fixed price. Upstairs there's a useful delicatessen and bread shop, which also sells wonderful, brown-bread-only sandwiches.

Seven Sheaves
East West Centre, 188 Old St, EC1 (251 4076)
MACROBIOTIC
Mon-Fri 11.00am-8.00; Sat 11.00am-3.00.
Food £6. Wine £3.
For those who know what a macrobiotic menu is, I need only say that this one conforms strictly to the rules; for those who don't, it's best described as a menu with no meat, dairy food or eggs, but lots of grains, pulses, wholemeal, vegetables, seaweed, fruit and fish. Lest that sounds too dull, I should add that much of it is crisply fried, enhanced by pickles and marinades and not half as dreary as it sounds. In the hands of imaginative chefs in fact, a macrobiotic meal can be (and is here) quite exciting.

HOLBORN & THE CITY

Try the pan-fried homemade soba-flour noodles, the pan-fried vegetables with tofu and prawns, the fish salad, the fruity desserts and cakes with tofu cream, the real ales, herb teas or grain coffee. For converts to the regime this was (at the time of writing) the only macrobiotic restaurant in London. The Community Health Foundation (of which it is a part) caters for the rest of the body (and mind).

TRANSPORT

(All details subject to change. Phone 01-222 1234 at anytime, day or night to check details. Some routes shown do not operate every day of the week.)

Tube: Holborn, Farringdon, Moorgate, St Paul's, Mansion House

Buses: 5, 8, 19, 22, 25, 38, 55, 68, 77a, 170 (Mon-Fri, but not evenings), 172, 188, 239 (Mon-Fri, but not evenings), 501 (Mon-Fri only, but not evenings)

Night: N84, N89, N98 — to Holborn

Or: 5, 18 (Mon-Sat only, but not evenings), 19, 38, 45, 46 (Mon-Fri, but not evenings), also Sat morning, 55, 63, 168a (Mon-Fri only), 221 (Mon-Fri only, except evenings), 243 (Mon-Sat only, but not Sat evenings), 259 (Mon-Sat only) — to Clerkenwell

Or: 8, 9, 11, 15, 21 (Mon-Sat only), 22, 25, 43 (Mon-Sat only), 76 (Mon-Sat only), 133, 501 (Mon-Fri, except evenings), 502 (Mon-Fri, except evenings)

Night: N89, N91, N94, N95, N97, N98 — to Bank

COOKE 8

Stand by the Bank or the Stock Exchange on a busy workday morning, and you will actually be looking at the two greatest temples of this country's financial power, you can feel it too as men scurry by, folders bulging under their arms. Walk less than half a mile eastward to Aldgate and Whitechapel and the world of high finance might be a million miles away; this is the place to come for discount houses, street market bargains and soggy chips rather than blue ones. Naturally the eating places reflect this contrast too. City men love steaks and grills, and possibly to revive the hard-worked grey matter, they want oysters and grilled fish too. Many start work hours before the rest of London, so an early lunch is not unusual. East of the City is the home of the Cockney's fish and chips and eels, pies and mash, Jewish gefilte fish and salt beef, Pakistani birianis and curries. It used to be a good place for Chinese restaurants too, (especially around the Docks), but they have been superseded now by Soho's more up-to-date ones.

LUXURY

The Beaufort Restaurant
Great Eastern Hotel, Liverpool
St, EC2 (283 4363)
FRENCH
Mon-Fri 12.30-2.30.
Food £30. Wine £5.15.
*This is one of BR's top
restaurants and the most
exclusive of the Great
Eastern's three restaurants;
spacious, plushy and
expensive. You can wait for
your fellow diners in a small
cocktail bar by the dining
room, and nibble small,
brightly coloured, lozenge-
shaped titbits while you study
the menu. The a la carte is
fairly traditional high quality
food served simply (smoked
salmon, grilled Dover sole,
chicken Maryland or filet de
boeuf with Bearnaise sauce).
The seasonal specialities are a
little more dressed up; Parma
ham filled with asparagus tips,
pheasant braised with foie
gras and brandy. This is the
place to be taken to by
someone who likes eating food
without having to have
anything explained to him,
and without having to admire
the cuisine with every
mouthful. There's a fine wine
list too.*

Bill Bentley's Bishopsgate
Swedeland Court, 202
Bishopsgate EC2 (283 1763)
FRENCH
Mon-Fri 12 noon-3.00.
Food £24. Wine £5.25.
*This dark, handsome and
expensive restaurant is
situated discreetly at the end
of a long, narrow alley just
opposite the southern flank of
Liverpool St Station and
behind the recently
refurbished Dirty Dick's. The
ground floor is an oyster bar,
the restaurant proper is below,
in the ancient, brickwalled
vaults. Black oaken barrels
loom large; some (behind the
bar) hold port and sherry; the
tun in the entrance hall is a
phone booth. The menu lists
straightforward, city man's
food; Parma ham, poached
eggs Benedictine, snails,
potted shrimps and of course,
native oysters (no 3s at £3.50
for six); fish and meat share
the menu fifty-fifty (this is not a
totally fish restaurant like the
other Bill Bentley's). Trout,
turbot and sole or steaks,
cutlets and roasts are given a
French touch with the sauces.
The cheese board is good, the
wine list is dear.*

Gallipoli
7-8 Bishopsgate Churchyard,
Bishopsgate (Off Old Broad St)
EC2 (588 1922/3)
INTERNATIONAL & TURKISH
Mon-Fri 12 noon-3.00; Mon-Sat
6.00-2.00am (with dancing
until 3.00am) Cabarets at 10.30
and 1.00am.
Food £24; £15.25 per head set
dinner plus show. Wine: £7
(lunch); £8.95 (dinner) £8.95.
*An odd little Turkish pillbox
stands in the middle of the
pedestrian precinct forming
part of Bishopsgate
Churchyard; it is the conning
tower of a largish,
subterranean ex-Turkish bath
built by Elphick in 1895 and
transformed into a restaurant
in 1967. The florid, tiled decor
makes an excellent setting,*

(even the kitchens have elaborately decorated tiles). The night time shows are famous for the belly dancers; the menu is mainly international but naturally Turkish food predominates. Favourite dishes include biryan Gallipoli (fillet of lamb braised in white Trakya wine), dolmalar (aubergines, courgettes, pimentoes and vine leaves, each stuffed with minced lamb) and kebabs served with yoghurt.

Great Eastern Hotel
Liverpool St, EC2 (283 4363)
The hotel contains three quite separate and different restaurants. Each merits a separate entry. Each caters for a different type of clientele both regarding price and the type of food, as well as opening times. They are called:
1. The City Gates *(See Budget Section)*
2. The Entrecote *(See Budget Section)*
3. The Beaufort Restaurant

Shares
12-13 Lime St, EC3 (623 1843/4)
Mon-Fri 11.30am-3.00.
Food £13.50 (4 course set menu), £12 (3 course set menu), early lunch (11.30-1.00) £8.00. Wine £5.50.
One of the partners owning this smart, newish restaurant (it opened in late 1980) was once a City man himself, the other (Terry Boyce) cooked at Carrier's for 15 years. Their past experiences combine to make Shares comfortable and attractive, with one of the most

tempting and practical menus to be found in the City. It changes monthly and is not too long. All the main dishes are cooked a la minute, the favourites being breast of duck glazed with a variety of sauces, or steaks and cutlets served with a variety of herbed or spiced butters. For starters there is always seafood pancake filled with a mixture of shellfish meat and glazed with a hollandaise sauce. The sweets include the petit pot de chocolat made famous at Carrier's. Brokers who start work around 7am are offered a special, early, two course 'brunch' so that they can be back at work by one.

Bloom's
90 Whitechapel High St, E1 (247 6001)
KOSHER JEWISH
Sun-Thu 11.00am-10.00; Fri 11.00am-2.30.
Food £16. Wine £4.50.
Bloom's once had a snack bar where the impecunious and hurried customer could eat frankfurters, salami or super salt beef sandwiches, gefilte fish, chopped liver, salads and other Jewish delicacies, without the hassle of ordering a table, being subjected to the slam-bang service and paying quite a bit more even though the food is rather good and the tablecloths snowy white. Now, thanks in a mysterious way to VAT, there is take-away only at the deli counter and, as

Whitechapel High St is no place for a picnic the choice is: take it away, leave it, or eat in the not-cheap restaurant. Complaining about this to a Jewish friend he laughed and quoted an old Jewish tag; 'Bloom's?' who goes to Bloom's?, only 'Goyim naches', meaning only non-Jews would take the trouble. Take the trouble to go there though if you like well cooked, strictly kosher food. It's handy for Petticoat Lane and the Whitechapel Art Gallery too. Another Bloom's at 130 Golders Green Rd, NW11.

The City Gates
Great Eastern Hotel, Liverpool St, EC2 (283 4363)
ENGLISH
Breakfast Mon-Fri 7.00am-10.00am; Sat & Sun 8.00am-10.00am. Lunch Mon-Sun 12 noon-3.00. Dinner Mon-Fri 5.00-10.00; Sat & Sun 6.00-10.00. Set prices for all meals; (VAT & service incl) Breakfast £3.50 per head; lunch £4.95. Dinner £5.75, also a la carte. Wine £4.25.
British Rail's catering department, since it has been under the guidance of Prue Leith, has improved beyond belief, especially in the hotels. At this one the food was always rather good; now it's very good. The idea of turning their handsome, large, domed dining room into a carvery is excellent and at lunch it's packed (with ladies as well as men). The carvery is below the dome and staffed by chefs who will cut fine roasts (including hot ham) or grill succulent steaks and chops

just as you ask for them. Waiters bring the first and third courses to you, you fetch the main course from the chefs yourself. There is also a great choice of salads, desserts and cheese. There are special reductions for children. At breakfast you serve yourself from the carvery, with eggs and bacon, fried bread, toast or croissants, juices and tea or coffee etc.

Clifton Restaurant
126 Brick Lane, E1 (247 3108/ 377 9402)
INDIAN
Mon-Sun 12 noon-1.00am. Food £10. Wine £3.25.
The street outside is a teeming outdoor market at weekends, where you can buy anything from a bicycle to a live puppy; it is also the main street of Whitechapel's Indian Quarter, so for tourists and locals alike the Clifton is pretty popular. The walls inside are covered with highly professional, spray-gunned murals of sexy Indian houris (this is a Muslim restaurant); one nymph reclines in an oyster shell on what looks like a bed of frog's spawn but is, in fact, pearls. The more frequented back room depicts a tiger among the beauties. The menu is lengthy, listing items like tandoori pheasant, quail and chicken livers. The latter is well recommended. Service is brisk but unhelpful; a pity when the choice is so vast. There is another, slightly smarter Clifton in Ludgate Hill, EC4.

Crazy Horse
50 Stoke Newington Rd, N16
(249 4895)
CYPRIOT
Mon, Tue, Wed 12 noon-12
midnight; Thu, Fri & Sat 12
noon-2.00am; Sun 12
noon-1.00am.
Food £10. Wine £4.
*Dalston may not be everyone's
idea of somewhere to visit for
the night life but at weekends
this particular corner is
buzzing with live music and
song and even (on special
occasions) belly dancers. The
Turkish cinema across the
road supplies many of the
customers at this bright and
friendly restaurant; the rest
are local droppers-in. The best
idea for a first visit is the £5 a
head meze which comprises
little samples of pretty well
everything on the menu and is
more than generous. The
kebabs and mullet are very
good. There are traditional
Greek stews, charcoal grilled
steaks and chops as well, and
the baclava and cheesecake
are homemade. The clean
kitchen in on full view to the
customers. Pretty vases of
fresh flowers decorate each
table and robust paintings of
white horses in the Wild West
cover the walls.*

Dickens Inn
St Katherine's Way, E1 (488
1226 & 481 1786)
ENGLISH
*There are three different
restaurants on each of the
three floors, each with
different hours and prices.*

The Tavern Room
Mon-Sun 11.00am-10.00.

Food £4. Wine £6.50 (1 1/2
litre bottle) or 70 p a glass.
Open for snacks
between, as well as during,
licensing hours.

The Pickwick Room
Mon-Sun 12 noon-3.00,
7.00-10.00; closed Sun night.
Food £22 a la carte; set price
menu £8.50 per head. Wine
£5.25.

The Dickens Room
Mon-Sun 12 noon-3.00,
5.00-10.00; closed Sun night.
Food £16. Wine £5.25.
*The whole building is a
carefully reconstructed ex-
brewery warehouse, built
possibly in the mid 16th
Century, moved 70 yards from
its original site, stripped of its
Victorian skin of bricks and
decked out as an 18th Century
Inn just a few years ago. The
place can therefore hardly be
described as totally authentic,
but it certainly has a delightful
atmosphere. Students of
architecture will admire the
beams; for boat-lovers there
are the views of the yacht
basin and the floating museum
ships moored just alongside.
The balconies on each floor
also have magnificent views,
by night as well as day.
Families with children can eat
outside at large sturdy tables,
untrammelled by any traffic
other than passing boats. It
really is a splendid place to
bring tourists or nostalgic old
salts; I should also add that the
food is genuinely good,
authentic, traditional fare,
though it's not that cheap, and
in high summer the place can
be very crowded.*

132

The Tavern Room is run like a wine bar with self service during licensing hours and as a snack bar between times. They specialise in Real Ales, spirits from the wood, sherries from the cask and very good seafood such as cockles, mussels and shrimps, also quiches, salads, pates and cheese. There's sawdust on the floor and, in keeping with that, plastic cutlery and paper plates. Very expensive coffee too in plastic beakers.

The Pickwick Room (on the first floor) is a sea of stripped pine; pine tables, pine chairs and pine sideboards. Waitresses wear long, Laura Ashley gowns. The table d'hote menu lists daily specials of a Dickensian kind such as steak and kidney pie, bubble and squeak, Irish stew and cutlets, and the a la carte has noble roasts and grills but veers into the 20th century occasionally with baked seafood, stuffed avocados, and stuffed aubergines. Like the Dickens Room above, this restaurant is popular with local business men as well as with the better-off class of tourist.

The Dickens Room on the top floor has a pine decor similar to the room below, but this restaurant is devoted to fish. You can select what you like from the slab in Captain Cuttle's display; there are many maritime nick-nacks on the walls, and even better views than from lower down. Starters include potted shrimps, whitebait, oysters and smoked salmon. Main courses are made from a variety of grilled, fried or poached fish, with plenty of different sauces and garnishes. There are good salads, very plain desserts, and cheeses to finish with.

The Entrecote
Great Eastern Hotel, Liverpool St, EC2 (283 4363)
FRENCH
Mon-Fri 12 noon-2.30pm.
Set price. Food £6.30 per head. Wine £5.15.
This is another bright idea from Prue Leith based on a simple but successful formula borrowed from Les Entrecotes of Paris. The menu offers no choice, just the same salad, steak, chips, dessert or cheese every day, for a set price. Here the salad is served in deep bowls with walnut oil dressing. The steak is of course an entrecote and generous with it. The cheeses are either stilton or brie; the dessert is always apple flan with an orange glaze, cream and coffee are included. The wine can be had by the half or quarter bottle. The setting is splendid — a traditional grand hotel dining room, white cloths, red carpet and chandeliers, with paintings of London's past Lord Mayors on the walls. The waitresses are all cheerful, local Cockney ladies.

Gow's
81 Old Broad St, EC2 (588 2050)
ENGLISH
Mon-Fri 12 noon-3.00.
Food £15. Wine £3.50.
Gow's is an endearingly shabby, large windowed, old fashioned fish restaurant just

by Broad St Station. It was established in 1885 and until very recently the Gow family had their own fish shop alongside. It is now owned by Balls Bros (see list for their wine bars in the City) but little else has changed. It still has a mostly male clientele, a dark mahogany bar and brown anaglypta wall paper. Dusky oil paintings of fish hang above, and two white haired and white overalled ladies make the coffee and work out the bills in a little booth. It must be one of the last places in London still to serve smoked haddock and poached eggs for lunch. The oysters are Helfords; whitebait and various good smoked fish are other good starters. The sole, plaice, halibut, turbot and skate are fried or grilled in enormous helpings and a savoury melange of 'fruits of the sea' is highly recommended. There are a few meat dishes for those who prefer meat to fish.

Le Marmiton
4 Bloomfield St, EC2 (588 4643)
FRENCH
Mon-Fri 12 noon-3.00.
Food £20. Wine £5.
The chef here is a Breton, with his own farm back home; not surprising then if some of the dishes here have a Breton flavour. He makes a delicious cold mousse of sea scallops and roulades filled with Bayonne ham; a selection of several different fillets of smoked fish or his own pates are among the starters. Steaks have a kidney sauce, escalopes of veal come with hot Roquefort sauce. The

cheeses are all French and well presented. It looks scruffy from outside, but inside, with its little bar, bright tablecloths and busy kitchen in full view, the impression is one of friendliness, speed and efficiency.

The Tower Hotel
St Katherine's Way, E1 (481 2575) for all three restaurants, each of which is described on a separate sheet. They are:
1. **The Picnic Basket** (See budget section)

2. **The Carvery**

3. **The Princes Room**

The Carvery
Tower Hotel, St Katherine's Way, E1 (481 2575)
ENGLISH
Mon-Sun lunch 12 noon-3.00; dinner 5.30-10.00; Sun 6.00-10.00.
Food £15.90 (set price of £7.95 per head). Wine £5.55 red £5.75 white or rose.
Taking a somewhat doom-laden theme from its neighbouring pile, (the Tower of London), the portraits on the Carvery walls are all of people who have been either incarcerated or beheaded there. The windows, which look out over St Katherine's Dock, are curtained with strong, shiny chains. Even the tables look as though they are made of blood-stained wood. Never mind, they and the leather-upholstered chairs accompanying them are full, daily and nightly, with customers eager to gorge themselves with as much roast

meat as they like. The central counters are laden with hot and cold roasts of ribs of beef, and legs of lamb and pork. You carve (the beef is roasted to three different degrees of doneness) your own helpings. Waitresses serve first and second courses.

The Princes Room

Tower Hotel, St Katherine's Way, E1 (481 2575)
ANGLO/FRENCH
Mon-Sun 12.30-3.00, except Sat lunch, 6.30-9.30.
Food £20 (set menus including wine at £10.75, £12.75 and £14.75 per head). Wine £5.90.

The view from this sober, luxurious and dignified modern dining room (decor by Richard Designs) is of a fine sweep of the Thames and Tower Bridge. This is the most expensive of the Tower Hotel's three restaurants, and it is busiest in the evenings. The menu is mainly French, though the odd English speciality, such as a Barnsley chop, does creep in. It is adventurous too; you'd look in vain elsewhere on the City's environs for brioches filled with morilles, leek and clam soup, sea bass baked in a bed of rock salt or swordfish steaks. Meat dishes tend to be slightly more conventional, and rich; there are some delicious sorbets to end with and the wine list, as befits a hotel owned by a brewery (Thistle and Newcastle Brown), is impressive.

Cooke's

41 Kingsland High St, E8 (254 2878)
ENGLISH
Mon-Sat 10.00am-6.00; Mon, Fri and Sat 8.30-11.00; closed Thu.
Food £3. Unlicensed

There's no point in pretending that the steak and kidney pies made here are the best in London; or that the hot stewed eels in a sea of green parsley sauce and the cold stewed ones set in a crystal white jelly could compete with anything served by the Roux brothers, but Cooke's is the epitome of an old-fashioned, working class eel and pie house and as such deserves to be visited. It should also have a protection order on it, so that the decor can be preserved for ever. Note the mirrors fixed by small intertwined brass eels, the art deco tiles, the marble tables and oaken benches and the tank of live eels by the terrazzoed threshold while you sample a traditional Cockney plateful of hot pie, hot eels, licqour and mash, washed down with a nice cup of tea. They do a brisk take-away trade as well.

The Picnic Basket

Tower Hotel, St Katherine's Way, E1 (481 2575)
ENGLISH
Breakfast Mon-Sat 7.30am-11.00am; Sun 8.00am-11.00am. Lunch, tea, dinner Mon-Sun 12 noon-12.45am.
Food £8. Wine £5.55 red,

£5.75 white/rose.

There is a vernal, conservatory look to this pretty snack/lunch/tea room in the otherwise rather severely modern Tower Hotel. It has green bamboo furniture and wallpaper and palm-tree pillars with golden leaves a la Dorchester. The view (at ground level) is of Tower Bridge. The menu is simple; salads, soups, omelettes, grills, burgers, and fried chicken, with sandwiches and desserts, hot drinks and a licensed bar. (Residents, but not passers-by, can order drinks in a hotel at any time of day. The licensing laws operate as in any restaurant otherwise). This makes a nice civilised rendezvous for tourists or local City workers, situated as it is between the Tower of London and St Katherine's Dock.

The Ringside
22 Kingsland Rd, E2 (739 1838)
AMERICAN
Mon 12 noon-6.00am; Tue-Fri 12 noon-1.00am; Sat 7.00-2.00am; Sun 2.00-1.00am. Food £6; set lunch £1.25 per head (12 noon-4.00) Wine £3.50.

This restaurant is rather a godsend in an area which seems otherwise to be devoted solely to the furniture trade and 'shoe factors'. The boxing posters indicate that the owner is an ex-boxer, Vic Andretti (one time lightweight champion); the heavy brass lamps were saved from nearby Spitalfields fruit and veg market; the menu reflects Vic's fondness for American hamburgers, though they also

do chops and steaks and 'the best roast dinners in London' for Sunday lunch at a set price of £4.75. The £1.25 daily set lunch is a great bargain — salad, burger and chips or pork chop, chips and peas. The decor, in keeping with the burgers, has a hint of the saloons seen in Westerns; wooden, balustraded and butch.

Sea Shell
392 Kingsland Rd, E8 (254 6152)
FISH
Tue-Fri 12 noon-2.00, 5.00-10.30; Sat 11.30am-10.30. Food £3.50. Unlicensed

This is a fish and chip shop, or, to put it more elegantly, a 'fish bar and restaurant'. It is admittedly not that unusual to find fish and chips hereabouts, but as this one serves outstandingly good fish and chips it deserves a place in this guide. Visitors from plushier Lisson Grove will already know of the Sea Shell there; this one is identical, except that here the frying is better, or so this frier asserts. Clad from boater to moccasins in dazzling white, Don (the frier) flips first class fillets into flour, batter and good clean oil. Two lady assistants powder them with salt and anoint them with vinegar as tenderly as they would handle a baby; (this service is performed for customers with very dirty hands). Enormous plaice, halibut and sole are cooked on the bone. The restaurant at the back is spartan, but spotless.

Throgmorton Restaurant
27a Throgmorton St, EC2 (588 5165 & 588 1495)
ENGLISH
Mon-Fri 11.45am-3.00 (restaurants); 8.30am-4.00 (Buffet Bar upstairs); 11.30am-3.00/5.00-8.00 (Bar Sinister).
Food £12. Wine £4.50.

Lyons owns this vast, Edwardian warren which occupies the ground floor and basement of a building one block wide. It sits right behind the Stock Exchange and the Bank is but a hundred yards away. At lunchtime it is loud with the roar of male voices and every one of the 160 places in The Grill and the 90 seats in The Oak Room is full. The service from real, old-fashioned nippies (two-thirds of whom have all been here all their working lives) is so fast that they can usually manage two and a half sittings so it's worth waiting for a table. (But remember lunch starts very early in the City). The Grill serves marvellous rump steaks, chops, cutlets, chips and peas; you can see the grill in the centre of the restaurant. The Oak Room is more for steak and kidney pie, roast beef and fish and chips. The two snack bars are also pubs, with wines and real ales. They serve salads, toasted sandwiches and quiches. Buffet Bar open for light breakfast (toasted sandwiches, bacon rolls, coffee).

TRANSPORT

(All details subject to change. Phone 01-222 1234 at anytime, day or night to check details. Some routes shown do not operate every day of the week.)

Tube: Aldgate, Aldgate East, Liverpool St, Tower Hill

Buses: 5, 10, 15, 22a, 23, 25, 40, 42, 44 (Sun am only), 78, 95 (Sun am only), 253

Night: N84, N95, N98 — to Aldgate

Or: 5, 6, 8, 8a (Mon-Fri only, except evenings), 9, 11, 22, 22a, 35, 47, 48, 55, 67, 78, 149, 243a (Sun only), 279a (Sun only), 502 (Mon-Fri only, except evenings)

Night: N83, N84, N91, N94, N97 — to Liverpool Street

CARRIER'S

No one could say that Islington is bursting with good restaurants but the few that can be recommended offer an interesting range of styles and prices; there's something for everybody, from Carrier's haute cuisine to tip-top fish and chips. You can make a casual meal of truly ethnic Turkish kebabs or dress up for a sophisticated, expense account entrecote, all within a square mile north of the Angel.
Further afield, and perhaps where you'd least expect to find them there are real treasures; breakaways like Gerhard's or Anna's Place who survive thanks to the faithful local clientele and lower rents.
There's nowhere particularly elegant or luxurious for tea or breakfast and nowhere stays open very late, but for pubs or bars with live music, cabaret or even theatre, Islington is one of the best places in London; a pioneer in the field.

LUXURY

Anna's Place
90 Mildmay Park, N1 (249 9379)
FRENCH
Tue-Sat 7.15-10.15.
Food £27. Wine £3.95.
As you might expect from a Swedish owner, there's grablax on the menu and the place is not just spotless but really pretty with it. What is less to be taken for granted is the standard of cooking which is not just good but amazingly so. Inventive too, and now that Anna's brother has been replaced by two extremely skilful English cooks, there is a touch of la nouvelle cuisine. Do try their new gravlax en croute with dill-flavoured hollandaise; filet of sole stuffed with crab and pike; noisettes of lamb with three purees (spinach and pear, apricot and celeriac). You get tiny tartelette shells filled with other savoury purees to nibble while you order, which softens the blow of 95p cover charge; marvellous home-made bread and wonderful sorbets, but rather steep prices on the wine list, even if it is a good one.

Carrier's
Camden Passage, N1 (226 5353)
INTERNATIONAL
Mon-Sat 12.30-2.30; 7.30-11.30.
Food £41.40 (dinner) £35.58 (lunch) Wine £3.75 (1/2 litre)
Said to be the only restaurant in which the Queen Mother has ever eaten, this one, owned and still closely supervised by the renowned cookery writer Robert Carrier, opened in 1966. Since then the menu has not changed drastically, though sauces have been lightened and the presentation made even more elegant thanks to a minute whisper of la nouvelle cuisine. The saffron soup, Japanese beef, calves liver with avocado and lemon posset remain top favourites on the four course table d'hote menu. There is nothing a la carte, but there is a shorter, cheaper three course lunch and supper menu. The wines are excellent, the surroundings charming and the service discreet.

Four Seasons
69 Barnsbury St, N1 (607 0857)
FRENCH
Mon-Fri 12.30-2.30; Mon-Sat 7.00-11.00.
Food £28. Wine £4.90.
Alain cooks and Joyce makes you warmly welcome in their tiny, six-tabled restaurant, with the open plan kitchen in full view as you enter. If it's summer time, and not raining you can sit out in the garden under shaggy, fringed umbrellas. The menu, which changes every two and a half months, lists home made pate and cured meats from the Grisons (Switzerland). Fish is bought daily (from the new Billingsgate) and top quality meat comes likewise from Smithfield. Sauces tend to be rich and unusual (cepes with the veal, blackcurrants with the lamb, moutarde de meaux with the filet de boeuf). Leave room for a syllabub packed with brandy. Note that it's easy for parking, open Bank Holidays and offers a three course set lunch for £9.80. Excellent wine list.

MID-PRICE

Due Franco
207 Liverpool Rd, N1 (607 4112)
ITALIAN
Mon-Fri 12 noon-3.00; 6.00-12
midnight; Sat 6.00-12 midnight
Food £15. Wine £3.75.
*Two Francos, ex-waiters from
the Portofino and both from the
same village near Parma, own
and run this Italian restaurant
well away from the trendy
Passage, but handy for locals
from Barnsbury. The menu is
doggedly Italian and the great
thing is that they make their
own pasta. This, as a main
course, makes a good
inexpensive meal; or you could
be more extravagant and try
the lamb steak grilled with
rosemary, the saltimbocca or
the escalope 'mont blanc'. The
cheeses, like the wines, are
mostly Italian. The ambience is
jolly, with friendly, helpful
service; the decor is simple —
red tablecloths, peasant
chairs.*

Frederick's
Camden Passage, N1 (359
2888)
INTERNATIONAL
Mon-Sat 12.30-2.30; 7.30-11.30.
Food £20. Wine £3.75.
*Businessmen from the City
come here by the limo-ful,
confident of finding the sort of
food that helps deals to go
smoothly. It is in fact a very
thriving, professional and well-
designed restaurant. Larger
and prettier rooms
(culminating in a handsome
garden) have been added over
the 10 years of its existence.
The longstanding favourites
are the deep-fried mushrooms,
the steaks and chops from the
charcoal grill, the game dishes
and the five well chosen
cheeses (blue brie, chevre,
whole stilton, mild cheddar
and camembert). There is an
enormous wine list and
magnums are a speciality
which are particularly
recommended for parties.*

Gerhard's
125 Church St, Stoke
Newington, N16 (254 8860)
GERMAN
Tue-Sat 7.00-11.00.
Food £16. Wine £2.50.
*I think people must come here
as much for (perhaps more for)
the ambience as for the food,
for this is a temple of pure
kitsch, mightily embellished by
the disarming charm of its
handsome young German
proprietor Gerhard, and totally
unlike anywhere else in the
neighbourhood, which is, to
put it mildly, unspeakably
dreary. Having got over your
initial surprise at the stuffed,
lifesize, cuddly toy bears,
leopard with cubs, and marble
cupid piddling into a small
fountain in the bar and coffee
after-dinner nook downstairs,
settle into button-backed sofas
upstairs and enjoy the deep-
fried mussels, sauerbraten with
rich trimmings, Wiener
Schnitzel, grilled bananas and
'fruit orgy'. The very battered
wine list displays prices (of
mostly German wines) which
are so low as to appear out of
date, but they aren't.*

Julius
30 Upper St, N1 (226 4380)
INTERNATIONAL

Mon-Sat 12.30-2.30; 7.30-11.45.
Food £16. Wine £3.85.
Julius, the white-coated owner-chef greets you in person from behind the counter of his little glassed-in kitchen. Everything on the menu is cooked to order or, as he, with his continental training would say, 'a la minute'. Only the specials — casseroles or roast — are cooked beforehand and these change daily. Ceviche makes a good starter, or a home-made pate; salmon trout, veal cutlet and filet of beef are recommended to follow, but do leave room for some top-class cheese and (or) one of Julius's own delicious desserts. The restaurant is small but pretty and the wine list impressive. Choose from some of those labelled by the door or let the efficient waiter guide you.

M'sieur Frog
31a Essex Rd, N1 (226 3495)
FRENCH
Mon-Sat 7.00-11.30.
Food £22. Wine £3.85.
Open for dinner only and bistro-like by nature, this is the favourite neighbourhood restaurant for many of Islington's residents. It is owned and run by the Rawlinson family who skilfully bring France to London with dishes such as moules mariniere, pigeon or poussin farci and coquilles St Jaques au Chambery. They are generous with the choice of good fresh vegetables and keep an excellent French cheese board. The menu changes every two months. The wine list is interesting because it's a very personal one - mostly French with several bargains and the odd Californian wine for fun. The decor is simple, clean and cheerful, with a snug little bar to wait in.

Portofino Restaurant
39 Camden Passage, N1 (226 0884)
ITALIAN
Mon-Sat 12.30-2.30; 6.30-11.30.
Food £20 (min ch £4.50) Wine £3.70.
Aquilino Consigli opened this, the first restaurant in Camden Passage, in 1962 and since then it has gone from strength to strength, providing its patrons with high quality Italian food in such generous portions that few bother with dessert (though the zabaglione is a great favourite). Antipasti from the trolley, calves liver, gigot steaks and skate with capers are other popular dishes; dolcelatte is the solitary but excellent cheese. There are different specialities each day, with game in season. Most of the wines are Italian and the list offers a comprehensive range of the best from that country. Warm, low lighting; yellow and cognac tableclothes; comfort and good service give the place a reassuring feel.

Villa Dei Pescatori
45 Camden Passage, N1 (226 7916)
ITALIAN/FISH
Tue-Sat 12 noon-3.00, 6.00-11.30, Sun 12 noon-3.00.
Food £16. Wine £3.70.
The ramifications of families running Italian restaurants in Islington extend to this one for here the proprietor is brother-in-law to one of the Due

Francos. The speciality is fish of every kind, starting with smoked eel, snails or oysters and ending with lobsters, sole or salmon. For confirmed meat-eaters there is steak or chicken and soups or pasta are offered as an alternative first course. Brown bread makes a welcome appearance on the table as well as white, and the waiters are helpful in telling you what is special that day — advice which, in my experience, is well worth taking. In keeping with the fishy theme the heavily beamed ceiling is veiled in netting, with glass floats, life-belts, ship's lanterns and a wheel even, decoratively hanging about.

BUDGET

Roxy Diner
297 Upper St, N1 (359 3914)
AMERICAN
Mon-Fri 12 noon-2.50; Sat & Sun 12 noon-12 midnight.
Food £4. Wine £3.45 (lunch) £3.65 (dinner).
Mainly for burgers, but the blackboard lists different 'specials' each day and these may be fish, stews or chops. Good salads and chips or jacket potatoes are the usual accompaniments. The prices are higher at night, but they do make child-sized burgers (or rather, small, cheaper burgers to suit children). Another bonus is the roast beef Sunday lunch. Popular for its cheapness and cheerfulness, the Roxy is unpretentious, clean, large, light and airy with greenery, bentwood chairs and check plastic tablecloths.

Sultan's Delight
301 Upper St, N1 (226 8346 & 359 2503)
TURKISH
Mon-Sat 12 noon-2.30; 6.00-12.30am; Sun 6.00-12.30am.
Food £9. Wine £3.80 (Carafe).
After 10 years the original, authentic and decorative Turkish charcoal grill is sagging a little and the outside of this very popular restaurant looks somewhat scruffy, but inside the murals (of stencilled patterns and harem scenes) are kept crisp and bright and the cooking is still better here than it is at any of the other Turkish restaurants in this area. Try the very fresh, vegetabley borek with the great variety of meze; order kebabs to take away and don't miss out on the pastries and puddings, which are all made on the premises. The wine list consists mostly of Turkish wines; the Buzbag is particularly recommended by Jason, the friendly proprietor.

Trattoria Aquilino
31 Camden Passage, N1 (226 5454)
ITALIAN
Mon-Sat 12.30-2.45; 6.30-11.00
Food £10 (min ch £3.50 evgs).
Wine £3.95 (litre).
This is the best place in Islington for a lunchtime plate of spaghetti and a glass of wine; other pastas are consistently good and the fish, escalopes, chicken dishes in various forms, grills and roasts are very good value. Everything is freshly cooked, cheerfully and swiftly served and nicely presented. Evenings are more leisurely and rather

more crowded. The trattoria is furnished in a conventional Italian style (rustic furniture, red check tablecloths) and is under the same ownership as the Portofino (qv) a few doors further down the Passage. The latest speciality at Aquilino is the giant pizza (Four Seasons) made with home-made dough.

The Upper St Fish Shop
324 Upper St, N1 (359 1401)
FISH
Mon-Sat 11.00am-2.00;
5.00-10.00.
Food £2 (takeaway) £3.80 (eat there). Unlicensed
Habitues of Kosky's fish shops in the East End will find here a brand-new, fire-engine-red shop run by a third generation member of the old firm. Alan Conway really knows the trade and his shop makes a welcome appearance for, odd as it may seem in a largely working-class borough, good fish and chips have so far been hard to find. This one is slightly up-market, by selling halibut and sole as well as the more usual cod, skate and haddock, with lemon wedges as well as pickled onions, wallys and vinegar. The shop itself, with clean tables, mirrors, panelled wood and greenery is nice enough to linger in if you don't want to takeaway. Tea, coffee and soft drinks are also served.

Young's
19 Canonbury Lane, N1 (226 9791)
CANTON & PEKINESE
Mon-Sat 12 noon-3.00;
5.30-11.45; Sun 12 noon-3.00;
6.00-11.00.

Food £10. Wine £3.85.
Young's opened in December 1979 and is Islington's first (and so far only) modern Chinese restaurant. The staff come from Hong Kong via some of Soho and Queensway's most successful eating places, bringing with them recipes for teppan dishes as at Pang's and the delicious lemon-fried chicken breasts of the original Poon's. For drink there is a choice of suitable French wines and two or three kinds of Chinese tea. Special dishes and banquets should be ordered in advance. The decor is clean, cool and unobtrusive and the service civil and attentive.

TRANSPORT

(All details subject to change. Phone 01-222 1234 at anytime, day or night to check details. Some routes shown do not operate every day of the week.)

Tube: Angel, Highbury & Islington
Buses: 4 (Mon-Sat only), 19, 30, 38, 43 (Mon-Sat only), 73, 104 (everyday except Mon-Fri evenings), 171, 172, 214, 277 (Mon-Sat only), 279 (Mon-Sat only), 279a (Sun only)
Night: N96, N96

LE KOOTIER

Camden here describes the area around Primrose Hill, Regent's Park and Chalk Farm, and not the much wider extent of the London borough. Camden became fashionable in the late 60s as an attractive villagey area; Regent's Park, the Canal, the Lock, and the Zoo have also made an impact throughout London and not just in this locality. The street markets, the Greek Cypriot and Irish communities, the shops and pretty, early Victorian terraces, all combine to make Camden appealing. One of the results has been the influx of people originally from other parts of London, who could not afford to live more centrally, and who do not wish to live in Establishment residential areas. The social services here are particularly good, the council notoriously left-wing, and the area one of contrasts. Thus the reputation for trendiness; the wholefood shops, the delicatessens, the converted and painted houses; the view of outsiders that the residents are connected somehow with the 'arty' world; and the everlasting allegiance of the residents themselves.

MID-PRICE

Chalcot's Bistro
49 Chalcot Rd, NW1 (722 1956)
FRENCH
Tue-Fri 12.30-3.00; Tue-Sat
7.00-11.00.
Food £16. Wine £4.70.
*This is a small French
restaurant, tucked away from
the main roads of Primrose
Hill, whose owner, Colin
Thompson, is also the chef.
The atmosphere is of a small
converted barn, and although
nominally a bistro, it is much
more sophisticated than we
have come to understand by
that term. It is small enough to
make it vital to book. The food
is quite rich and traditionally
French. The wine list is short
but carefully chosen. Every
care is taken to make eating
here a relaxed and memorable
occasion.*

Chalk And Cheese
14 Chalk Farm Rd, NW1 (267
9820)
FRENCH
Tue-Sat 7.00-11.00; Sun 12
noon-3.30.
Food £12. Wine £3.75 (set
menu: £3.95 per person)
*Totally unostentatious, all
white, slightly clinical and not
very full, this restaurant makes
a virtue of its service and
attention to detail. The choice
is not huge, but each dish is
carefully presented. On
Sundays there is a set three-
course lunch which is very
good value at £4.50 — it is
advisable to book. The
proximity of Camden Lock and
the Roundhouse theatre make
this restaurant a useful place*
to know for a pleasant meal in
the area. It is also open by
prior arrangement for pre-
theatre meals.

**Ferdinand's Cocktail
Restaurant**
48 Chalk Farm Rd, NW1 (267
5939)
FRENCH
Tue-Sun 12 noon-3.00, 6.30-12
midnight; closed Mon.
Food £16. Wine £3.75.
*This is a Camden gem. A
converted cafe, the cocktail
bar and restaurant now
occupy this small corner site.
The American-style bar,
tastefully decorated, blends
with the more sophisticated
restaurant upstairs. The choice
of cocktails is appetising, and
while you sip your drink your
order can be taken and
prepared. Immense care is
taken over the food and the
customer's well-being. The
menu offers both rich and
simply cooked dishes,
examples of the former being
crepe cardinale (with seafood
in a lobster cream sauce), or
chicken gastronome (stuffed
with liver pate in a white wine
and vegetable sauce). The
vegetables are excellent. Don't
be disappointed: book ahead.*

Froops
17 Princess Rd, NW1 (722
9663)
SCANDINAVIAN
Mon-Sat 7.00-11.30.
Food £16. Wine £3.75.
*This is now a restaurant with
regional specialisation. It is in
the basement, with an
unassuming front door that
you should enter with
confidence. Cleanliness and*

airiness are achieved underground here. The menu includes items you would not easily find elsewhere, such as reindeer (delicious), all sorts of smoked fish, smorgasbord (for two) and gorgeous, unusual puddings. For sheer originality and variation you should try this.

The Gallery Boat
Opp 15 Prince Albert Rd, NW1 (485 8137)
PEKING/CHINESE
Mon-Fri 12 noon-2.30, 6.00-11.30; Sat-Sun 12 noon-11.30.
Food £15 (min). Wine £5.
This is a restaurant with a romantic setting — on a boat moored on the Regent Canal, within site of London Zoo. Down from the road along a canopied covered staircase decorated with fairy lights, you board the boat on the canal. The service here is friendly and quick, the tables are private, and it is not necessary to book for lunch. The menu features 'live' lobsters, which may or may not be alive!. The Peking cooking is spicy and less bland than the glutinous Cantonese we have come to understand as British Chinese. This restaurant is a treat that has to be paid for. Menus for two start at £17 per head and go up to £12.50. Individual main dishes are about £3.50, and 12% service is always added. The food is good, the atmosphere exceptional, but the price too high.

Lemonia
154 Regent's Park Rd, NW1 (586 7454)
GREEK
Mon-Sat 6.00-11.30.
Food £15. Wine £4.50.
This is a Westernised Greek-Cypriot restaurant. This means that more attention is paid to the food and service than is normally the case amongst Camden Greek restaurants. The cuisine is good and fresh. There is a high noise level which is supposed to engender cheerfulness. It is necessary to book. There is little privacy at the tables and the lighting is low. It is well worth a visit.

Mustoe Bistro
73 Regent's Park Rd, NW1 (586 0901)
ENGLISH
Tue-Fri 6.30-11.15; Sat 1.00-3.00, 6.30-11.15; Sun 1.00-3.00, 6.30-10.45.
Food £14. Wine £4.50.
Mustoe's is very much a product of its owner and his strong personality. He has complete influence over the restaurant, although his presence is not always guaranteed. Some might describe him as chauvinistic. The tables are all very private, each in its own compartment separated by wooden partitions. The menu is quite short with imaginative variations on standard fare, such as Shrewsbury Lamb. The fish is good. There is an unexciting range of starters but the puddings are worth saving up for.

Odette's
130 Regent's Park Rd, NW1
(586 8766)
FRENCH
Mon-Sat 7.30-10.15; Mon-Fri
12.30-2.15; closed Sun.
Food £21. Wine £4.
*Walking into Odette's you
know that food and all that
goes with it is cared about
here. This is not a big
restaurant, but tall ceilings,
tables sufficiently far apart,
pastel (mostly green)
paintwork and all the
decoration create an airy
impression of comfort and
ease. The menu is imaginative,
and the choice is
sophisticated. There is little
that is plain or simple — for
example, you must choose
between delicious crisp fried
Camembert, Arbroath smokies
or trout in champagne. Book.*

Le Routier
Camden Lock, Commercial
Place, NW1 (485 0360)
FRENCH
Mon-Sun 12.30-2.30, 7.00-10.45.
Food £17. Wine £4.75 (litre).
*This is the Camden restaurant
whose reputation was
established most quickly,
firmly and outside the locality.
In a wooden cabin next to
Regent's Canal, the
atmosphere of a French
Routier restaurant is retained
by functional furniture and
plastic tablecloths but
enlivened by flowers and
bright colours. The menu
offers a good choice of fairly
rich food. French sauces and
stuffings are well represented,
in the usual coquilles,
avocados and fish provencale,
but English roasts are also
available. The food is not
absolutely exquisite, but very
pleasant. You would be well
advised to book.*

BUDGET

Andy's Kebab House
81a Bayham St, NW1 (485
9718)
GREEK
Mon-Sun 12 noon-2.30; Mon-
Fri 6.00-11.15.
Food £9. Wine £3.75.
*Camden has a large Greek
and Cypriot community. This
is one of many such
restaurants, but it is a good
one, with tablecloths! You step
directly into the dining room
from the noisy street. The
decor is purely functional, as
in most basic Greek
restaurants. The kitchen
extends away from the back of
the room, so it is possible to
see what is being cooked. The
service is pleasant enough and
quick. The menu is basic
Greek-Cypriot, and the food is
better than in most tavernas in
Greece.*

Manna
4 Erskine Rd, NW3 (722 8028)
VEGETARIAN
Tue-Sun 6.30-12 midnight.
Food £8.50. Wine £4.50.
*This is one of the earliest
London wholefood restaurants,
in Primrose Hill, which used to
be known as slightly trendy,
arty and carefully
unconventional. Manna
survived. Refectory pine
tables, menu chalked on a
blackboard, lots of people,
little privacy — all are part of*

147

the atmosphere. It is not unusual to wait a short while for a table. Most dishes are described very straightforwardly, but are presented more attractively, taste delicious and come in huge portions. The soup is always good, and the choice of salads is excellent. The rice is, of course, brown. Don't forget that everything is vegetarian, even if it sounds as if it is not. The service is good.

Le Petit Prince
5 Holmes Rd, NW5 (267 0752)
FRENCH/ALGERIAN
Tue-Sun 12.30-2.30, 6.15-11.30
Food £9.50. Wine £3.95.
This is a small bistro that uses couscous as its staple, as do so many French restaurants run by Algerians. The bistro atmosphere signifies no great comfort or privacy, but cheerfulness and good value. This is the most unusual place in Kentish town. It is possible not to eat couscous, but the standard French dishes are more expensive and will take you over budget. The main selection lies in the choice of meats to accompany the couscous (£2.40 to over £4).

Moditis Restaurant
83 Bayham St, NW1 (485 7890)
GREEK
Mon-Sat 12.30-2.30, 6.00-11.30.
Food £8. Wine £3.80.
Next door to Andy's (see above), this is a more downmarket restaurant. There are no tablecloths. The food is perfectly adequate Greek, the atmosphere workmanlike. It is the general character of the place and the friendly, lively

service that make this worth visiting for a cheap meal.

Tilley's Eats
208 Camden High St, NW1 (485 4506)
ENGLISH
Mon 6.30-10.45; Tue-Wed 6.30-11.00; Thu-Fri-Sat 6.30-11.15; Sun 1.00-5.00.
Food £8. Wine £3.55.
To say that this is a straighforward place to eat would be an understatement. If the cooker is too full to accommodate the variety of vegetables you have chosen, you will be told. The proprietor, George, takes care of the cooker, explains his space problems and chooses the music himself. He does not have much help. This means service is not quick. It is, however, friendly and the portions are worth waiting for. Choose a pie (fish, steak or chicken and ham, £1.55) as a main course to keep within budget. There are also many grilled meats and a huge mixed grill (£3.85). The vegetables are plain and not overcooked. Soups and other starters and fruit pies or trifle will make sure you don't go hungry.

Trattoria Lucca
63 Parkway, NW1 (485 6864)
ITALIAN
Mon, Tue, Wed 12 noon-3.00, 5.30-10.00; Thu, Fri, Sat 12 noon-3.00, 5.30-11.00.
Food £10. Wine £3.50.
A busy, successful Italian restaurant. There is much bustle, created by the lively truly Italian waiters; you miss out on this part of the fun if

you sit in the room at the back. But you can choose a table with privacy. The service is quick and expert. To keep the bill low, choose carefully, because it is quite possible to spend much more than £10. The menu has standard Italian dishes, and daily specials are always available. Zabaglione recommended. There is usually no need to book.

TRANSPORT

(All details subject to change. Phone 01-222 1234 at anytime, day or night to check details. Some routes shown do not operate every day of the week.)

Tube: Camden Town, Mornington Crescent (closed Sat & Sun)

Buses: 3, 24, 27, 29, 31, 46, 53, 68, 74, 134, 137, 214, 253

Night: N90, N93

MOTHER HUFF'S EATING HOUSE

Although not considered a part of central London, the range of food available in this area is comparable to that of Chelsea, or possibly even Soho. This can partly be explained by the sheer size of the area, but has more to do with the affluence and cosmopolitan nature of the population. Hampstead may be radical, but it's not short of a bob or two either.
A considerable part of the area's charm lies in its rejection of the inner city norms of rectangularity and newness — everything in Hampstead is curvaceous and aged, not least the geography. This characteristic is borne out in the restaurants, where warm wood panelling and weatherbeaten furniture tend to be the keynote as opposed to spotlit prints or expensive interior design. So there is a refreshingly homely quality to quite a few of the restaurants (Oakley's Diner, Pippin, Turpins, Mother Huffs, Retsina Kebab) that combines simple human intimacy with an absence of the desperate urge to impress the customer at all costs.

LUXURY

Capability Brown
351 West End Lane (794 3234)
FRENCH
Mon-Sat 12 noon-2.00,
7.00-11.30.
Food £30. Wine £3.
Capability Brown specialises in serving French food in smart and tasteful surroundings. The room is a crisp combination of green and white, and is liberally dotted with plants. The food tends towards cuisine minceur, which means there are some distinctly original notions (melon and grapefruit cocktail with fresh mint) but also some dishes that are unnecessarily complicated. But even if some of the more adventurous things are flawed, everything is immaculately finished and garnished and the service is satisfactory.

Chateaubriand
48 Belsize Lane (435 4882)
FRENCH
Mon-Sat 7.00-12 midnight.
Food £25. Wine £4.75.
This is a small and intimate French restaurant, with wooden surfaces and dark reds predominant. It's a good place for a tete-a-tete. The waiters are alert and friendly but not so sycophantic that they won't make suggestions. The short menu contains few surprises. The devilled whitebait were a bit soggy, but the soupe de poissons was rich and fishy. They concentrate, obviously, on meat, and both their tournedos and Chateaubriand are tender and succulent. They bring a generous and varied dish of mixed vegetables, and there is a small, effective wine list.

Keats
3-4 Downshire Hill (435 3544)
FRENCH
Mon-Sat 7.30-11.00.
Food £40. Wine £8.
Certainly the best restaurant in Hampstead, Keats offers classic French cooking in a sumptuous room liberally sprinkled with paintings and books. Apart from the ordinary restaurant service, they have gourmet meals and feasts at holidays, such as last year's ten course Christmas dinner. The menu changes with the seasons, but you can always rely on a generously apportioned, subtly delicious meal. But then, at these prices...

Villa Bianca
1 Perrins Court (435 3131)
ITALIAN
Mon-Sun 12 noon-2.30,
6.30-11.30.
Food £25. Wine £4.90.
A supposedly classy Italian place that has, in fact, seen better days, Villa Bianca now offers food that, for its quality, is on the pricey side. The sauces are generally thin, and give the impression of having only recently been introduced to whatever they are anointing; and the salads are disappointing. The desserts are some compensation, and include fresh fruit salad, orange in caramel sauce and chocolate gateau. The Verona Antica in Heath St is a better bet.

MID-PRICE

The Cosmo Restaurant
4-6 Northways Parade (722 2627)
AUSTRIAN
Mon-Sun 12 noon-10.45.
Food £14. Wine £2.50.
The Cosmo has all the stolidity that one associates with traditional Austrian food and design. The large, relaxed restaurant is given the atmosphere of an ancient hotel by the wooden panelling and high ceiling. The menu offers many Germanic dishes amid the more ordinary steaks and chicken; home-made brawn, wiener schnitzel, calf's liver Berlinoise, extrawurst, sauerbrauten with red cabbage. The apfelstrudel with whipped cream is exquisite. Very popular with emigres and Austrian matrons in spectacular hats, you will hear little English. An eccentric and friendly restaurant that deserves greater popularity.

Fagin's Kitchen
82 Hampstead High St (435 3608)
FRENCH
Mon-Sun 12 noon-2.30, 7.00-11.30 (Sun closing 11.00)
Food £20. Wine £4.
Fagin's Kitchen offers Gallic richness instead of the expected Dickensian gruel minceur, warm wood and candlelight in place of the rigours of the workhouse. The food is robust, but not lacking in subtlety. The regular menu is supplemented by daily specials. Succulent moules marinieres, spinach and bacon salad, duck in orange, meaty charcroute Alsacienne (pork, bacon, sausage and sauerkraut in gravy), and thick creme brulee with an impeccably brittle crust. They serve cocktails with Dickensian names (quite a conceit, that) and have a useful wine list. Ask for more.

La Gaffe
109 Heath St (435 4941)
FRENCH
Tue-Sun 12.30-2.30, 6.30-11.30.
Food £18. Wine £3.50.
A restaurant where the exotic decoration is matched by the colourful owners, who if you are lucky will argue loudly throughout your meal. There is an extraordinary alcove with gilt plasterwork, skylight and murals, and generally the feel is of being below decks on some strange ship. The food is fairly conservative and competently cooked, but never brilliant. There are soups, pate, escalope de veau, spaghetti a choix, chicken kiev, dover sole, Paillard de boeuf and a small selection of puddings. A place to have fun in.

Gourmet Rendezvous
263 Finchley Rd (435 0755)
CHINESE
Mon-Sun 12 noon-2.30, 5.30-11.30.
Food £12. Wine £3.50.
The Gourmet Rendezvous is one of those Chinese places whose decor looks a bit like the set for Ali Baba and the 40 thieves — shiny embroidered pictures, pagoda style woodwork and tinkling Chinese music. But the food

brings you back to earth pretty quickly. Most of the dishes have a listless, dry quality. The Peking duck is stringy, and the roast crab overcooked and difficult to eat. The soups appear to be made by dropping things into Bovril. But the service is good and I'm sure it's possible to find things on the large menu that are good.

Gulistan
75 Heath St (435 3413)
INDIAN
Mon-Sat 12 noon-2.30,
5.30-11.00; Sun 12 noon-11.00.
Food £14. Wine £3.95.
This is a small and dignified place, free of the excesses of bad taste in decor that spoil so many Indian restaurants. The room is dark, there are plain mirrors behind the bar, and the tables are crisply covered in white. They have all the usual Tandoori things, and the chicken is even more succulent and flavoursome than is usual with this method. There are many different chicken and beef curries to try; Bindi gosht, beef curry with okra, is particularly good, as is Kashmiri chicken, a fruit curry. The flavours are full but delicate — I know someone who compares it favourably with Khan's.

Oslo Court
Prince Albert Rd (722 8795)
INTERNATIONAL
Mon-Sat 12.30-3.00, 6.30-11.30;
Sun 12 noon-3.00.
Food £24. Wine £4.50.
This elegant and comfortable restaurant, situated in the eponymous block of flats, is justifiably renowned for its wine list, which is both comprehensive and select. The wine waiter is an expert. The varied menu just holds its own in comparison, especially the seafood. The choice ranges from parma ham and melon to stuffed salmon trout, from asparagus to moussaka. An excellent place for wine buffs and learners alike, and for anyone who simply wants to drink as well as they can eat.

Simply Steaks
66 Heath St (794 6775)
INTERNATIONAL
Mon-Sat 7.00-12 midnight; Sun
12.30-2.00, 7.00-11.00.
Food £20. Wine £2.50.
Simply Steaks has but one aim; to ensure that you eat and enjoy high quality steaks. This singlemindedness makes it fascinating, and there's nowhere on the menu where you can escape the tyranny of flesh; there are but two different soups and a choice of salads to go with the various steaks. You can have 'em plain, with bearnaise sauce, stilton, ham and mushroom stuffing, anchovies or Mexican style, and they know all about seignant and well-done. A small selection of puddings, and that's it. Very satisfying, especially for carnivores without guilt.

The Third Man
13 Englands Lane (No telephone)
AUSTRIAN
Mon-Sun 6.00-11.00.
Food £16. Wine £4.80.
European food, other than French, tends to be good value (see Cosmo) and The

Third Man is no exception. It is a square room in light wood with tables covered in red and white check tablecloths, lit by candles in winebottles. The food is substantial and tangy; Bismarck herring, salad rolled in ham to start, goulash with sausage and fried egg, Paprika chicken with noodles, apfelstrudel, cheese and Austrian desserts. It's all full-bodied and leaves you with a full body. And if you see a shadow flit by, it'll be Harry...

Turpins
118 Heath St (435 3791)
ENGLISH
Tue-Sat 7.00-11.00; Sun
12.30-2.30; closed Mon.
£20. Wine £3.85.
The old house in which Turpins is situated provides warm and pleasant surroundings for food that veers unhappily from the solid (pies with various fillings such as duck and cherry; Sirloin steak) to the gimmicky (lamb with mangoes in pastry). The vegetables though are excellent, and there are some interesting desserts. If they would only take it easy on the complex and unusual combinations the food would be considerably better.

Verona Antica
108 Heath St (435 6397)
ITALIAN
Mon-Sat 12 noon-2.30,
6.30-11.30.
Food £14. Wine £3.50.
A compact place that provides pretty good Italian food, brought to you promptly by some very attentive waiters. The tables are arranged like a train buffet car (remember those?) with an aisle stretching away down the middle from the entrance and its enticing food display and bar. They have orthodox starters (delicious whitebait), a selection of pasta, and steaks, chicken and veal to follow. The desserts are fine, especially the profiteroles which lurk in crude chocolate. A good place to eat Italian fast, well and not too expensively.

BUDGET

Falafel House
95 Haverstock Hill (722 6187)
ISRAELI
Mon-Sun 6.00-11.30.
Food £8. Wine £3.50.
The Falafel House is a deservedly popular haven for those who value properly cooked Middle Eastern food, as opposed to greasy indeterminate doner kebabs. It's small and gently lit and usually quite full, which makes it a lively place to come to. From a slab of a menu that Moses would have approved of, you can choose from humous, taramasalata, falafel, avgolemono (a tangy Greek chicken soup with egg and lemon), a variety of salads (Greek, Oriental) and kebabs. They also do a sampler meal with a little of everything, or you can eat all you want for £7.50.

Maxwell's
76 Heath St (794 5450)
AMERICAN
Mon-Thu 6.00-12 midnight; Fri-Sat 6.00-1.00am; Sun 12.30-12 midnight.
Food £8. Wine £3.50.
From a tiny entrance you duck down some steps to the cavern-like restaurant. A long bar down one side dispenses drinks and cocktails. The food which consists of American staples (burgers, club sandwiches, salads, waffles, cheesecake) is all quite adequate, except for the burgers which can be dodgy. But then there are surprisingly few places that can cook something as simple as a hamburger consistently well. Rock music, alert and quickish service; not a bad deal.

Mother Huff's Eating House
12 Heath St (435 3714)
ENGLISH
Mon, Tue, Wed 12 noon-3.00; Thu-Fri 12 noon-3.00, 7.30-11.00; Sat 7.30-11.00; closed Sun.
Food £8. Wine £3.95.
This oblique little place hides itself in a loft up some stairs from an entrance concealed in an antique market off Heath St. The high, pitched roof, skylights and solid but worn furniture lend the air of an artist's studio. The menu is short and nothing is expensive, but the food manages to be both simple and expert despite this. There are crusty chicken and mushroom pies, delicate and crisp salmon fishcakes, chicken Kiev, and a range of excellent, fresh salads. It is an

unusual and tasty place.

Pippin
83 Hampstead High St (435 6434)
WHOLEFOOD
Mon-Sun 10.30am-11.45.
Food £8. Wine £3.75.
Pippin is quintessential Hampstead - a sloppy, studiedly informal canteen-style joint bedecked with flyers for organic growth therapy and vegetarian socialist flatmates, with wonky ancient wooden furniture and a stone flag floor. The food is only slightly dessicated, which is pretty good for a place of this kind — there are various casseroles, salads, curries, latkes, and a range of cakes, cheesecakes and pies for pudding. You can fill up effectively here without poisoning yourself, and enjoy the casualness of it all.

Pizza Express
64 Heath St (435 6722)
ITALIAN
Mon-Sun 11.30am-12 midnight.
Food £8. Wine £3.20.
Another of the popular chain's outlets, the pizzas here, coming piping hot from the large oven that dominates the proceedings, are as crispy of crust and moist of filling as they are elsewhere. You can choose your own filling from the usual variety, and there are fairly good gateaux and cheesecake for pudding. Good value.

Retsina Kebab
83 Regent's Park Rd (722 3194)
GREEK
Mon-Sat 6.00-11.30.

Food £8. Wine £2.50.
Retsina Kebab is a tiny, homely Greek place run by a husband and wife team. With only five or six tables you will probably find yourself sharing but that's part of the fun. They offer all the usual things, quality humous, taramasalata, a range of lamb kebabs, sheftali, and baklava and coffee to finish up with. The surroundings are as simple as the food is excellent; wood panelled walls and a somewhat unusual ceiling made of bottle corks. It all adds up to great value for money and a very enjoyable meal.

Harry Morgan's
31 St John's Wood High St (722 1869)
JEWISH
Tue, Wed, Thu, Sat 12 noon-3.00, 6.00-10.00; Fri 12 noon-3.00; Sun 12 noon-10.00; closed Mon.
Food £10. Wine £4.50.
Harry Morgan is basically a Soho salt beef bar sufficiently gentrified to fit into plush St John's Wood High St, North London's answer to Beauchamp Place — which means no signed boxers' mug-shots. It is bright and clean with much wood panelling and formica. The borscht, served hot or cold in a glass, is delicious, and there is chicken soup, gefilte fish, tongue, steak, veal, goulash, excellent latkes, apple strudel, creme caramel and sorbets for pudding. A little expensive because of the location, but worth it.

Lee Ho Fook
5-6 New College Parade (722 9552)
CHINESE
Mon-Sun 12 noon-11.30.
Food £10. Wine £4.
The sun beams in through the south facing windows of this large restaurant, brightening the front and making the red tablecloths glow. The surly waiters are the kind that make you feel pretentious (if you are not Chinese) for even being in a Chinese restaurant, but the food is fine, especially the range of Tim Sum. These are small steamed delicacies such as stuffed mushrooms, beef balls, and tiny prawn rolls, that come in individual bamboo steamers. At 65p each, four or five of these make a varied, substantial and cheap meal.

Mandarin
279c Finchley Rd, NW3 (794 6119)
CHINESE
Mon-Sun 12 noon-2.30, 6.00-11.00, closed Sun lunch.
Food £10. Wine £4.50.
The Mandarin is crisp, modern and welcoming, the immaculately varnished sliding doors leading to a high ceilinged room with some remarkable, if garish, embroidered pictures. I was cheerfully served with sweet and sour fish Mandarin style, simple but delicate. Apart from the Mandarin specialities there is a large selection of special, seasonal dishes such as Szechuan hot crispy beef, and stir-fried frogs' legs. It is a friendly and unpretentious place, and some care has gone into creating an interesting

interior.

Oakley's Diner
98 West End Lane (328 3308)
ITALIAN
Mon-Sat 9.30am-11.00.
Food £10. Wine £3.95 (litre).
*This is a useful place to know.
It's open all day, welcoming,
has a huge and varied menu,
it's cheap, and they serve
breakfast. Despite the
American name, the food and
owners are Italian, a fact that
doesn't easily escape
observation because of the
high spirits of the staff who
miss no opportunity to envelop
you in a joke. There is a
standard range of Italian
meats, including very tender
liver, and delicious al dente
courgettes and mushrooms.
You get huge helpings and
there is ice cream and coffee
if you can manage it.*

TRANSPORT

**(All details subject to change.
Phone 01-222 1234 at anytime,
day or night to check details.
Some routes shown do not
operate every day of the
week.)**

Tube: Warwick Avenue,
Maida Vale, St John's
Wood, Swiss Cottage,
Belsize Park,
Hampstead

Buses: 6, 8, 16, 16a daily, but
not evenings or Sun),
46, 176

Night: N94 — to Maida Vale

Or: 2, 2b, 13, 31, 46 — to
Finchley Road

Or: 24, 46, 268 — to
Hampstead Heath

Or: 210, 268 — to
Hampstead

PETER EVANS' EATING HOUSE

Eating out South of the River is both a frustrating and a rewarding experience. Frustrating because in a very large area there are very few good places to eat, rewarding because every now and again one discovers an oasis of culinary delight amidst the desert of fish and chip shops and kebab houses (not, I hasten to add, that I have anything against these particular establishments, simply that I wouldn't recommend them for an evening out!). Such delights include the excellent La Barca, *almost submerged beneath Waterloo Station, the* RSJ Restaurant, *so called because of the rolled steel joist around which it is built,* Peter Evans' Eating House, *and a number in Greenwich, foremost of which is* Le Papillon. *Much of the eating south of the river to the east exists in pockets, for example around the South Bank, to satisfy the visiting culture seekers, strung along the banks of the Thames to cater to the tourist, and clustered around the Royal Naval College at Greenwich. There are doubtless many hidden gems which have been missed, for which our apologies both to them and* to those who would have savoured their fares. Let us know where you are and we will visit for the next edition!

LUXURY

Le Papillon
57 Church St, Greenwich, SE10 (858 2668)
FRENCH
Mon-Sat 12.30-2.30, 7.00-10.30; closed Sat lunch.
Food £26. Wine £4.75.
This is undoubtedly the best restaurant in Greenwich, with prices to match. The interior is sophisticated; the service immaculate; the food imaginatively cooked. The Pork Pate was unusual, and quite delicious, as was the Salade Papillon. To follow we had Coquilles St Jacques, with limes, and live lobster! The vegetables were fresh and crisp, the sweet trolley tempting, with the usual array of French tartes and mousses. Combine a tour of the old bookshops and the tourist sites with a truly memorable meal here.

MID-PRICE

The Anchor
Bankside, SE1 (407 1577)
ENGLISH
Mon-Fri 12 noon-2.00, Mon-Sat 7.00-10.00.
Food £19. Wine £3.75.
This justly famous riverside pub dates back to Shakespeare's time; and recent renovations have laid bare the original brick walls and beams and a minstrels' gallery. The prices are rather inflated, but this is due no doubt to the summer tourist trade; customers otherwise are local businessmen in three piece suits (with appetites to match). Their specialities are Roast Rib of Beef, carved from a central table, and Mrs Thrale's Steak & Mushroom Pudding. Then there is Mrs Boswell's sweet trolley, a truckle of English Cheddar and Stilton; finally coffee and mints. The menu is colourful, relating the history of the pub and its connections with Dr Johnson.

The Angel
101 Bermondsey Wall East, Rotherhithe, SE16 (237 3608)
ENGLISH
Mon-Fri 12.30-2.00; Tue-Sat 7.30-10.30.
Food £16. Wine £3.55.
One of the 'Chaucer Inns' group (elsewhere in this area at The Geoffrey Chaucer, Westminster Bridge Rd, SE1, and the Grove Tavern, 522 Lordship Lane, East Dulwich, SE22) The Angel is chiefly famous because of its position in what is, at the moment, dock wasteland. It has a pleasant interior with a bar downstairs, serving standard pub fare, with a restaurant on top, with magnificent views across the Thames. The food is unexceptional, just what one expects from any reasonable steak house. Starters range from pate and melon, to whitebait; main courses from the full range of steaks (inevitably overdone, so order

blue if you mean rare) through lemon Sole, Steak and Kidney Pud, Baked Trout and Moussaka. The Koulibiak, a mixture of various fishes in pastry, is a good choice if you like fish. As in so many of these places, the vegetables and the desserts are best avoided; instead, order the coffee, sit back and enjoy the view.

Ristorante La Barca
80-81 Lower Marsh, SE1 (261 9221)
ITALIAN
Mon-Sat 12 noon-2.30, 7.00-11.30; closed Sat lunch.
Food £20. Wine £4.
The setting is rustic Italian: bare brickwork and beams, and typically Italian service — brusque but good-natured. We were introduced to La Barca as 'one of the best Italian restaurants in London' and arrived with high expectations. The menu is extensive, with all the usual dishes, as well as some more interesting ones not so often found. We started with the hot spicy prawns — frozen prawns in a tasteless tomato sauce — and the pasta with basil, which lacked the delicate flavouring required in such a dish. The baked eggs, however, were excellent; as were the squid. The liver and bacon too were cooked to perfection, and the vegetables were crisp and fresh. Such are the size of the portions that all we could manage for dessert was a shared crepe a la barca, served from a sweet trolley laden with equally tempting homemade puddings. Though I can't agree that this is one of

the best restaurants in London, it is certainly worth a visit; and as with so many of the restaurants in this area it offers excellent value for money. It is always full, so you would be well-advised to book.
Also at 541 King's Rd, SW6.

Marmara Restaurant
166 Evelyn St, SE8 (692 5557)
TURKISH
Mon-Sun 6.00-12.30
Food £15. Wine £4.75.
A somewhat dull interior enlivened by the smiling geniality of the Turkish owners who maintain their country's tradition of hospitality. You can choose from amongst all the well-known, and some less well-known, traditional Turkish dishes — though variety is not a facet of Turkish cuisine. For starters choose Dolma or Imam bayildi, aubergine stuffed with onion and tomato and baked in the oven. All the main dishes are cooked on a charcoal grill, and if you like the flavour this produces, then you can't do much better than their Bobrek (lamb kidneys), Pirzola (lamb chops), or best of all the Pilic Izgara (breast of chicken on a skewer with green peppers, tomatoes and mushrooms).

Mogul Restaurant
10 Greenwich Church St, SE10
INDIAN
Mon-Sun 12 noon-3.00, 6.00-11.30.
Food £13. Wine £3.90.
Although south of the river east is an area rich with Indian restaurants, this is the only one to merit a mention. Almost everything about it is unusual

for an Indian restaurant;
devoid of flock wallpaper, it is
in a cellar with white walls
and individual tables in
vaulted alcoves, where
intimacy is possible, unless
one has to share the table. This
may well happen, as the
Mogul is popular and often
full. The menu is without the
normal roll-call of vindaloos,
madras and pahls; it is made
up rather of an interesting
selection of Biryani and
Tandoori dishes, lamb or
chicken. The Chicken Chat —
with a hot sauce of lemon,
butter and mint — makes a
particularly good appetizer;
follow with any of the Biryanis,
the Ghost Piaza — succulent
lamb in hot spices — or the
Chicken Chilli Massala. A
word of warning however:
avoid the wines and stick to
lager or water.

Peter Evans' Eating House
31 Tooley St, SE1 (403 6059)
INTERNATIONAL
Mon-Fri 12 noon-3.30,
5.30-10.00.
Food £15 (Buffet Bar £7). Wine
£5.
Run, as one may guess from
the name, by Peter Evans and
his charming wife, there is
little here that is predictable —
from the lemon yellow interior
to the imaginative menu. Set in
a converted warehouse, built
in the 1840's, and now a listed
building, you can watch your
meal being prepared in the
open plan kitchen. Eat either
at the Buffet Bar — choosing
from a selection of
sandwiches, stilton, prawn,
pate etc., served on fresh
granary bread; with soup

before, and fool or trifle after
— or in the main restaurant,
where you can choose from
one of the most inventive
menus south of the river. Try
such delights as Steak, Kidney
and Sherry Pie, or Java Beef
Devils with spiced peanut and
lime, though it is probably
best to avoid the curry unless
you like it mild. The starters,
by comparison, are rather
mundane, but perfectly
acceptable: the Gravad Lax
(Scandanavian Cured Salmon)
is especially worth trying.
Though I am told by those who
eat here regularly that the
standard is variable, I would
still rate this as one of the
'gems' of the area.

Royal Festival Hall
Restaurant
Royal Festival Hall, South
Bank, SE1 (928 2829)
INTERNATIONAL
Mon-Sat 12 noon-3.00,
6.00-10.30; closed Sat lunch.
Food £18. Wine £4.10.
The restaurant here attracts
businessmen at lunchtime,
concert goers in the evening,
not it seems the most
discerning diners. The food is
expensive and unimaginative,
the service defiant. Our waiter
was not apologetic when he
spilled the vegetables across
the table. But there is a
marvellous view of the
Thames; and it does provide a
convenient fuelling station for
music lovers. There is a
concert menu (£7.95) which
changes fortnightly, as well as
an a la carte selection.

RSJ Restaurant
13a Coin St, SE1 (928 4554)
FRENCH
Mon-Sat 12 noon-2.00,
7.00-11.30; closed Sat lunch.
Food £16. Wine £3.90.
*One of the few restaurants in
this area to rate a mention in
the 'other' guides, RSJ —
Rolled Steel Joist, 'for want of
anything better to call it', as
the charming waitress told us
— is something of a
disappointment. RSJ has an
ordinary, not unpleasant,
interior, with seating upstairs
and downstairs, slightly
irritating background music,
potted plants and chocolate-
brown paint. The menu is
equally unspectacular, though
it does offer one or two
interesting items — calves'
livers with leeks and limes, for
instance, which turned out to
be rather tasteless. The main
complaint was the
temperature of the food,
tending to the tepid; the deep-
fried camembert was good,
but chilly, as was the vol au
vent. The highlight was
undoubtedly the halibut: firm
and juicy with a delicious
hollandaise sauce. The
vegetables were crisp and
fresh, but, again, betrayed
signs of having stood around.
The wine list is lengthy and
reasonably priced, but unlikely
to produce any surprises. It
would be unfair, however, to
suggest that RSJ is a bad
restaurant; for its price it
offers good value, and you are
unlikely to meet with any
disasters. If you live in the
area, or if you have visited the
nearby National Theatre, you
would do well to stay this side
of the river, rather than seek
the more expensive, and no
better, eateries further north.*

South Of The Border
8 Joan St, SE1 (928 6374)
ANGLO/FRENCH
Mon-Sat 12 noon-2.30,
6.00-11.30; closed Sat lunch.
Food £16. Wine £4.20.
*Sited in an old mattress factory
off Waterloo Cut, the decor is
unusual - old furniture, and
polished wood floors. The
menu changes every couple of
months, and includes such
delights as Escargot Cassolette
(snails, hazelnuts and
mushrooms in a wine and
garlic sauce with a pastry lid),
and Poached Egg Tartlets
(eggs poached in red wine
and garnished with bacon and
onions in pastry tartlets). Main
courses include smoked
mackerel, grilled and served
with a mint and yoghurt sauce,
which is tasty, as is the
smoked loin of pork, with hot
sour cream paprika sauce.
There is in addition a dish of
the day.*

BUDGET

The Station Grill
2 Braganza St, SE17 (735 4769)
INTERNATIONAL
Mon-Sat 12 noon-3.00,
5.00-10.00.
Food £9. Wine £3.80.
*This, as the rather dreary
name would suggest, is an up-
market caff; a place in which it
would be wise to avoid the
house wines. The cooking is
plain and, on the whole, good.
I started with the prawn*

cocktail, but the prawns were frozen and the cocktail over-vinegary. The Shashlik a la Russe was very tasty; and the pancakes were delicious. Pink and green flock wallpaper adds a touch of colour. I would not recommend anyone to travel any distance to come here, but it is quite adequate, and considering the dearth of decent places to eat in this area, a welcome supplement.

Trattoria La Spezia
35 Railway Approach, London Bridge, SE1 (407 0277/0749)
ITALIAN
Mon-Sat 12 noon-11.30.
Food £10. Wine £3.30.
The waiters here are notoriously difficult — the customer is never right — but then this is true of a good many London restaurants, and anyway the food is very good, and reasonably priced. The menu is extensive: soups, pasta, egg, fish and meat dishes; an array of salads and a tempting selection of desserts — crepes suzette and zabaglione (for two), for instance. Stick to something simple: the home-made soup perhaps, or Cappeletti in brodo, pasta served in chicken broth. Follow with calves' livers cooked in butter, lemon and white wine, or jugged hare.

TRANSPORT

(All details subject to change. Phone 01-222 1234 at anytime, day or night to check details. Some routes shown do not operate every day of the week.)

Tube: Waterloo, Vauxhall, London Bridge, Elephant & Castle, Lambeth North, Oval

Buses: 5, 177, 501, 513, 18, 501, 513, 77, 77a, 168a, 76, 4, 68, 149, 168a, 171, 239, 42, 78, 35, 48, 95, 133, 109, 172, 184, 44, 88, 170, 507, 155, 8a, 10, 40, 44, 2, 2b, 36, 36a, 36b, 185, 159, 12, 53, 70, 1, 176, 21, 43, 47, 70, 188

BUZKASN

Despite the knocks south-west Londoners have taken over the years we stand defiant! Restaurants hereabouts may be thin on the ground but if you're lucky enough to find one it's likely to be a rare outpost of excellent value and surprising quality. Thai in Tooting, Afghan in Putney plus a sprinkling of English, Chinese and Indian hotspots, in all of which the food is taken seriously. French restaurants predominate, however, and a number of these are certainly not to be sniffed at. So, armed with your A-Z, wallet, and preferably your own transport, head off over Putney or Wandsworth bridge and explore. If it's warm, have a pint of Young's by the river and work up an appetite in the fresh air.

164

LUXURY

Alonso's
32 Queenstown Rd, SW8 (720 5986)
FRENCH/ITALIAN
Mon-Sat 12.30-2.30, 7.30-11.30; closed Sat lunch.
Food £25. Wine £4.25.
Cosmopolitan and eclectic menu with a leaning to the exotic. Three or four course meals at set prices — £11.25 or £12.25 per person. Hawaian ribs, mango and crab, Andalusian mushrooms with caper sauce. An enormous choice of main courses: venison, chinese duck, tandoori chicken, fillet en croute etc...all sounding delicious but of variable quality. Puddings however taste as good as they sound, chocolate and Tia Maria mousse, champagne syllabub. Ritzy, continental surroundings and service.

Chez Nico
129 Queenstown Rd, SW8 (720 6960)
FRENCH
Mon-Fri 12.30-2.00, 7.15-10.45.
Food £25. Wine £6.50.
Family run, serious eating academy. Nico Ladenis is both patron and chef and serves an unbeatable meal for at least half the price of La Gavroche and others in the Michelin, 'Good Food...' gaggle. The cost of your starter as well as VAT and service is included in the price of your main course. Essential to start with is the Ragout de coquille St Jaques, scallops in leak and cream sauce, or various terrines and expertly composed salads — notably goat's cheese and walnut. A word of warning regarding the main course: do not advise the patron on how you would like your beef/lamb cooked; to quote the menu, it is served rare/pink and M. Ladenis knows best, I can assure you. Excellent fillet of beef, lamb chops in garlic puree, sliced duck with fruit salad, white of chicken with foie gras in cream sauce. Irresistible, exotic puddings including passion fruit sorbet and Armagnac parfait with marrons glaces. Highly recommended. No music. No salt and pepper. Booking advised.

The Galley
The Square, Richmond (940 9183)
FISH
Mon-Sat 12.30-2.30, 7.30-11.30 (approx)
Food £25. Wine £4.45.
Not really this reviewer's dish of whitebait, but trying hard to be a proper fish restaurant. Usual fishy delights: oysters, mussels, sea food pancakes with hollandaise sauce, sole, lobster etc for those on expense accounts. Don't be alarmed when the patron asks you for your name — it isn't a market research survey, he just wants you to feel at home. Nautical furnishings, incongruous top 20 sounds.

Gino's
15-17 Hill Rise, Richmond (940 3002)
ITALIAN
Tue-Sat 12.30-2.30, 6.30-11.30.
Food £25. Wine £5.50.

Chi chi Italian dive. White-tiled opulent Mediterranean interior calls to mind a warmer climate (and a healthier bank balance). Prosciutto, homemade soups and pasta for starters. Steaks, liver, escalopes and seafood to follow, their names taking you on a grand tour of Italia. Stupendous view of Thameside Richmond. Next stop Capri!

Oh Boy!
843 Garratt Lane, SW17 (947 9760)
THAI
Mon-Sun 7.00-10.30.
Food £25. Wine £3.60.
Thai in Tooting! An exotic concept, but one that really succeeds. The sheer friendliness of the staff coupled with the unusual preparation of some delicious food makes this a notable find. Delicate and unfamiliar tastes abound: Sudsahkon (seafood soup with chili and lemongrass), unbeatable satay, followed by their speciality Oh Boy Steak sat — thin strips of fillet steak grilled at your table on an iron, charcoal-fired dish and served with vegetables, rice and three different spicy sauces. A veritable treat.

MID-PRICE

Les Amoureux
156 Merton Hall Rd, SW19 (543 0567)
FRENCH
Mon-Sat 7.30-10.00.
Food £16. Wine £3.70.
Popular, family run restaurant. Relaxed and homely atmosphere with a no-nonsense menu to match. Starters include watercress salad with bacon and croutons, fresh black pudding, moules mariniere, all tastily prepared and garnished. Main courses: duck casserole, calves kidneys, blanquette of lamb, vegetables included. Easy-going service, a place where they're happy if you take your time over dinner.

Barnaby's Restaurant
39a Barnes High St, SW13 (878 4750)
FRENCH
Tue-Fri 12.30-1.45, Mon-Sat 7.00-10.30.
Food £15. Wine £4.55.
Excellent food a mere boule's throw from the Thames. In fact it's food first, decor nowhere: but all the more enjoyable for that. Crab bisque, pates, mousse de foie with a hot cream sauce. Unusual main courses : lamb's brains with butter sauce and capers, skewered monkfish, chicken stuffed with avocado. Attentive service. Cover etc included.

Buzkash
4 Chelverton Rd, SW15 (778 0599)
AFGHAN
Mon-Sun 12 noon-3.00, 6.00-11.30.
Food £20. Wine £3.95.
Afghan food is more delicately flavoured than Indian although similar spices are used: chili, garlic, ginger, cardoman and saffron. From a selection of lamb, chicken and prawn dishes, try Ghadoola, Afgan style mixed grill of chicken, lamb chop, ground fillet of lamb and king prawn,

marinated in spices and cooked in a charcoal oven. The puddings too are well worth experimenting with, particularly Firni, Afghan rice pudding topped with pistachios and almonds. Pleasant service in cheerful room festooned with Afghan carpets and weaponry. Parties of up to 25 welcome with due notice. Highly recommended.

Cassis
30 Putney High St, SW15 (778 8668/0829)
FRENCH
Mon-Sat 12 noon-2.00, 7.00-11.00, closed Sat lunch.
Food £20. Wine £3.50.
Delectable eaterie. Cafe-style interior with 40's French waitresses who take their task seriously. Select and varied menu: delicious snails en croute with creamy mushroom sauce, garlicky gambas and soupe de poissons followed by red mullet with fennel, turbot, entrecotes, duckling etc. Set menu good value at £6.75. Superb trolleyful of patisseries, wash them down with a glass of marc. La vraie chose!

Henrietta's
162 Lower Richmond Rd. SW15 (788 3844)
ANGLO-FRENCH
Mon-Sat 7.30-12 midnight; Sun 1.00-3.00.
Food £14. Wine £3.70.
Newly opened, flashy Anglo-French joint. Spacious, sunny interior with patio for summer eating. Set three course meal includes such temptations as baked onion tartlets with anchovies, mushrooms and ale soup followed by roast chicken

in lime and tarragon marinade, pork with Calvados and apple and vegetarian moussaka. Original pudding selection features fresh orange tart and baked banana with cream, honey and cinnamon. Very good value Sunday lunch. Booking advised.

Memsahib
22 Lower Richmond Rd, West Hill, SW15 (874 3593)
INDIAN
Tue-Sun 6.00-11.00.
Food £14. Wine £4.50.
I freely admit to having lost all faith in the popadom until I went to the Memsahib. In fact, all the food was cooked and presented to the very highest standard. Lamb shislick, fish tandoori, samosas etc, all warmly recommended and the prawn curry even tasted of prawns on a Sunday night! Relaxed, non-Indian atmosphere made more genial by a charming but quirky patron who won't budge you from your table before 2.00am. Cocktails.

No Name Place
143 St John's Hill, SW11 (228 3043)
FRENCH
Tue-Sat 12 noon-3.00, 7.30-11.00; closed Sat lunch; Sun 12.45-3.00.
Food £20. Wine £4.
Trendy, up-and-coming haunt of South Londoners in search of Cuisine Minceur. Fight your way through dense shrubbery and savour escargots, smoked mackerel, pates followed by roast Aylesbury duck, lambs liver, tarte maison and profiteroles. Three course

Sunday lunch for £5.75. Very popular — you're advised to book.

Red Lion
18 Red Lion St, Richmond (940 2371/938 1961)
CHINESE
Mon-Wed 12 noon-2.00, 6.00-11.30; Thu-Sun 12 noon-2.30, 6.00-12 midnight.
Food £18. Wine £2.40 (½ litre carafe).
Peking cooking. The crispy duck with pancakes and yellow bean sauce is worth the trip alone. Prawns fried with sesame seeds, oriental soups, lemony chicken. Set menu £6 for one person (includes cripsy duck). Business-like unpretentious decor but fearful muzak. Sip hot saki and be transported from Richmond's nightmarish one-way system.

River Bistro
15 Barnes High St (876 1471)
FRENCH
Mon-Sat 7.00-12 midnight.
Food £18. Wine £3.85.
Busier than Barnaby's across the road and equally appetising. Candlelit and atmospheric. Where to impress the au pair girl. Juicy escargots and usual choice of starters including a good soupe de poissons. Share a chateaubriand for two (£11.25), finely cooked sole, turbot etc. Good cheeseboard.

Wei Hai Wei
7 The Broadway, White Hart Lane, SW13 (876 1165)
CHINESE
Mon-Sun 6.30-11.00.
Food £15. Wine £3.80.

The name of this restaurant makes perfect sense if you try saying 'White Hart Lane' in Chinese. Bright, businesslike interior, deadpan service of Peking style duck, giant prawns and the usual eastern delights. Set dinners for two or more persons at £4.10 and £6.40. Banquets on demand featuring elaborate whole fish dishes and Mongolian hotpot. Muzak free, no-nonsense establishment.

Wild Thyme
96 Felsham Rd, SW15 (789 3323)
INTERNATIONAL
Tue-Sat 12 noon-2.30, 7.00-11.00; closed Sat lunch.
Food £16. Wine £5.25.
Seasonal specialities: stuffed mushrooms with brains, prawns with quails' eggs; other main courses — steak and oyster pie, hare, pigeon and sweetbread pie. Hungarian chef. Private rooms. Excellent rhubarb crumble. Garrulous patron.

Yesterday
12 Leopold Rd, SW19 (946 4300)
ENGLISH
Tue-Fri, Sun 12.30-2.30; Tue-Sat 7.30-11.15.
Food £15. Wine £3.95.
Reasonably priced, wholesome food in a sunny brick-built interior. Definitely on the local businessman's lunch roster. Home-made soups, casseroles, roasts, fish pie. Leave space for ample English puds. Set three-course Sunday lunch: £5.95 adults, £2.95 children. Booking advised.

BUDGET

Mrs Beeton's Restaurant
58 Hill Rise, Richmond (948 2787)
ENGLISH
Mon-Sun 10.00am-5.00. Wed, Thu, Fri, Sat 6.30-11.00.
Food £6. Unlicensed.
Cosy, high calorie cake and wholefood establishment. Manned by worthy Richmond ladies, a different couple, a new menu every day. Hard seats, nourishing soups, baked flans, cheesy vegetables and other filling fare. Prices vary according to cook of the day. Open for tea.

The Refectory
6 Church Walk, Richmond (940 6264)
ENGLISH
Tue-Sat 10.00-12 noon (for coffee); Tue-Sun 12 noon-2.15; Thu, Fri, Sat 7.30-8.45 (last orders)
Food £8. Wine £3.10 (1/2 litre) white; £2.80 (1/2 litre) red.
Hidden in a leafy Richmond backwater another establishment offering honest English sustenance and an intriguing selection of English and Australian wines. Lentil potage, seafood flan, rumbledethumps! Interesting and substantial puddings such as coconut treacle tart and steamed honey and ginger pud. Outdoor tables available — interior bright and cheerful. Suitable for children and reasonably priced. Booking advised.

Sree Krishna South India Restaurant
194 Tooting High Street, SW17 (672 4250)
INDIAN
Mon-Sun 12 noon-3.00, 6.00-11.00 (Fri & Sat closing 12 midnight).
Food £10. Wine £4.10.
Modestly appointed but top-notch South Indian restaurant. Predominantly vegetarian — lashings of dal, lentils etc. Masala Dosai (spiced pancake with potato stuffing), vegetable curries. Half a pint of their excellent lassi is recommended to cool the palate. Held by locals to be the best value outside Bombay.

TRANSPORT

Some routes shown do not operate every day of the week.)

Tube:	East Putney, Richmond, Clapham Common
Buses:	14, 22, 30, 37, 39, 74, 85, 93 — to Putney (High St)
Or:	33 (Mon-Sat only), 37, 72, 73 (Sun only) — to Barnes
Or:	7, 27, 33 (Mon-Sat only), 37, 65, 73 (Sun only), 290 — to Richmond
Or:	19, 28, 39, 44, 77a, 170 (Mon-Sat only), 220, 249
Night:	N68, N88 — to Wandsworth
Or:	19, 39, 44, 45, 49, 170 (Mon-Sat only)
Night:	N88 — to Battersea
Or:	35, 37, 88, 137, 155 (Mon-Sat only)
Night:	N81, N87 — to Clapham

A GUIDE TO
London's
BEST
Restaurants

PART 2

Action Space Cafe
16 Chenies St, WC1 (637 8270)
Mon 12 noon-2.00; Tue-Thu 12
noon-9.30; Fri-Sat 12 noon-12
midnight.
*Cheap and cheerful arts centre
cafe concentrating on
vegetarian and wholefood
meals, but great place to go for
coffee, tea and cakes.*

Almeida Theatre Cafe Bar
La Almeida St, N1 (359 4404)
Tue-Fri 11.00am-3.00,
5.30-11.00; Sat 11.00am-11.00;
Sun 12.30-10.30.
*Tea place with cake and
pastries, tea and coffee.*

Amalfi
31 Old Compton St, W1 (437
7284/1907)
Mon-Sat 8.30am-11.00.
*Italian restaurant which makes
its own cakes and pastries.*

Arthur's Restaurant
60 Long Lane, EC1 (600 8243)
Mon-Fri 5.30am-2.30.
*Really rough but genuine
restaurant with breakfasts (and
lunches) chalked on
blackboards. Heart of
Smithfield, hence the early
start. Black puddings and fried
slice (of bread) highly
recommended.*

Bacon And Eggs
South Molton St, W1.
Mon-Fri 7.00am-5.00; Sat
7.00am-3.00.
*Family-run caff in the middle of
posh pedestrian precinct,
serving one of the best
breakfasts in London.*

Bar Creperie
21 Covent Garden Market,
WC2 (836 2137)

10.00am-12 midnight.
*Good coffee and croissants in
warm, friendly basement cafe.*

Bendicks
195 Sloane St, SW1 (235 4749)
Mon-Fri 9.00am-5.30, 3.30 on
Sat.
Chocolatier with restaurant.

Bonne Bouche
2 Thayer St, W1 (935 3502)
Mon-Fri 9.00am-6.00; Sat
9.00am-5.00.
*Patisserie serving fresh cakes,
tarts and savoury snacks.*

Boswells Coffee House
8 Russell St (240 0064)
Mon-Sat 9.00am-7.30.
*Compact, new coffee house
close to the Market.*

La Brasserie
272 Brompton Rd, SW3 (584
1668)
Mon-Fri 8.00am-11.45; Sat
10.00am-11.30; Sun
11.00am-11.30.
*Breakfast and brunch are the
meals to go for in London's
best designed brasserie.*

Brooke's
68 Old Brompton Rd, SW7 (584
8993)
Mon-Sun 11.00am-12 midnight.
*Scones with your tea in light
airy surroundings.*

Brown's Hotel
Dover St and Albermarle St
(two entrances) W1 (493 6020)
Mon-Sun 7.15-10.00am for
breakfast (from 8.00am Sun);
3.00-6.00 for afternoon tea.
*Afternoon tea is probably the
best in London.*

BREAKFAST & TEA

Cafe de la Gare
19 York Rd, SE1 (928 9701)
Mon-Fri 8.00am-11.00; Sat
8.00am-3.00.
French style cafe.

Cafe Snack Bar
58 Cross St, N1.
Mon-Sat 8.00am-6.00.
*Good, cheap freshly cooked
sausage, egg and chips; steaks
and mixed grills; clean and
friendly.*

Cafe St Pierre
29 Clerkenwell Green, EC1
(251 6606)
*A delightful sunny corner in a
somewhat bleak area where
breakfast can be obtained from
7.30am onwards — coffee,
croissant, toast, jams but
nothing cooked. Tea from 3.00
— rich, creamy, home-made
cakes and pastries.*

Camisa
16 Pond St, NW3 (794 4712)
Mon-Fri 8.00am-7.00; Sat
8.00am-2.00.
*Italian cafe next to Hampstead
Classic serving good, basic
English breakfast and an
excellent cup of cappuccino.*

La Capannina
5 Vigo St, W1 (734 8353)
Breakfast from 8.30am, tea
from 3.00-5.00, Mon-Fri.
*Italian restaurant offering
superb Continental and cooked
breakfasts and cream cakes for
tea.*

Chandos Snack Bar
60 Chandos Place, WC2 (836
0060)
Mon-Fri 7.30am-3.30.
*Superb sandwiches, pastries,
omelettes, toast, offer good*

light breakfasts.

Charing Cross Hotel
Strand (839 7282)
Tea available all day.
*This is a BR Hotel, so watch out
for that tea.*

Charlotte Restaurant
221 West End Lane (794 6476)
Mon-Sat 7.30am-8.30.
*Tables have board printed for
chess or draughts.*

The Cherry Top
Paddington St, W1.
Mon-Fri 7.00am-4.00; Sat
7.00am-11.00.
*Working man's caff which
attracts office workers. Great
cooked breakfasts served all
day.*

Chubbies
22-23 Liverpool St, EC2 (283
3504)
Mon-Sun 7.00am-6.00.
*Has saved many a hungry
traveller from starvation. Great
fried breakfast.*

Churchill Hotel
30 Portman Square, W1 (486
5800)
From 7.00am (7.30am Sun) for
breakfast, 3.30-5.30 for tea.
Tea by piano.

The Crazy Crepe
107 Aldgate St, EC1 (253 2428)
*Breakfast served until noon,
good standard English fare —
bacon, egg, sausage etc. Tea
from 2.00 with crepes of
course, and very tempting
cakes.*

Crumbs
48 Holborn Viaduct, EC1 (236
8970)

172

Mon-Fri 7.00am-4.00.
Very busy self-service restaurant, already bustling at 7.30am with City workers enjoying breakfast. Good value lunches, too.

Cunard International Hotel
Shortlands, W6 (741 1555)
Gallery restaurant open 24 hours a day, every day.
Continental breakfast, cakes, snacks served all day.

Danish Coffee House
16 Sloane St, SW1 (235 8521)
Mon-Sat 9.30am-5.00.
Downstairs in the Danish Shop, self-service place offering delicious gateaux, coffee and tea — as well as light meals.

Danish Coffee Room
146 Regent St, W1 (734 7784)
Mon-Sat 9.30am-5.00, (Thu to 6.15)
Bright, clean, airy, self-service place in Jaeger offering light meals, cakes, pastries, Danish open sandwiches.

Le Detour
5 Camden Hill Rd, W8 (937 9602)
Mon-Sun 9.30am-11.00.
Open for breakfast with fresh coffee and the best croissants in town. At tea find delicious french cakes and tartes.

Diana's Diner
39 Endell St, WC2 (240 0272)
Mon-Fri 7.00am-3.30.
Full breakfasts — even porridge — served at this owner-run cafe. Meals at lunch.

Dorchester
Park Lane, W1 (629 8888)
Mon-Sun 3.15-5.45.
Afternoon tea takes on a new meaning in ornate lounge of this world-famous hotel.

Dunkin' Donuts
2 Ludgate Circus Buildings, Farringdon St, EC4 (248 6260)
Open 24 hours a day, every day (except Sunday; closed midnight to 8.00am Monday)
Freshly baked each morning (you can watch the cooks between 2.30am and 5.30am) and eat doughnuts all day long. Prices from about 20p to 45p, round, long, with or without holes in, filled with jam, nuts, fruit, real cream. Ideal for tired hacks and tourists' children. Drink: coffee, tea, hot chocolate or soft drinks.

Farmer Brown
4 New Row, WC2 (240 0230)
Mon-Sat 7.30am-7.00.
Friendly little cafe with cooked breakfasts, massive rolls, cakes and pies in the afternoon.

Farquharsons
1b Hampstead High St (435 8278)
Mon-Sat 9.00am-12 midnight;
Sun 10.00am-12 midnight.
Cosy little tea shop.

Fleur de Lys
13a Gloucester Rd, SW7 (589 4045)
Mon-Sat 8.15am-5.30.
Pastries made on the premises, including some fancy treats like iced pretzels.

General Trading Company
144 Sloane St, SW1 (730 0411)
Mon-Fri 9.30am-5.00; Sat 9.30am-1.30.
Shop-housed cafe, always crowded, serving elaborate

snacks.

The Goodfare Restaurant
26 Parkway, NW1 (485 2230)
Mon-Sun 8.00am-7.00
(sometimes closed Sun)
A basic caff with all the usual breakfast items, but unusual because it is run by Italians, so good lunches too.

Grandma Lee's
Bridge St, W1 (839 1319)
Mon-Sun 7.00am-9.00.
Amazing American-style self-service place offering great muffins, buns, cookies and huge (and expensive) sandwiches.

Habitat Cafe
206 King's Rd, SW3 (351 1211)
Mon-Fri 10.00am-5.00 (Wed 5.30) Sat 10.00am-4.30.
Clean cafe living up to Habitat tradition of pine and serving good cakes and pastries.

Hampstead Patisserie and Tea Rooms
9 South End Rd, NW3 (435 9563) Tue-Sat 9.00am-8.00; Sun 9.30am-8.00.
Fresh, buttery croissants, fairly good coffee. They also do poached or scrambled eggs on toast for breakfast.

Harrods Georgian Restaurant
Knightsbridge, SW1 (730 1234)
Mon-Fri 3.30-4.30; Sat 4.00-5.30.
Help yourself to as much as you want from a feast of cakes, pastries, bread, butter and jam, scones and clotted cream, trifles and tea accompanied by the pianoforte. All for £2.95!

Harrods Health Juice
Knightsbridge, SW1 (730 1234)

Mon-Fri 9.00am-5.00; Wed 9.30am-7.00; Sat 9.00am-6.00.
Sweet and sour juice, sometimes thickened with yoghurt, strawberry, pear, celery, carrot. Mix and match.

Harvey Nichols One-O-Nine
Knightsbridge, SW1 (235 5000)
Mon-Sat 9.30am-5.30 (Wed till 6.30)
Self-service continental breakfast. Delicious cheesecake, blackcurrant or strawberry.

Hatchetts Salt Beef Bar
5 Clerkenwell Rd, EC1 (251 2587)
Mon-Fri 7.30am-7.30 (Mon & Fri closing 3.30) Sun 10.00am-3.00.
Jewish restaurant/deli.

Hilton International, Kensington
179 Holland Park Avenue, W11 (603 3355)
Breakfast 7.00am-11.00am.
Very good value — as much as you can eat for set price. Continental £2.90 or English £3.95 including coffee, tea and fruit juices.

The Holiday Inn
King Henry's Rd, Swiss Cottage, NW3 (722 7711)
Mon-Sun 7.00am-10.30am.
The super-fast, super-efficient breakfast of an international chain.

Hyde Park Hotel, Park Room
Knightsbridge, SW1 (235 2000)
Mon-Sat 7.00am-11.30; Sun from 7.30am.
Very pretty room offering traditional afternoon tea.

Indian Tea Centre
343 Oxford St, W1 (449 1975)
Mon-Sat 11.00am-8.00.
English afternoon teas served, but Indian snacks better.

Kenwood House, The Coach House
Hampstead Lane, NW3 (348 8876)
Mon-Sun 10.00am-5.30.
Large self-service cafeteria in the grounds of Kenwood House. Cakes, scones, toasted buns, tea, coffee and fruit juice.

Louis' Patisserie
32 Heath St, NW3 (435 9908)
12 New College Parade, Finchley Rd, SW3 (722 8100)
Mon-Sat 9.30am-5.50.
Delicious Hungarian pastries, cakes and coffee.

Lyons Corner House
450 Strand (930 9381)
Mon-Sun 8.00am-8.00.
Spacious, brightly-lit tea and coffee house.

Lyric Theatre
King St, W6 (741 7693)
Mon-Sat 10.00am-7.30.
Lively theatre bar, large terrace open in the summer for taking tea or coffee with flapjacks and fine fudge cake.

Maison Bertaux
28 Greek St, W1 (437 6007)
Mon-Sat 9.00am-6.00.
Little patisserie selling exquisite cakes and pastries and definitely the best croissants in London. Tea room above the shop. Tasty cheese tartlets at lunch-time.

Maison Bouquillon
22 Vivian Avenue, NW4 (202 3354)
Mon-Sat 9.30am-5.30 (Sun till 3.30)
Delectable cakes and pastries including pain chocolat and cheese croissants. A few tables in the shop if you want to have coffee. Best of all their fruit tarts — strawberry, blackcurrant, apricot etc.

Maison Pechon Patisserie Francaise
127 Queensway, W2 (229 0746)
Mon-Sat 8.00am-5.00.
Busy shop selling wide range of bread, cakes and pastries. Cafe in the back serves good coffee with choice of pastries. They also do English breakfast from 9.15am.

Maison Sagne
105 Marylebone High St, W1 (935 6240)
Mon-Fri 9.00am-5.00, Sat till 12.30.
Very pleasant tea shop; cakes and pastries baked on the premises. Choice of Indian or China tea.

Maison Sagne
105 Marylebone High St, W1 (935 6240)
Mon-Fri 9.00am-5.00; Sat 9.00am-12.30.
Charming tea shop with charming service.

Marine Ices
8 Haverstock Hill, NW3 (485 8898)
Mon-Sat 10.00am-10.00.
Not an ordinary tea, but a fantastic choice of ice cream in every conceivable flavour and combination to eat there or take away as your mid-afternoon snack.

Maxwells
16-17 Russell St, WC2 (836 0303)
Tea served 3.00-5.45.
Finger sandwiches, cream pastries, scones served to background rock and swing in hamburger joint.

Muffin Man
12 Wright's Lane, W8 (937 6652)
Mon-Sat 9.30am-6.00.
Mouth-watering home-made cakes, dainty cucumber and tomato sandwiches, tempting Devon cream teas in cosy tea shop adjoining craft shop.

Neal's Yard Tea Rooms 6 Neal's Yard, WC2 (836 5199)
Mon-Sat 10.30am-5.30; Wed till 3.30; Sat till 4.30.
Ground floor bakery, tiny first floor tea room, both offering savouries and rich cakes.

The Nosherie
12 Greville St, EC1 (242 1591)
Mon-Fri 8.00am-5.00.
From 8.00am onwards. Though it's not strictly kosher you won't get bacon; but there are eggs all ways, toast, fruit, coffee.

Old Burlington
140 Old Burlington St, W1 (734 6177)
Mon-Fri 6.45am-5.00.
Italian caff offering wonderful breakfasts, set price or a la carte.

Paris Croissant
369 Oxford St, W1.
Mon-Sat 8.00am-8.00.
Take-away only, but a range of croissants — with chocolate, raisins, cheese, etc — not found anywhere else in London,

made on the premises.

Parson's
311 Fulham Rd, SW10 (352 0651)
Mon-Sun 12.30-12.30am.
Good cakes and ices, tea and coffee in light lively place.

Pasticceria Cappuccetto
8 Moor St, W1 (437 9472)
Mon-Sat 8.00am-7.30.
Excellent patisserie prepared on premises, along with croissants and Danish pastry.

Patisserie Valerie
44 Old Compton St, W1 (437 3466)
Mon-Sat 8.30-7.00.
Busy take-away and sit-down patisserie popular with arty set, students, Continentals and little old ladies.

Peppermint Park
13 Upper St Martin's Lane, WC2 (836 5234)
Sunday 11.30am-3.00.
Perhaps more brunch than breakfast — but the best (possibly the only) place to try real American breakfast food, like waffles with maple syrup.

Quality Chop House
94 Farringdon St, EC1 (No phone)
Open from 6.30am onwards this is one of the best places in the city to have breakfast; porridge, kippers, haddock as well as eggs, bacon and sausage. Toast or lovely thick wedges of real bread and butter.

Raoul's
13 Clifton Rd, W9 (289 7313)
Mon-Sat 9.00am-6.00; Sun till

5.30.
*Light airy shop/cafe near Little
Venice. Wonderful pain au
chocolat, truffles, creamy
pastries, bread, croissants,
chocolate eclairs; and good
toasted sandwiches and
quiches.*

Ritz Hotel, Palm Court
Piccadilly, W1 (493 8181)
Mon-Sun 3.30-5.30.
*Formal atmosphere, but really
good old-fashioned tea. Set
price £5.20.*

Russell Hotel
Russell Sq (837 6470)
Mon-Sat 7.00am-10.00am, 3.30-
6.00; Sun 8.00am-10.00am,
3.30-6.00.
*Extravagant Victorian building
and marbled interior. Beautiful
high-ceilinged dining room.
Never mind the patisserie, eat
the architecture.*

Savoy Hotel
Strand, WC2 (836 4343)
Mon-Sun 4.00-7.30.
*Newly created Thames Foyer
offers a pleasant setting in
traditional style for afternoon
tea. Cucumber sandwiches like
credit cards.*

The Selfridge Hotel
Orchard St, W1 (408 2080)
Lounge open 10.00am-11.00
*Offers a welcome break for
tired shoppers. Sink into comfy
chairs for filling set afternoon
tea — dear but good — or just a
cuppa.*

Troubadour Coffee House
265 Old Brompton Rd, SW5.
Mon-Sun 11.00am-3.00,
3.30-11.00.
Marble table tops, wooden

*floor, good croissants and
pastries. More substantial
breakfast served between
11.00am-12.30.*

Valenti's Tearoom
52 Red Lion St, WC1 (405 0130)
Mon-Fri 8.00am-5.00.
*Creamy cakes, pizzas,
croquembouches, all made on
the premises. Lunch time
snacks.*

Waldorf Hotel
Aldwych, WC2 (836 2400)
Mon-Sun 3.30-6.00.
*The Palm Court is the 30s style
setting for afternoon tea.*

Young Vic Coffee Bar
66 The Cut, SE1 (633 0133)
Mon-Fri 10.30am-8.30; Sat
4.30-8.30.
*Trendy wholefood-type place
providing good cakes, tea and
coffee.*

WINE BARS

Almeida Theatre Cafe Bar
1a Almeida St, N1 (359 4404)
*Very interesting hot and cold
dishes to go with various good
wines. Cakes and pastries, tea
or coffee at weekends. Phone
for everchanging details of
live jazz and cabarets.*

Archduke
Concert Hall Approach, SE1
(928 9370)
*Famed for its upstairs room
where sausages created from
recipes all over the world are
served with mash. Live jazz
and blues each evening.*

The Arches
7 Fairhazel Gardens, NW6

(624 1867)
In what was once a bakery, this charming wine bar serves excellent food — soups, pates, hummous; grilled mackerel with gooseberry sauce, turkey in lemon sauce, served with salad. Black grape brulee, chocolate roulade to follow. Menu changes daily. Mulled wine in winter. Live music on occasions.

L'Artiste Muscle
1 Shepherd Market, W1 (493 6150)
Set in the heart of Mayfair this bar is on the ground floor and cellar. Tables on pavement outside. Daily dishes, steaks and salads.

Bas & Annie's
58 New King's Rd, SW6 (731 2520)
Graphic red and white facade. Ground level restaurant with more interesting cocktail bar downstairs.

Blakes
34 Wellington St, Covent Garden, WC2 (836 5298)
Open every day, coffee is served throughout the afternoon. Restaurant downstairs where menu changes weekly; live music nightly.

Le Bouzy Rouge
221 King's Rd, SW3 (351 1607)
Small cellar bar in which regulars gather to hear live music. Blackboard menu, which changes daily. Good selection of wines.

Bubbles Wine Bar
51 North Audley St, W1 (499

178

0600)
Comprehensive wine list including Australian and New Zealand wines. Large seating area downstairs, and in front of the bar, and two small rooms upstairs for quiet conversation. Home-made pates (duck liver, tarragon, and chicken liver), wide range of English/French cheeses and hot dishes available lunchtime and evening.

Campbell's Wine Bar
61 Tooley St, SE1 (403 5775)
Extensive menu that includes Chicken a la King with rice, Moussaka or Lasagne with salad, fresh fruit salad, and a selection of cheeses. The house wine is excellent value at £2.95. Wine also sold wholesale by the case.

Carlos 'n' Johnny's
268 Fulham Rd, SW10 (352 0379)
This is one of the most unusual bars in London. Items suspended from the ceiling include a two-ton bear and an aeroplane. Mexican food served until midnight.

City Boot
7 Moorfields, High Wall, Moorgate, EC2 (588 4766)
One of the original London wine bars. Noted for its good game pie.

Clowns Cocktail Cafe
136 Upper Richmond Rd, SW15 (789 7043)
Toy clowns, plants and pictures clutter the bar. Menu includes a selection of salads, steaks, burgers and 'Clown alternatives' (chunky

sandwiches, toasted specials);
'Clown Sweet Dreams' to
finish.

Cork And Bottle
44-46 Cranbourne St, WC2
(734 7807)
*Arrive early to ensure a nook
where you can sit back, listen
to the guitar player and enjoy
the excellent food and wine.*

Corks
3 Harrington Rd, SW7 (589
6502)
*Food is home-cooked and
worth every penny. Meeting
place for the beautiful people.*

Cozy Griffs
11 Sun St, EC2 (247 9445)
*Hot lunches follow City
traditional line, with a few
novelties such as the steak
sandwich and crab claws.
Open till 8.00 for cold food.*

Dalys
210 Strand, WC2 (583 4476)
*Spacious wine bar with
excellent range of cheeses.
Good simple food with large
helpings of home-made
quiches and pies.*

Draycott's
114 Draycott Avenue, SW3
(584 5359)
*Spill out onto the pavement
from this elegant, trendy wine
bar, serving salads, quiches,
pates etc and one hot dish of
the day.*

French's Wine Bar
55 East Hill, SW18 (874 2808)
*One of the few wine bars
where one can eat after 11.00;
the menu includes rainbow
trout and a good selection of*

desserts including waffles.

Gangsters
488 Caledonian Rd, N7 (607
7125)
*Candlelit cellar bar with open
fires, plants, gangster prints
and friendly staff. Menu
includes 'things that fly, swim
and move' — roast chicken
with honey and lemon, fillet
steaks stuffed with fresh
oysters, fish bouillabaisse.
Vegetarian dishes also
available. Live music and
extensive wine list.*

Georges Wine Bar
The Market, Covent Garden,
WC2 (836 1662)
*Once part of the old Covent
Garden cellars, this small bar
is full of character. Extensive
menu includes salads, lasagne,
cannelloni and daily specials.*

Grapes
The Mall, Camden Passage,
N1 (359 4960)
*Congenial atmosphere, good
food and wine and live
classical jazz. Roast beef and
jazz on Sundays, newspapers
too.*

Heath's Wine Bar
34 Rosslyn Hill, NW3 (435
5203)
*Interesting, varied menu
including daily specials. Jazz,
solo pianists and guitarists
nightly.*

Jimmies Vinotheque
Kensington Church St, W8
(937 9988)
*In the old converted stables of
Kensington Barracks this
unusual venue has an
excellent wine list. Lunchtimes*

are very busy: worth a visit for the charcoal grills and Chicken Kiev. Live music each evening.

Julie's Wine Bar
137 Portland Rd, W11 (727 7985)
Two bars each having its own separate character. Downstairs is functional with wood furniture and mirrors, upstairs is more informal. From 7.00-10.30 there is food served: a hot dish and salads and quiches.

Korky's
319-321 King St, Hammersmith, W6 (741 2458)
Busy, lively bar. Blackboard menu includes steak and kidney pie, assorted home-made quiches, eye-catching display of salads and desserts. Live music or DJ evenings.

Logans Wine Bar
238 Upper Richmond Rd, SW15 (778 2340)
Small cafe-style bar with checked tablecloths. Lunchtime and evening menu, also 'Daily Specials'. Saturday brunch. Live music Saturday nights.

Loose Box
136 Brompton Rd, (also at 7 Cheval Place) (584 9280)
Upstairs generous portions of cold rare beef, hot seafood vol au vents and rabbit followed by a wicked chocolate cake. Downstairs cauliflower au gratin and cottage pie. The wine list is broad European.

Marlows Wine Bar
Marlow House, Lloyds Avenue, EC3 (481 1168/488 3868)
Large basement serving lunches only; smoked salmon mousse, one hot special and shoofly pie among other things.

Ormes
67 Abbotville Rd, SW4 (673 2568)
Home-made soups and garlic mushrooms; large selection of wines to choose from. Tables outside.

Peachey's
205 Haverstock Hill, NW3 (435 6744)
Victorian-style wine bar and restaurant. Original food; menu changes daily.

Railway Tavern
16 Liverpool St, EC2 (283 3598)
Has the best food in its Wine Bar. Filled with railway memorabilia and packed to bursting, lunch time.

Russkies
6 Wellington Terrace, W2 (229 9128)
Small cellar bar with plush Edwardian decor across from the Russian Embassy. Different menu every day.

Scandies Wine Bar
4 Kynance Pl, SW7 (589 3659)
Small, friendly wine bar on two floors — restaurant downstairs. The menu includes cassolet, chilli con carne, salads and specialities of the day. Sunday roast (£1.50). Guitarist plays Thursday and Saturday evenings.

Shampers
4 Kingly St, W1 (437 1692)
Very popular wine bar with small upstairs room and larger basement area. Very good cold buffet and good selection of inexpensive wines.

Smithy's Wine Bar
28-32 Britannia St, WC1 (278 5659)
Notable a) for its charcoal grilled steaks and chops and b) for its space (was once a horse-bus garage, stables and smithy, hence the name) Help-yourself-salads; pates and cheese. Mulled wine in winter; same ownership's wine warehouse (Kings Cross Wines) adjacent, to choose drink from.

Tiles
36 Buckingham Palace Rd, SW1 (834 7761)
Bistro bar, blue and white tiles on the floor, trendy wine list. Home-made, changing menu, including spicy scotch egg, smoked salmon and bread, chicken liver and walnut pate, fisherman's pie, fruit crumble, stilton...

Tracks
17a Soho Sq, W1 (439 2318)
This busy bar opens early in the morning serving coffee and croissants. Extensive wine list. Good selection of food; game pie and assorted salads. Large pots of coffee.

PUBS

The Albion
10 Thornhill Rd, N1 (607 1769)
Lunch only, home-cooked pies, curries, salt beef, liver and bacon to be eaten in the garden in summer or by a coal fire in the bar in winter. Hot pies only on Saturdays.

Avenue Bar
134 Shaftesbury Avenue, W1 (437 6553)
Pleasant, spacious and comfortable pub with mock Edwardian decor. Ideally sited for the West End theatres. Consists of one bar only and serves good hot lunches.

Barmy Arms
Riverside, Twickenham, Middx (892 0863)
An old nautical pub which was originally a school house. Roast lunches available. Outside patio.

Blue Posts
6 Bennet St, SW1 (493 3350)
A cosy, traditional pub which has a permanent display of paintings by local artists for sale. English carvery upstairs serves very good selection of food.

Bunch Of Grapes
16 Shepherd's Market, W1 (499 1563)
Set in Shepherd's Market, Victorian interior with a village pub atmosphere. Lunchtime restaurant upstairs where you pay a set price and eat as much as you like.

Cheshire Cheese
145 Fleet St, EC1 (353 6170)
*Named after Dr Johnson's
favourite cheese (he lived
round the corner). Rooms on
several floors of this genuinely
17th Century pub serving
traditional British food; steak
and kidney pudding, roast
beef and chops.*

Crown
Aberdeen Place, NW8 (289
1102)
*Large sprawling Victorian pub
known as Crocker's Folly.
Good bar food, live music
every night and a wide range
of real ales.*

Denmark
102 Old Brompton Rd, SW7
(373 2403)
*Wide choice of food: good
cold meats, quiches and
salads. Delicious duck, good
pies.*

Dukes Head
8 Lower Richmond Rd, Putney
SW15 (788 2552)
*Situated on the river with
unrestricted views of the
waterfront from the lounge.
Excellent lunch menu, all
homemade.*

Finch's (Kings Arms)
190 Fulham Rd, SW3
*Where arty crowds and city
gents rub shoulders quite
happily. Good food and lovely
engraved glass partitions.*

The Fox and Anchor
115 Charterhouse St, EC1 (253
4838)
*Meeting place for buyers and
butchers of Smithfield Market.
Open from 6.00am-3.00pm.*

*Serves colossal amounts of
food at moderate prices.*

The Grenadier
18 Wilton Row, SW1 (235 3074)
*Originally the Officers' Mess
for the Duke of Wellington,
and frequented by King
George. More recently it has
featured in a number of films
and radio shows. A la carte
menu at lunch and dinner;
snacks lunchtime.*

Island Queen
87 Noel Rd, N1 (226 5507)
*Situated in the middle of a
terrace this is a popular local
with excellent food. French
restaurant upstairs.*

Jack Straw's Castle
North End Way. (435 8885)
*Huge and attractive old pub
by Whitestone Pond.
Restaurant upstairs; bar snacks
down.*

King's Head
115 Upper St, N1 (226 1916)
*Plain, not fancy food at the bar
or at tables in the
restaurant/theatre space
behind the bar, with first-rate
fringe theatre shows to follow.
Jazz and folk in the bar (see
papers).*

Kings Head and Eight Bells
50 Cheyne Walk, SW3 (352
1820)
*Pleasant restored Victorian
pub with good game and pies.*

Ladbroke Arms
54 Ladbroke Rd, W11 (727
0051)
*18th Century bar. Forecourt
with an abundance of plants
and hanging baskets. Good*

food; original salads and tasty chicken curry.

Mayflower
117 Rotherhithe St, SE16 (237 4088)
Riverside pub built in the 16th Century, and a favourite with letter writers, as it's the only pub licensed to sell British and American stamps. 'Daily special' served at lunchtime (three-course meal at the bar). Good a la carte menu.

Olde White Hart
191 Drury Lane, WC2 (242 3135)
Large boisterous pub convenient to Covent Garden and West End theatres. Jazz every evening. Restaurant.

Pontefract Castle
Wigmore St, W1 (486 3551)
Bars on different levels with food served upstairs at lunchtime when it is almost impossible to move. Candlelit wine bar downstairs.

Prospect Of Whitby
57 Wapping Wall, E1 (481 1095)
Famous dockland Thames-side pub, mentioned by Pepys. Caters for tourists rather than locals, with posh restaurant food.

Rossetti's
23 Queens Grove, NW8 (722 7141)
Modern Italian owned pub/restaurant serving Italian food, lunch and dinner, all week.

The Samuel Pepys
Brooks Wharf, 48 Upper

Thames St, EC4 (248 3048)
A nautical pub on three levels dedicated to Samuel Pepys. A stone flagged bar in the basement six feet below water level. Veranda overlooks the river. Snack bar and restaurant with two menus (£5.95 inc wine, and £10.95).

Sherlock Holmes
10 Northumberland St, WC2 (930 2644)
Close to Trafalgar Sq and the Embankment this pub keeps alive the memory of Sherlock Holmes. Restaurant upstairs.

Spaniards Inn
Hampstead Heath, NW3 (455 3276)
Large 17th Century pub opposite Hampstead Heath, very popular with large garden for summer use. Buffet bar downstairs, restaurant on the first floor, serving from a la carte menu, lunch and dinner.

Spice Of Life
6 Moor St, W1 (437 7013)
Lively three-storey West End pub offering a variety of entertainment. Upstairs lunchtime theatre. Live music Fri nights in wine bar downstairs. Lunchtime food very good.

Sun Inn
63 Lamb's Conduit St, WC1.
Unpretentious, crowded pub that serves a vast array of real ales. Good home-made food.

Swiss Cottage
98 Finchley Rd, NW3 (722 4747)
Well-known landmark with a

preservation order on it. Large selection of real ales and good food.

Three Pigeons
87 Petersham Rd, Richmond, Surrey (940 0361)
Spectacular views over the Thames. Good bar snacks. Restaurant.

Trafalgar Tavern
Park Row, Greenwich, SE10 (858 2437)
Near the Cutty Sark and Royal Navy College this pub is steeped in history. Famous for its dishes. Special children's room.

Warwick Castle
6 Warwick Place, W9 (286 6868)
Situated near the canal, this 150-year-old pub is a great favourite with locals. Real ale is served and bar lunches include home-made shepherds pie.

The Windsor Castle
114 Camden Hill Rd, W8 (727 8491)
Small busy pub — wooden settles, open fires and copper jugs on the wall. Three small bars and garden for summer. Good bar food — sandwiches, sausages, steaks and 'Daily Special'.

World's End
459 King's Rd, SW10 (352 7992)
A large high-ceilinged Victorian pub. Live music at weekends. Food lunchtime and evenings.

Barclay Bros
35 Whitehall, SW1 (930 7106)
All-night mirrored cafe. Stand with your back to the mirrors: the clientele are supposedly harmless, but look terrifying. Food is bearable and cheap.

The Cafe
36 Kensington High St, W8 (937 6968)
Mon-Sat; closes 4am.
Min charge £1.50.
Friendly hamburger joint.

Dunkin Donuts
2 Ludgate Circus Bldgs, Farringdon St, EC4 (236 7942)
All night cafe off Fleet Street, specialises in ice creams and home-made doughnuts. Good coffee and cheap.

Emmanuelle Restaurant
149 Finchley Road, NW3 (586 0069)
Mon-Sat; closes 6.00am.
Min charge £1.50.
Large sophisticatedly sleazy hamburger place.

Far East
13 Gerrard St, W1 (437 6148)
Open until 4.00.
Serves Chinese food.

Frank's Cafe
13 Hammersmith Road, W14 (602 1549)
Mon-Sat; closes 6.30am.
Min charge £1.10.
Also known as Rose Restaurant. Friendly, comfortable and clean.

Great British Success
85 Gloucester Rd, Victoria

Station, SW7 (370 4404)
Closes 3.00am, opens 5.00am.
Unfriendly and boring food.

Kensington Hilton
179 Holland Park Ave, W11
(603 3355)
*Crescent Lounge open all
night for coffee and snacks.
Plush.*

Rodos
59 St Giles High St (836 3177)
Mon-Sat; closes 5.00am.
*Good Greek food in the
shadow of Centre Point.*

Toddies
241 Old Brompton Rd, SW7
(373 8217)
Mon-Sat; closes 6.00am.
*Professional African
restaurant. Good food.*

Up-All-Night
325 Fulham Rd, SW10 (352
1998)
Mon-Sat; closes 6.00am.
Min charge £1.50.
Boring but clean.

Witchity
253 Kensington High St, W8
(937 2654)
Mon-Sat; closes 7.00am.
Min charge £3.
*Part of disco-club. Waiters in
black and white.*

Wurst Max
75 Westbourne Grove, W2
(229 3771)
Mon-Sun 10.00-4.00am.
*Very amusing place to go in
the middle of the night for a
German hot sausage, chewy
rye bread, sauerkraut, wiener
schnitzel and soup. Summer
night-flits sit outside on neo-
white garden furniture and*

*ignore the jolly lederhosen
musak.*

All My Eye & Betty Martin
Chelsea Wharf, Lots Rd, SW10
(352 6015)
Mon-Sun 7.30-11.30.
*Nightclub/restaurant
overlooking the Thames with
varied entertainment: jazz,
rock, cabaret, etc.*

The Beachcomber
Berkeley St, W1 (629 7777)
Mon-Sat
*Polynesian-style decor.
Dancing from 8.30 to live
music. £14.40 for three course
meal and coffee.*

Bunjies
27 Litchfield St (240 1756)
Mon-Sat 12.00-11.45pm. (Music
from 8.15 every night.) Open
Sun 5.00-12 midnight.
*Folk music cellar with
beatnik/vegetarian vibe. Beard
vital.*

The Click
533 King's Rd, SW10 (352
7161)
*Cabaret, raised dance floor,
comprehensive selection of
wines and cocktails. Wide
range of American-style food
available.*

Embassy
7 Old Bond St, W1 (499 5794)
*Disco every Mon-Sat
9.00-3.00am, Sun 8.00-1.00am.
Membership £50 under 25s;
£75 over 25s, Admission Mon-
Fri £4 guests, £6 non-
members, Sat £5, £6, Sun £5, £7
including free food and drink.*

Live acts and disco every night. All acts on stage at 12.30am. Restaurant Mon-Sat £8 set menu inc. door charge if booked in advance.

Foobert's
18 Foubert's Place, Carnaby St, W1 (734 3630)
Open all week 9.00-3.00am; Sun 2.00am.
Disco, wine bar and restaurant, with extensive menu. Open for lunch and dinner. Membership available.

Gargoyle Club
69 Dean St, W1 (437 6455)
Striptease revue at 12.30am. Dancing and dining from 10.30-3.30am.

Harveys
17c Curzon St, W1 (409 0142)
Luxurious nightclub open from 8.00 until breakfast (breakfast is served). Cocktail bar, restaurant, dancing and cabaret at midnight.

Heath's
34 Rosslyn Hill (435 5203)
Mon-Sat 12 noon-3.00, 7.00-11.00. Sun 7.00-10.30.
Jazz, solo pianists and guitarists nightly.

L'Hirondelle
Swallow St, (off Regent St) W1 (734 6666)
8.30-3.30am.
Small club with dancing to two bands. Cabaret at 11.00 and 1.30am. No membership and entrance fee but non-diners pay a cover charge of £4.75. Good menu and cabaret.

Kennedy's
316 King's Rd, SW3 (352 0025)

Mon-Sun 11.00-1.00am.
Hamburgers and cocktails with live music, 8.30-1.00am. Solo or duo acts: pop, jazz, blues and the odd cabaret act.

Legends
29 Old Burlington St, W1 (437 9933)
12.30-3.00 lunch, 6.30-8.00 happy hour, 7.00-12 midnight Mon-Thu; 8.00-1.30am Fri & Sat.
Membership £150 pa plus free admission, or £40 pa plus admission £3. Non-members £3 weekdays, weekends £4. Restaurant with disco. Dress optional.

London Hilton
22 Park Lane, W1 (493 8000)
Mon-Sat free entry disco 9.00-3.00am.
Good standard of dress required. Also roof restaurant with French cuisine and live music. (£35-£45 for two).

Mort's
279a Old Brompton Rd, SW5 (373 5524)
Restaurant and downstairs discotheque. Low ceiling, atmospheric, licensed to 2.00am.

Noufaro
187 Chiswick High Rd, W4 (995 6870)
GREEK/INTERNATIONAL
Mon-Sat until 2.00am.
Live music, cabaret, Greek dancers and singers.

La Pergola
138 Cromwell Rd, SW7 (370 1363)
Italian club/restaurant with good food. Live music until

3.00am (every day). Advisable to book.

Ronnie Scott's
47 Frith St, W1 (439 0747)
Mon-Thu £6, Fri & Sat £7.
Mon-Thu 8.30-2.00am, Fri & Sat
8.30-3.00am.
*Excellent jazz, charming service, a la carte menu —
steaks, chicken, pasta, salads. Drinks expensive.*

Stringfellows
16/19 St Martin's Lane, WC2
(240 5534)
Disco Mon-Sat 10.00-3.00am,
Sun 9.00-3.00am.
Glass dance floor, black suede walls and good light show. Open daily for lunch and dinner. Expensive. Cocktails from 6.00 onwards.

Terrace Restaurant
Dorchester Hotel, Park Lane,
W1 (629 8888)
Mon-Sat. From 7.00-10.00
pianist; 10.00-1.00am three
piece band and dancing.
Pre and post theatre three-course menu £12.50 (exc. wine); and the menu surprise, a six-course 'nouvelle cuisine' menu £45 for two (exc. wine).

Thursdays
38 Kensington High St, W8
(937 7744)
Mon-Sat 9.00-3.00am.
No membership required. Restaurant on balcony overlooking dance floor.

Tiddy Dols
2 Hertford St, W1 (499 2357/8)
6.00-2.00am every night.
Cabaret from 7.00-2.00am. Selection of menus from light supper to a la carte.

Vecchiomondo
118 Cromwell Rd, SW7 (337 7756)
6.00-2.30am
Italian food and dancing. Lively atmosphere.

Xenon
196 Piccadilly W1 (734 9344/5)
Mon-Sat 9.00-3.30am.
Three bars including piano cocktail bar. Light and water shows, wild animals appear on stage, dance routine, magicians, jugglers and tumblers. No membership. Nightly admission. Mon, Tue £3, Wed, Thu £4 and Fri, Sat £5. The piano bar is open from 12 noon until 9.00 for cocktails, light food and afternoon tea.

STOP PRESS

A La Pizza
51 Fulham Broadway, SW6
(381 2042).
ITALIAN
Mon-Thu 12.00-12.00; Fri-Sat
12.00-1.00; Sun 2.00-12.00.
Food £6. Wine £3.50 (carafe)
*Bland, basic pizzeria but it
comes up with the goodies.
Standard and large pizzas with
variations on the pizza chain
offerings. Amongst a choice of
20 or so there are vegetarian,
chicken surprise, savoury meat
and tropical pizzas. Fine baked
tatties with different sauces
and fillings as well as
American-style milk shakes.*

Arlecchino
8 Hillgate St, W8 (229 2027)
ITALIAN
Mon-Sun 12 noon-3.00,
6.00-11.30.
Food £15. Wine £3.75.
*Small, busy restaurant, with
red flock wallpaper, and
efficient waiters, the pasta is
excellent — fettucine all'
Alfredo, spaghetti carbonara.
There is sole for the fish lover,
and a broad selection of meat
dishes for the carnivore. For
dessert a trolley is wheeled
out: have the orange in a rich
and delicious syrup.*

Maharaja
50 Queensway, W2 (727 1135)
INDIAN
Mon-Sun 12 noon-12 midnight.
Food £16. Wine £3.90.
*When I want a curry and can't
find anyone to accompany me,
I come here. The waiters are
charming, the brightly-
coloured food company
enough. The special dishes
'are cooked in Tandoori the
Grill of the Eastern Palaces' —*
*Keema Nan, stuffed with meat,
Shish Kebab, and a delicious
Chicken Musalam, cooked in
spices with a cream sauce.
The cauliflower bhajee is
interesting. There is a small
selection of English dishes for
those who merely want the
atmosphere of an Indian
restaurant. Tinned fruits.
Coffee with Turkish delight.*

New Bengal
187-189 Queensway, W2 (229
1640)
INDIAN
Mon-Fri 12 noon-3.00,
6.00-11.30; Sat, Sun 12
noon-11.30.
Food £7. Wine £4.50.
*The New Bengal, tucked away
at the tail end of Queensway,
is very good value, and
deservedly popular. The menu
is typically extensive — Birani,
Parsee, Pliau and Persian
dishes, and excellent
vegetable dishes such as Alu
Gobi and Tarka Dhal. The
choice of desserts — tinned
fruits, ice-cream or Indian
sweets, such as Rus Malai and
Gulubjaman — is, again
typically, rather unimaginative;
but good strong coffee follows.
There is an extensive wine list,
although it seems a shame to
drink a good wine with curry.
The service is courteous; and
in the evenings candlelight
and red tablecloths make the
restaurant more cheerful. For
good straightforward average
quality Indian food, at below
average prices, the New
Bengal has few rivals.*

Afghan
Buzkash

African
Calabash, The
Toddies (African/English)

American
Bones
Boulevard
Bruno's All Day Diner
Carlettes
Cassidy's
Chicago Pizza Pie Factory,
The
Coconut Grove
Drones
Garfunkel's
Grunts
Hamburger Heaven
Hard Rock Cafe
Joe Allen
Maxwells
New York Cafe
Pappagallis Pizza Inc.
Pizza on the Park
Ringside, The
Rock Garden
Roxy Diner
Sloane's
Smiles
Surprise
Tango
Tootsies
Widow Applebaum's
Wolfe's

Anglo/French
Bendicks
Bistro Vino
Brinkley's
Company
Connaught Rooms
Dan's
Foxtrot Oscar
Henrietta's
Julie's
Justin de Blank
Mildred's
Monkeys

Princes Room
William F

Austrian/Swiss/German
Cosmo Restaurant, The
Gerhard's
Third Man, The
St Moritz
Swiss Centre, The

Canadian
Adam's

Chinese
Chelsea Rendezvous
China Garden, The
Choy's
Chuen Cheng Ku
Crystal Palace
Diamond Restaurant
Gallery Boat, The (Peking)
Golden Duck
Good Earth
Gourmet Rendezvous
Green Jade
Ho Lee Fook
I Ching
Ken Lo's Memories of China
Lee Ho Fook
Ley Ons
Lotus Garden
Mama San
Mandarin (NW3)
Mandarin (W8)
Mandarin Kitchen
Mr Chow
New Lee Ho Fook
(Cantonese)
Poons (Cantonese)
Red Lion
Sailing Junk
Shangri La
Shu Shan II
Tiger Lee
Wei Hai Wei
Young's (Cantonese)

English
Anchor, The
Angel, The

CUISINE INDEX

Annabelle's
Aunties
Bagley's
Baron of Beef
Belle Epoque, La
Bill Bentley's
Bumbles
Carvery
City Gates, The
Cooke's
Dickens Room
Drakes
English House
Filling Station Bistro, The
Fingal's
Francesca's Cafe
Gow's
Grange, The
Holland Street Restaurant
Hungry Horse, The
Lockets
Massey's Chop House
Maypole, The
Mother Huff's Eating House
Mrs Beeton's Restaurant
Mustoe Bistro
Oodles
Overtons
Pickwick Room
Picnic Basket
Porters
Quality Chop House
Red Onion Bistro, The
Refectory, The
Reflections
Richoux
Rules
Salad Days
Scats
September
Sheeky's
Simpson's in the Strand
Staveley's
Tate Gallery Restaurant
Tavern Room
Thomas De Quincey
Throgmorton Restaurant
Tiddy Dols Eating House
Tilley's Eats
Tudor Café

Tudor Rooms
Turpins
Wags
Waltons
Wild Thyme
Yesterday

Fish
Alcove
Antoine's (Wheeler's)
Bentleys
Carafe, Le
Foleys
Galley, The
Geales Fish Restaurant
Manzis
Quai St Pierre, Le
Scotts
Sea Shell (E8)
Sea Shell Fish Bar (NW1)
Sweetings
Trattoria Dei Pescatori
Upper Street Fish Shop, The
Villa Dei Pescatori

French
Alonso's (French/Italian)
Amoureux, Les
Anna's Place
Ark
L'Artiste Affame
L'Artiste Assoiffe
Au Bon Accueil
Bagatelle
Balzac Bistro
Bar Creperie
Barnaby's Restaurant
Beaufort Restaurant
Bewicks
Bill Bentley's
Bistingo, Le
Bistro Vino
Boulestin
Brasserie, La
Brasserie Des Amis
Brasserie St Quentin
Bubbs
Cafe Creperie
Cafe des Amis du Vin, Le
Cafe Jardin

CUISINE INDEX

Capability Brown
Capital Hotel Restaurant
Carlo's Place
Cassis
Chalcot's Bistro
Chalk and Cheese
Chanterelle
Chateaubriand (NW3)
Chateaubriand, Le (W1)
Chef, Le
Chez Gerard
Chez Moi
Chez Nico
Chez Solange
Chez Victor
Cliche, Le
Connaught Restaurant, The
Corse, La
Crazy Crepe, The
Croisette, La
Daphne's
Detour, Le
Didier
Dominic's
Dorchester Grill Room
Eaton's (French/Russian)
Ebury Wine Bar
Entrecote
L'Epicure
L'Escargot
L'Estanquet
L'Etoile
Fagin's Kitchen
Ferdinand's Cocktail
Restaurant
Fontana, La (French/Italian)
Four Seasons
Francais, Le
Fringale, La
Gaffe, La
Gamin, Le
Gastronome One
Gavroche, Le
Gavvers
Inigo Jones
Jacaranda
Jonathan's
Keats
Lacy's
Langan's Bistro

Langan's Braserie
Ma Cuisine
Magno's Bistro
Mange Tout, Le
Marmiton, Le
Menage a Trois
Mes Amis
Mijanou
Mirabelle
Mon Plaisir
Monsieur Thompson
Mr Garraways
M'sieur Frog
My Old Dutch
Neal Street Restaurant
Newport
No Name Place
Obelix
Odette's
Odin's Restaurant
L'Opera
Oscar's Brasserie
Papillon, Le
Penny's Place
Petit Prince, Le
(French/Algerian)
Poissonnerie de l'Avenue
Pomme d'Amour
Poulbot, Le
Poule Au Pot, La
P'tit Montmartre, Le
Relais des Amis
River Bistro
Routier, Le
Rowleys
RSJ
Savoy Restaurant
Steak Nicole, Le
Suquet, Le
Tante Claire, La
Thierry's
Toque Blanche, La
Trois Canards, Les
Vie En Rose, La

Greek/Turkish
Andy's Kebab House
Anemos
Averofs
Beoty's

CUISINE INDEX

Bitter Lemons
Costas Grill
Crazy Horse
Efes Kebab House
Hellenic, The
Kalamaras
Kolossi Grill
Lemonia
Little Acropolis
Marmara Restaurant
Moditis Restaurant
Othello Psarapoula
Retsina Kebab
Savvas Kebab House
Semiramis
Sultan's Delight
White Tower Restaurant

Indian and Pakistani
Agra, The
Al Khayam
Baba Bhelpoori House
Clifton Restaurant
Clive's India
Diwana Bhelpoori House
Gaylord
Ganpath
Gurkhas Tandoori Restaurant,
Gulistan
Holy Cow
India Club Restaurant, The
Khan's
Khyber
Kundan
Last Days of the Raj
Maharaja
Majlis
Mehran Indian Restaurant
Memsahib
Mogul Restaurant
Noojahan
Rama Sita
Salloos
Sharuna
Shezan
Sree Krishna South India
Restaurant
Standard, The
Star of India

Tandoori Ashoka
Uddins Manzil
Veeraswamy

International
Basil Street Hotel Restaurant
Carlton Tower Rib Room
Carrier's
Chelsea Kitchen
Fountain, The
Frederick's
Gallipoli (International/
Turkish)
Granary, The
Ivy
Julius
Leeks
Leith's Restaurant
Motcombs
Nineteen
Oliver's
Ormonds
Oslo Court
Parkes
Peter Evans' Eating House
Pomegranates
Popote, La
Pot
Ritz, The
Royal Festival Hall Restaurant
Salamis
Savoy Grill Room
Savoy Restaurant
Shares
Simply Steaks
Station Grill, The
Stockpot
Tuttons
Witchity
Yodelling Sausage, The

Italian
A La Pizza
Alcove
Al Gallo d'Oro
Amalfi
L'Amico
Apicella
Arlecchino

192

CUISINE INDEX

Barbarella
Beccofino
Bersagliera, La
Bertorelli Brothers
Bistingo, Le
Blue's Trattoria
Bussola, La
Canaletto
Casa Porrelli
Cecconis
Chanticleer
Chez Franco
Como Lario
Concordia Notte
Don Luigi
Due Franco
Eleven Park Walk
Famiglia, La
Fatso's Pasta Joint
Franco Ovest
Gatamelata
Gennaro's
Gino's
Girasole, Il
Gondoliere
Gran Paradiso
Leoni's Quo Vadis
Lugger, The
Luigi's
Mario's Pizza Express
Mimmo d'Ischia
Mimmo e Pasquale
Mio Sogno
Montpeliano
Nassa, La
Oakley's Diner
Perla, La
Pizza Express (NW3)
Pizza Express (WC1)
Pizza Express (W2)
Pizza Vino
Pontevecchio
Portofino Restaurant
Ristorante La Barca (SW6)
Ristorante La Barca (SE1)
Sale e Pepe
San Frediano
Scala, La
Spaghetti House (SW1)
Spaghetti House (WC2)

Tiberio
Topo d'Oro
Trattoo
Trattoria Aquilino
Trattoria Bernigra
Trattoria la Spezia
Trattoria Lucca
Trattoria Terrazza
Vecchia Milano
Verde Valle, Le
Verona Antica
Villa Bianca
Zia Sophia

Japanese
Ajimura
Gonbei
Masako

Jewish/Kosher
Bloom's (Kosher)
Carroll's
Harry Morgan's
Nosherie, The

Mauritian
Dodo Gourmand, Le

Mexican
Texas Lone Star Saloon
(Tex/Mex)

Middle Eastern
Byblos
Falafel
Phoenicia

Russian
Borshtch 'N' Tears
Luba's Bistro
Nikita's

Scandinavian
Froops

Spanish/Portuguese
Costa Del Sol
Hispaniola
Martinez

THE STUNTMAN

Restaurant and Wine Bar

''We were impressed by the crisp
good looks of the room, and by
the excellence of the food''

''A certain film world glamour is
noticeable both in the clientele
and in the menu…''

What's On In London

3 course gourmet lunch for £8.50 or try
our superb selection of a la carte dishes

7 Kensington High Street, London W8
For reservations: 937-0932

INDEX

TRANSPORT

Public transport operates to many parts of London throughout the night, so before you decide to spend pounds on a cab or risk using the car, find out what is available.

The last Underground trains leave the West End after midnight with some such as the Piccadilly Line from Piccadilly Circus as late as 12.30am. Most of the last journeys on the main bus routes leave central London in the half hour before midnight.

However some of the well know routes (such as the 11) run all night and their is also a network of special night bus services which operate throughout the night which should get you at least part of the way home. To check for details for routes and times phone London Transport's 24 hour Travel Information service on 01 222 1234.

There are still a few early morning trains on some lines in the British Rail network. Telephone your local enquiry bureau for details.

London Transport produce a useful comprehensive booklet with details of all the all-night buses and other public transport facilities which operate in the small hours. You should be able to get a copy from any of London Transport's Travel Information Centres or by post from the Public Relations Officer, 55 Broadway, London SW1H 0BD.

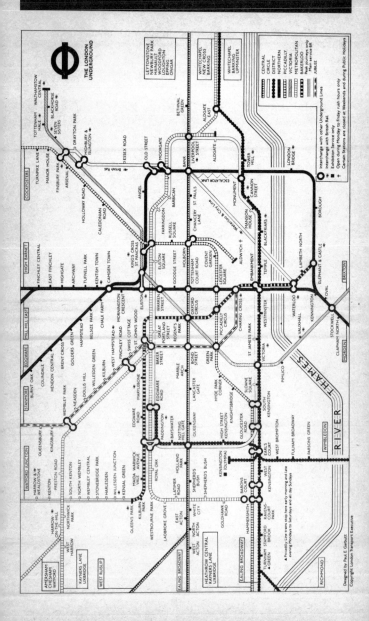